Signpost
Guides

LOIRE VALLEY

The best of the Loire Valley, from its glorious châteaux to its quiet backwaters, from the Orléans of Joan of Arc to the Ussé of Sleeping Beauty, and from the vineyards of Sancerre to the Gothic masterpiece of Chartres, with suggested driving tours

Andrew Sanger, Fiona Nichols,
Gillian Thomas and John Harrison

The
Globe
Pequot
Press

Thomas
Cook
Publishing

Published by Thomas Cook Publishing
A division of Thomas Cook Holdings Ltd
PO Box 227
Thomas Cook Business Park
Units 19–21
Coningsby Road
Peterborough PE3 8XX
United Kingdom

Telephone: +44 (0)1733 416477
Fax: +44 (0)1733 416688
E-mail: books@thomascook.com

For further information about
Thomas Cook Publishing, visit our website:
www.thomascook.com

ISBN 1-841571-55-5

Published in the USA by
The Globe Pequot Press
PO Box 480
Guilford, Connecticut 06437
USA

ISBN 0-7627-1251-1

Text: © 2002 Thomas Cook Publishing
Maps and diagrams:
Road maps generated from Bartholomew digital database © Bartholomew Ltd, 2002
Reproduced by permission of HarperCollins Publishers
City maps prepared by Polly Senior Cartography, © Thomas Cook Ltd

Publisher: Donald Greig
Commissioning Editor: Deborah Parker
Editor: Fay Franklin
Proof-reader: Jan Wiltshire
Written and researched by: Andrew Sanger, Fiona Nichols, Gillian Thomas, John Harrison
Managing Director: Kevin Fitzgerald

About the authors

Andrew Sanger is a well-established travel writer who has contributed many hundreds of travel articles to a wide range of British newspapers and magazines. He has also written over 20 guidebooks, most about regions of France, which have been translated into several languages. His most recent titles for Thomas Cook are *Signpost Guide Provence & the Côte d'Azur* and *Signpost Guide Burgundy & the Rhône Valley*. Andrew was editor of French Railways' travel magazine *Rail Europe*, and has twice been the winner of the prestigious annual Travelex Travel Writers' Award in London, in 1994 and 1996.

Fiona Nichols has contributed travel and lifestyle articles to magazines and newspapers in various parts of the world. She is a co-author of some dozen or so travel guides, and author-photographer of eight travel books. Fiona lives in the south of France, near the Spanish border, where she continues to write and photograph travel-related features and books. This is her first contribution to a Thomas Cook publication.

Gillian Thomas and John Harrison are freelance travel writers who started their careers in the BBC, where she worked in the Paris news office. Married, with three grown-up children, they are frequent visitors to France including camping, walking, cycling and canal-boating holidays. They wrote the *Signpost Guide Languedoc and Southwest France* for Thomas Cook.

Acknowledgements

Andrew Sanger would like to thank Rail Europe and the Regional Tourist Board of Centre-Val-de-Loire for their assistance. Gillian Thomas and John Harrison would like to thank Brittany Ferries and the tourist boards of the Central Loire Valley and Western Loire regions for their assistance. Fiona Nichols would like to thank all the Tourist Offices concerned, who were extremely kind and informative.

Contents

LOIRE VALLEY

Signpost
Guides

Titles in this series include:

- Andalucía and the Costa del Sol
- Australia
- Bavaria and the Austrian Tyrol
- Brittany and Normandy
- Burgundy and the Rhône Valley
- California
- Canadian Rockies, Alberta and British Columbia
- Catalonia and the Spanish Pyrenees
- Dordogne and Western France
- England and Wales
- Florida
- Ireland
- Italian Lakes and Mountains with Venice and Florence
- Languedoc and South-west France
- Loire Valley
- New England
- New Zealand
- Portugal
- Provence and the Côte d'Azur
- Scotland
- Tuscany and Umbria
- Vancouver and British Columbia
- Washington DC and Virginia, Maryland and Delaware

and

- Selected Hotels and Inns in North America
- Bed and Breakfast in France 2002

For further information about these and other Thomas Cook publications, write to Thomas Cook Publishing, PO Box 227, Thomas Cook Business Park, Units 19–21, Coningsby Road, Peterborough PE3 8XX, United Kingdom

About Signpost Guides

Thomas Cook's Signpost Guides are designed to provide you with a comprehensive but flexible reference source to guide you as you tour a country or region by car. This guide divides the Loire Valley into touring areas – one per chapter. Major cultural centres or cities form chapters in their own right. Each chapter contains enough attractions to provide at least a day's worth of activities – often more.

Star ratings

To make it easier for you to plan your time and decide what to see, every sight and attraction is given a star rating. A three-star rating indicates a major attraction, worth at least half a day of your time. A two-star attraction is worth an hour or so of your time, and a one-star attraction indicates a place that is worth visiting, but often of specialist interest. To help you further, individual attractions within towns or theme parks are also graded, so that travellers with limited time can quickly find the most rewarding sights.

Chapter contents

Every chapter has an introduction summing up the main attractions of the area or town, and a ratings box, which will highlight its appeal – some places may be more attractive to families travelling with children, others to wine-lovers visiting vineyards, and others to people interested in finding castles, churches, nature reserves, or good beaches.

Each chapter is then divided into an alphabetical gazetteer, and a suggested tour or walk. You can select whether you just want to visit a particular sight or attraction, choosing from those described in the gazetteer, or whether you want to tour the area comprehensively. If the latter, you can construct your own itinerary, or follow the authors' suggested tour, which comes at the end of every area chapter.

The gazetteer

The gazetteer section describes all the major attractions in the area – the villages, towns, historic sites, nature reserves, parks or museums that you are most likely to want to see. Maps of the area highlight all the places mentioned in the text. Using this comprehensive overview of the area, you may choose just to visit one or two sights.

One way to use the guide is to find individual sights that interest you, using the index, overview map or star ratings, and read what our authors have to say about them. This will help you decide whether to visit the sight. If you do, you will find plenty of practical information, such as the telephone number for enquiries and opening times.

Symbol Key

ℹ Tourist Information Centre

Ⓦ Website

⊘ Advice on arriving or departing

Ⓟ Parking locations

Ⓐ Advice on getting around

⊃ Directions

🏛 Sights and attractions

🍴 Eating

Ⓒ Accommodation

🛍 Shopping

⚽ Sport

Ⓐ Entertainment

Practical information

The practical information in the page margins, or sidebar, will help you locate the services you need as an independent traveller – including the tourist information centre, car parks and public transport facilities. You will also find the opening times of sights, museums, churches and other attractions, as well as useful tips on shopping, market days, cultural events, entertainment, festivals and sports facilities.

Alternatively, you can choose a hotel, with the help of the accommodation recommendations contained in this guide. You can then turn to the overall map on pages 10–11 to help you work out which chapters in the book describe the cities and regions closest to your touring base.

Driving tours

The suggested tour is just that – a suggestion, with plenty of optional detours and one or two ideas for making your own discoveries, under the heading 'Also worth exploring'. The routes are designed to link the attractions described in the gazetteer section, and to cover outstandingly scenic coastal, mountain and rural landscapes. The total distance is given for each tour, and the time it will take you to drive the complete route, but bear in mind that this indication is just for driving time: you will need to add on extra time for visiting attractions along the way.

Many of the routes are circular, so that you can join them at any point. Where the nature of the terrain dictates that the route has to be linear, the route can either be followed out and back, or you can use it as a link route, to get from one area in the book to another.

As you follow the route descriptions, you will find names picked out in bold capital letters – this means that the place is described fully in the gazetteer. Other names picked out in bold indicate additional villages or attractions worth a brief stop along the route.

Accommodation and food

In every chapter you will find lodging and eating recommendations for individual towns, or for the area as a whole. These are designed to cover a range of price brackets and concentrate on more characterful small or individualistic hotels and restaurants. In addition, you will find information in the 'Travel facts' chapter on chain hotels, with an address to which you can write for a guide, map or directory.

The price indications used in the guide have the following meanings:

€   budget level
€€   typical/average prices
€€€ de luxe

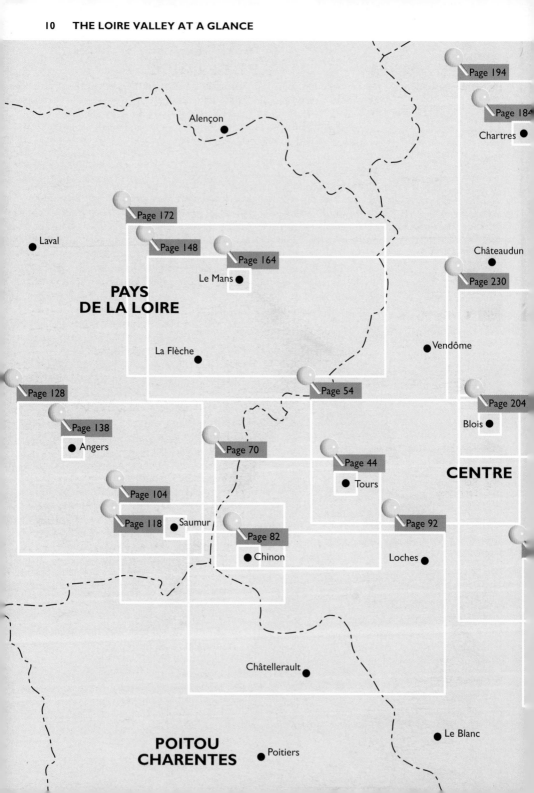

Page 194

Page 184

Chartres

Alençon

Page 172

Laval

Page 148

Le Mans

Page 164

Châteaudun

Page 230

**PAYS
DE LA LOIRE**

La Flèche

Vendôme

Page 128

Page 54

Page 204

Page 138

Blois

Angers

Page 70

Page 44

Tours

CENTRE

Page 104

Page 118

Saumur

Page 82

Page 92

Chinon

Loches

Châtellerault

Le Blanc

**POITOU
CHARENTES**

Poitiers

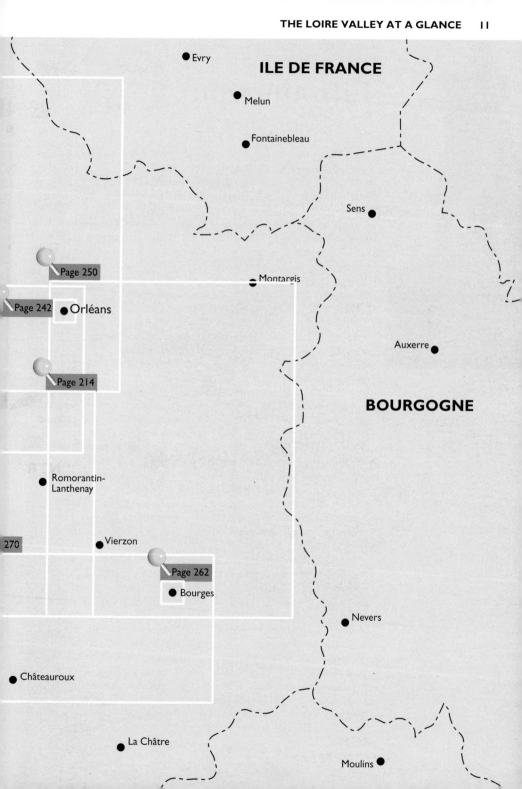

● Evry

ILE DE FRANCE

● Melun

Fontainebleau ●

Sens ●

● Montargis

Page 250

Page 242 ● Orléans

Auxerre ●

Page 214

BOURGOGNE

● Romorantin-
Lanthenay

270

● Vierzon

Page 262

● Bourges

● Nevers

● Châteauroux

● La Châtre

Moulins ●

Above
Statue of Joan of Arc, Orléans

Introduction

The Loire Valley today is one of the world's greatest tourist areas, enjoyed by visitors throughout the year. This is not just a recent phenomenon, however. Long before the advent of mass tourism, its mild climate and natural beauty attracted royalty and pleasure-loving nobility from far and wide.

These first visitors built mighty castles to protect themselves in an era of almost constant feuding. Then, in the 16th century, as life in France gradually became more peaceful and the influence of the Renaissance began to spread, the need for fortification declined. Instead comfort and decoration became the priorities. Beautiful country houses were built, carefully positioned to make the most of the landscape, and furnished sumptuously.

The legacy of those times is an astonishing mixture of châteaux open to the public. These range from ruined castles to elegant mansions that are still family homes. Most are architectural masterpieces with striking exteriors, often rich in detail. Some of the interiors are bare, some decorated with just a few token items which hint of their past, and some fully furnished – often overwhelmingly so to modern eyes! Adding further to the pleasure of a visit, many have extensive gardens that are a delight to stroll around.

In some châteaux the visitor is free to wander alone; in others a guided tour is compulsory. Some are further brought to life by imaginative *son-et-lumière* presentations. In many there is far more to see than can be absorbed in a single visit, especially if something particular catches the eye and sets the imagination racing; perhaps a dainty turret, a grand staircase, a secret door, a voluptuous portrait or a dank dungeon. Who knows what pageantry, feasting, intrigues and passion each château must have witnessed over the centuries?

But exploring châteaux is only one of the pleasures of a stay in the Loire Valley. The countryside may be largely flat but there are beautiful views to enjoy. The area is well endowed, too, with historic towns and tranquil villages, magnificent churches and a remarkable diversity of museums whose collections range as widely as masks, mushrooms, military tanks and – inevitably – wine. Most unusual of all is the underground life in some of the old *tuffeau* (tufa) caves, originally quarried to provide stone for building the châteaux but now used inventively as homes, museums or restaurants.

Throughout the area, there is accommodation to suit every taste, from grand château-hotels to small, family-run inns. Everywhere, too, the local love of good food, particularly fish and cheeses, is obvious, complemented of course by the excellent local wines. Pausing at wineries to do some sampling, and perhaps to invest in a case or two, is an essential part of most visitors' itinerary.

So the Loire Valley certainly deserves its popularity. Indeed, for most people, a single visit is never enough. Many return again and again, including the large number of Parisians who regard it as the ideal location for a holiday home.

Most important of all is the Loire itself, the longest river in France. Its influence on the areas through which it flows is reflected by the fact that no fewer than six of France's *départements* include it in their name: Loire, Haute-Loire, Loire-Atlantique, Indre-et-Loire, Maine-et-Loire and Saône-et-Loire. And countless towns and villages on its banks proudly call themselves 'sur-Loire'. Starting far to the south, high in the mountains of the Cevennes, it flows in a great semi-circle – first north, then west – to the Atlantic. On the way it is joined by more than a hundred tributaries, including several that are important rivers in their own right like the Cher, Vienne, Maine and Sarthe. By the time it reaches the area covered in this book, it is often as wide as a lake. For centuries much of the adjoining land was prone to devastating floods. Even in towns, people had to resort to boats, many were drowned and buildings were washed away. Today, however, its flow is much more controlled, thanks largely to the long embankments built beside it.

Until the arrival of railways, the Loire was an important highway, busy with cargo boats. Similarly the construction of bridges across it – often architectural gems in their own right, that remain to this day – put paid to the many little ferries that once linked its banks. Now, by comparison, the water seems quiet and tranquil – but ever picturesque. For the touring traveller in this region, that special combination of peacefulness and beauty is a recurring one, making for many enduring memories of time spent in discovering the delights of the Loire Valley.

Below
Saumur

Travel facts

Accommodation

France (*for Loire Valley websites, see pages 19–20*): *www.francetourism.com/* (French Tourist Office site in the US with useful accommodation and trip-planning pages); *www.fr-holidaystore.co.uk/tourops/* (UK tour operators specialising in France); *www.gites-de-france.fr/csomang/general* (Gîtes de France site); *www.logis-de-france.fr/us/index* (English-language pages of Logis de France site).

www.a-castle-for-rent.com is a novel website if you are looking for some stately accommodation. Amongst other details, it lists which châteaux may be rented either in their entirety or by the room.

Accommodation in the Loire Valley ranges from stylish 5-star hotels to country campsites, and everything in between. There are hundreds of small, moderately priced independent family-run hotels. A particular feature of the region is privately owned châteaux which take paying guests. Almost every little town, and many a tiny village, has at least one clean, adequately comfortable, unpretentious hotel (or sometimes, *restaurant avec chambres*, restaurant with rooms). Standards range from the extremely basic to the height of elegance. Pricing is normally for the room, not per person. A star system is in force, but some traditional hotels in both town and country fall short of even a single star, while others far exceed the requirements for the maximum grade '4-star Luxe'. Most are 2–3 stars. Self-catering *gîtes* – usually country cottages – are often a bargain, though facilities can be basic.

In this region, it is always wise to book ahead, and if you want to visit during high season (July–August), it's wise to plan everything a couple of months in advance.

The major international hotel chains are represented in the Loire region. The big French chains, all with several hotels in the region, include:

• **Campanile** – popular national chain of motels with restaurant, reliable, all identical, mid-price.

• **Formule 1, Etap Hotel, Balladins, Bonsaï, Liberté, Première Class** – all economy motels, modern but minimalist.

• **Ibis** – modern, functional, town hotels, mid- to low-budget.

• **Meridien** – smart, modern high-quality chain.

• **Sofitel** – luxurious modern hotels.

Useful French hotel and restaurant federations include:

• **Relais & Châteaux** – independently owned, top of the market, old-fashioned luxury and (especially those designated as *Relais Gourmand*) with excellent food. Free handbook from French Government Tourist Offices abroad. *www.relaischateaux.com*

• **Relais Routiers** – truckdrivers' stops; inexpensive roadside restaurants, often with a few basic rooms above. Recognisable by a blue and red circular sign outside.

• **Relais du Silence** – good-quality hotels in especially quiet locations. Bookable in France; *tel: 01 44 49 90 00.*

• **Logis et Auberges de France** – almost 5000 small, unpretentious, family-run independent hotels, nearly all with a good, inexpensive restaurant (half of them specialise in regional dishes); rooms are adequate, reasonably priced. Free handbook from French Government Tourist Offices abroad. *www.logis-de-france.fr/*

• **Château Acceuil** or **Chambres d'Hôtes en Châteaux et Demeures Privés** is an alternative B&B in the Loire where the 'guesthouses' are privately owned châteaux and mansions. Details of them can be found in a variety of handbooks available from local regional tourism authorities (CRTs) or from French tourist offices abroad.

• **Gîtes de France** are simple cottages rented as inexpensive self-catering vacation accommodation. They're bookable in the UK; *tel: 0990 360360, e-mail: info@gites-de-france.fr*. For more information, visit the Gîtes de France website, *www.gites-de-france.fr/*, which is in French and English and allows online booking of some gîtes.

• **Villages des Vacances (holiday villages)**, either for all the family or for children only, are popular with the French. Details from national and regional tourist offices.

Other options include:

• **Chambres d'Hôtes** ('guest rooms'), often announced by a simple handmade sign on a front gate, are homely bed & breakfast stopovers (often with evening meal too), usually in ordinary family homes in rural areas.

• **Meublés** (literally, 'furnished') are short-let apartments suitable for vacations. There are some in all the major towns. Contact local tourist offices for a list, and they can also make bookings.

• **Campsites** – France has over 11,000 approved campsites. They're graded with stars: anything above 2 stars will have hot showers and good facilities. *Camping à la Ferme*, campsites on farms, tend to be more basic. Four-star and the even better 4-star 'Grand Comfort' sites have excellent amenities, play area, a shop, and sports facilities, often including a swimming pool. *Castels et Camping*, mainly in superb locations, is a federation of top-quality camps (*www.les-castels.com*). There are good campsites within easy reach of the major châteaux.

Airports

Nantes Airport, although outside the area covered by this book, is the principal airport for the western Loire. It receives daily scheduled flights from London (Gatwick) and, in summer, from Montreal. A major local airport is **Angers-Marcé**, near Angers, with flights from 19 other French regional airports. The rest of the Loire valley region is within easy reach of Paris-Orly. (*See also pages 30–31, Getting to the Loire Valley.*)

Children

Children in France will strike their British, American and Australasian counterparts (and their parents) as very well-behaved and fairly strictly

disciplined. Children are expected to sit quietly at table and eat grown-up food. On the other hand, there are plenty of facilities and entertainments for kids and they are welcomed everywhere.

Climate

The Loire Valley is known as the 'Garden of France', and gardens need watering. Humid conditions and rain are possible all year. The region enjoys a long, warm summer, from around May to September, with daytime temperatures often reaching above 20°C. Autumn is bright, mild, and comfortably warm. Occasional heavy downpours are a feature of the later summer and autumn. Spring is mild and pleasant. In winter it can be damp, though not especially cold, and in the larger valleys, even milder.

Currency

France is part of the Euro zone. From early 2002, the French franc (FF) has been replaced by the Euro (€), divided into 100 cents. Euros are readily available from all ATMs (Cash Dispensers) outside banks, hypermarkets and in shopping centres using credit cards and bank cards displaying the appropriate international symbols. There's no limit on the amount of money in any currency that can be taken into or out of France.

Customs regulations

Non-EU citizens, aged over 15 and spending less than 6 months in France, may be able to reclaim VAT (*TVA* in French) on any items costing over about 35€ purchased for export. At the time of the purchase, present your passport and ask for a *bordereau* form. On leaving France, you should be sure to have the *bordereau* validated by French Customs.

• For travellers returning to the **UK and other EU countries** there are no restrictions except that all goods brought back must be for personal consumption and must be legal for private possession. In the UK, HM Customs & Excise still maintain (unenforceable) limits on the amount of alcoholic drinks and tobacco that will be considered reasonable 'for personal use'. These propose up to 90 litres of wine, 10 litres of spirits and 800 cigarettes. More information at *www.hmce.gov.uk*

• Travellers returning to the **USA** have an allowance on goods for personal use of up to $400, but most plants or foods are prohibited. You will find US Customs listed in the 'US Government' section of your local phone directory under the Treasury Department listing. You may also call US Customs in Washington, DC; *tel: (202) 927-6724.* For US Treasury customs information consult *www.customs.ustreas.gov/ travel/travel.htm*

Electricity

The power supply in France is 220 volts. Circular 2-pin plugs are used.

Entry formalities

Travellers from the UK, USA, New Zealand and Canada do not need a visa for visits of less than 90 days. Australians and South Africans must apply for a visa from a French Embassy.

Festivals

Mar:
• *Festival de Jazz*, Chartres;
• *Conteries Mars* (carnival and festival), Blois;
Easter Sat: Easter Vigil (at 2200), St-Benoît-sur-Loire;
Easter weekend: St-François Fair, Sully-sur-Loire;
Easter Mon: Easter Egg Festival, Pagode de Chanteloup.

Apr:
• International Guitar Festival, Vendôme;
• 24-hour motorcycle race, Le Mans.
End-Apr:
• Horsemanship Competitions, Saumur;
• Evening Carnival Parade, Cholet.
Whitsun:
• Wine Fair, Vouvray;
• Wine Fair, Sancerre;
• Rhododendron Festival, Châteaneuf-sur-Loire.

May:
Weekend nearest 1 May:
• *Fête du Crottin de Chavignol*, Sancerre;
• Harpsichord Festival,

• For **Australia** the allowance is up to $400-worth of goods, including 250 cigarettes and 1 bottle of an alcoholic drink. Foods and anything containing wood or plant material may be prohibited.
• For **New Zealand** the allowance is $700-worth of goods, including 200 cigarettes and 6 bottles of alcoholic drinks. Foods and anything containing wood or plant material may be prohibited.
• In general, goods for personal use or gifts up to $300 may be brought back to **Canada**. *Tel: 1-800-461-9999* for more information.
• **South Africans** can bring back up to 1 250 rands-worth of goods tax-free including 1 litre spirits, 2 litres wine and 400 cigarettes. Above that limit, an additional 10,000 rands-worth of goods is allowed but is taxed at 20 per cent for all goods.
For visitors entering France there are no limits on legal articles for ordinary personal use.
Information is provided by the French Customs Office on the French Embassy website in Washington DC: *http://info-france-usa.org/america/embassy/customs/cover.htm*

Drinking

The Loire Valley is famous for its fine wines, but everyday drinking in the region's homes and bars is similar to elsewhere in France. Even here, the Loire's great wines are reserved for special occasions or an evening out. Of the local wines, the commonest and least expensive are fruity white Sauvignon de Touraine and sweeter Rosé d'Anjou. Drink plays a vital part in life, but it is rare to see a local person drunk. The French do not usually drink with the intention of getting drunk at all, but to enhance appetite, conversation and companionship. In any bar or brasserie, not only alcoholic and soft drinks are served but also coffee (including decaffeinated), hot chocolate, tea and herb tea.

Drinks

de l'eau minérale – mineral water
gazeuese or *eau plat* – sparkling or still water
une bière – any name-brand German or Belgian beer
un demi or *une bière à la pression* – a glass of draught lager-style beer
un café – espresso (the French keep going with frequent shots all day)
un café-crème (usually *un grand crème*) – coffee with milk (the French usually drink this only for breakfast)
un déca – decaffeinated coffee
un thé (*nature, citron* or *au lait*) – tea (black, with lemon, or with milk)
une tisane – herbal tea
un chocolat chaud – hot chocolate
un Miky – cold chocolate drink
un kir – an aperitif of dry white wine and *crème de cassis* (blackcurrant liqueur)

Chartres;
5–6 May: *Grande Brocante* street market, Orléans;
7–8 May: *Fêtes Johanniques* (Joan of Arc festival), Orléans.

June:
• International Jazz Festival, Orléans;
• 24-hr motor race, Le Mans;
• International Classical Music Festival (at weekends), Sully-sur-Loire.
Last weekend in June: solstice bonfire and market, Chaumont-sur-Loire.
End-June:
• *Les Orientales* music festival, St-Florent-le-Viel;
• Touraine Music and Dance Festivals, region around Tours;
End-June–mid-July: Anjou Festival (one of France's main arts festivals), Angers and throughout Anjou.
June–Oct: International Garden Festival, Chaumont-sur-Loire.

July:
Loir Music Festival, Montoire-sur-le-Loir;
First weekend July: *Les Scénomanies* (street theatre), Le Mans.
Early July: *Les Affranchis* (festival of street entertainment), La Flèche;
Third weekend July: Carnival, Gien;
Last weekend July: Military Tattoo, Saumur;
July–Aug: International Organ Festival, Chartres.

Aug:
First weekend Aug: Rabelais Market, Chinon;
Mid-Aug:
• Wine Fair, Vouvray;
• World Folklore Festival, Montoire-sur-le-Loir;

Suze, Noilly Prat, Dubonnet and *Martini* – popular brand-name aperitifs
un panaché – shandy (mixed beer and lemonade)
un coca/un coca light – Coca Cola/Diet Coke
un diabolo menthe (green) or *diabolo grenadine* (red) – lemonade mixed with brightly coloured syrup
un jus d'ananas, jus de poire – pineapple juice or pear juice are both popular
un jus d'orange – bottled orange juice
une orange pressé – freshly-squeezed orange juice
une Orangina – fizzy orange drink
sirop – fruit-flavoured sweet drink served in either still or fizzy water
du vin (*rouge/blanc/rosé/doux/mousseux*) – wine (red/white/rosé/sweet/sparkling). No need to ask for dry – it's all dry unless you specify sweet.
un pichet/demi-pichet (*d'eau/de vin blanc/de vin rouge/de vin rosé*) – 1-litre carafe/half-litre carafe (of water/white wine/red wine/rosé wine)
See also Wines (*page 37*).

Eating out

Most French eating places offer a choice of about three *menus*, that is, *prix fixe* (fixed price) set meals, as well as the *à la carte* menu, a list of individually priced dishes. The price difference reflects not differences in quality but in the number of courses and difficulty of preparation. In general, to get the best out of a French restaurant, order one of the *menus*. Prices will usually be higher if you pick and choose from the carte. The day's menus are always displayed outside the restaurant.

Prices must include service and all taxes. It's not necessary to give any extra tip, though a few cents is often left for the waiter on a café table. *Vin compris* means wine included (usually about a quarter or third of a litre of house wine per person).
Away from resorts and big cities, it can be difficult to find something to eat outside normal mealtimes. The lunch break lasts from 1200 to about 1400. Sunday lunch, often taken *en famille* at a local restaurant, lasts until 1500. A little more flexibility comes into dinner hours, from 1900 to 2200, though 2000 is still

• Wine Fair, Pouilly-sur-Loire;
End-Aug: Wine Fair, Sancerre.

Sept:
8 Sept: pilgrimage, St-André-de-Cléry;
Mid–end-Sept: Annual Jazz Festival, Montlouis-sur-Loire.

Oct:
Rockomotives, Vendôme;
End-Oct: Oyster Fair, Sancerre.

Mid-Nov: Wine Fair, Vouvray.

24 Dec:
• *Messes des Naulets* (mass in dialect), different Anjou church each year;
• Christmas vigil and mass (at 2200), St-Benoît-sur-Loire.

Useful websites

France:
www.holidayfrance.org.uk/Default.htm – UK-based site of tour operators specialising in France.

www.focusguides.com/newsfrance.htm – UK-based site with French travel news, offers, links and features.

www.francetourism.com/ – French Tourist Office in US has useful accommodations and trip planning pages.

The Loire Valley:
www.loirevalleytourism.com (Centre-Val-de-Loire).

www.regioncentre.fr/tourisme/ (Centre region).

www.berrylindre.com (Berry and Indre).

the usual time to start dinner. Brasseries are bars that generally serve food at any time. A *salon de thé* serves pastries and other light snacks with tea or coffee.

Health

It's usually possible to see a general practitioner quickly without an appointment, or to phone to request a visit. For doctors, medicines and hospital treatment, payment must be made on the spot. Keep doctors' and pharmacists' receipts – you will need them when claiming reimbursement, whether through Form E111 (available to UK citizens: instructions on the form and accompanying leaflet) or from your travel insurance.

Information

• **UK:** Maison de France (French Government Tourist Office), *178 Piccadilly, London W1V 0AL. Tel: 0891 244123, fax: 0171 493 6594.*
• **Ireland:** Maison de France (French Government Tourist Office), *38 Lower Abbey Street, Dublin 1. Tel: 1 703 4046, fax: 1 874 7324.*
• **USA:** Maisons de France (French Government Tourist Offices), *676 N. Michigan Ave, Chicago, IL 60611-2819, fax: (312) 337-6339. 9454 Wilshire Blvd, Ste 715, Beverly Hills, CA 90212-2967, fax: (310) 276-2835. 444 Madison Avenue, 16th Floor (between 49th & 50th Street), New York, NY 10022-6903, fax: (212) 838-7855.*
• **Australia:** Maison de France (French Government Tourist Office), *BNP Building, 12 Castlereagh St, Sydney, NSW 2000. Tel: (61) 2 231 5244, fax: (61) 2 221 8682.*

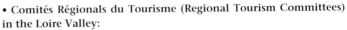

www.chartrescountry.com/eure/ (Chartres and its region).

www.berrylecher.com/cher/ (Cher département).

www.berrylindre.com/indre (Indre département).

www.loire-france.com/ (Loire, France).

www.tourism-touraine.com (Touraine district, Loire Valley).

www.chambordcountry.com (Loir-et-Cher département, Loire and Loir Valleys).

www.tourismloiret.com/loiret/ (Loiret département).

www.coeur-de-france.com – useful promotional site for Centre region; in French.

www.paysdelaloire.fr/ (Pays de Loire).

www.loiredeschateaux.com/ (Loire châteaux).

• **Comités Régionals du Tourisme (Regional Tourism Committees) in the Loire Valley:**
CRT Centre (covering central and eastern parts of the region): *37 ave. de Paris, Orléans. Tel. 08 10 24 02 40, fax : 02 38 79 95 10, e-mail: crtl.centre@crtlcentre.com, www.loirevalleytourism.com*
CRT Pays de la Loire (covering western parts of the region): *2 r. de la Loire, Nantes. Tel. 02 40 48 24 20, www.paysdelaloire.fr*

Maps

Tourist offices have free city and country maps printed in French and sometimes also in English. City brochures usually have a map of the city printed inside.

Michelin regional maps 244 (Pays de la Loire) and 238 (Centre Berry-Nivernais) cover most of the Loire Valley in detail. For Eure-et-Loir *département*, including Chartres, map 237 (Ile de France) is needed. The annual Michelin motoring atlas is useful for touring in the Loire region and further afield. The *Michelin Atlas Autoroutier* (Motorway Atlas) is a handbook detailing facilities, junctions, etc on the *autoroutes*. IGN regional maps are an alternative to Michelin, and IGN local large-scale maps are ideal for walking.

Museums

Basic opening times for most museums in the region are 0900–1200, 1400–1800, closed Mon or Tue and some national holidays, with many variations (sometimes with different opening times on different days and different months). Hours are often extended in July and August.

Opening times

Shops: typically Tue-Sat 0900–1200 or 1230, 1500–1900. Food shops may open earlier in the morning, but later in the afternoon, and some (especially *pâtisseries*) open on Sun am. In cities, tourist centres or resorts shops may keep longer hours or stay open all day every day.
Department stores: Mon–Sat 0900–1830 (often with one or more later evenings per week).
Hypermarkets: Mon–Sat 0900–2200.
Banks: either Mon–Fri or Tue–Sat 0900–1200, 1400–1700, with local variations. Banks always close on local and national holidays.
Petrol stations: usually around 0700–2200 daily.
Post offices: Mon–Fri 0800–1900, Sat 0800–1200. Stamps and envelopes can usually be bought from newsagents.

Insurance

UK citizens should travel with Form E111 entitling reimbursement of part of any medical expenses incurred, as well as travel insurance covering medical emergencies. All others are advised to have full medical cover as part of their travel insurance policy. For motorists, third-party insurance is compulsory. Comprehensive motor insurance issued by UK insurers is valid in the EU (a Green Card is no longer required, though some insurers wish to be informed that you are going abroad).

Regional Nature Parks

Regional Nature Parks control and oversee development in unique or threatened natural and cultural environments. The Loire region contains one Regional Nature Park, Loire-Anjou-Touraine, lying between Angers and Tours, and reaching south as far as Richelieu. For information, contact the Park's office at: *Maison du Parc, 7, r. Jeanne d'Arc, 49730 Montsoreau; tel: 02 41 53 66 00, fax: 02 41 53 66 09, e-mail: info@parc-loire-anjou-touraine.fr, www.parc-loire-anjou-touraine.fr*

Tourist offices: usually 0900–1200, 1400–1800 Mon–Sat. Longer hours, and no midday closing, in season.
Businesses: Mon–Fri 0900–1200, 1400–1800.
Bars: 0700 or 0800 to 2300 or 2400. Some stay open later, especially in resorts.
Restaurants: 1200–1400, 1900–2200. Most restaurants have one or more days off per week.
Churches: usually 0900–1700 daily.

Packing

Bring a hat, sunglasses, light clothes, cool footwear, plus a sweater and light raincoat. If you're planning to visit upmarket night spots or classical concerts, a smart dress or jacket or smart casual wear could be appropriate. It can be cool even on summer evenings, and if you are attending outdoor evening events such as a *son-et-lumière*, it's wise to be prepared. In winter, take a thick sweater and warm coat.

Postal services

Postcards and letters weighing up to 20g are charged at the same rate for all EU destinations, with delivery within a few days. Stamps are available in newsagents and tobacconists. Airmail rates for letters to other destinations are much higher and items have to be weighed at a post office (indicated by a PTT sign). Letter boxes are yellow.

Sport

River cruising – most of the Loire is too difficult for inexperienced sailors, but certain sections of the Loire, as well as the region's other rivers, provide plenty of scope for river cruising, especially along the Cher and the Loir. Several foreign and local hire companies and package operators provide craft and make all arrangements.
Walking – the region is criss-crossed by marked footpaths, especially through the forests and along the river banks. The Angers, Tours and Orléans tourist offices have information for ramblers.
Cycling – a relatively easy region for cycling, this is a popular way to explore along the major rivers and forests.
Golf – there are around 20 excellent golf courses in the Loire Valley.
Riding – there are several riding schools and centres, notably the National Riding School at St-Hilaire-St-Florent, near Saumur. For information on riding holidays, contact the **Association Régionale de Tourisme Équestre** at the following addresses:
for Val de Loire Océan region (western *départements*) – *La Senserie, 44522 La Roche-Blanche, tel: 02 40 98 43 66;* for Val de Loire Centre (central and eastern *départements*) – *Maison des Sports, 32 r. Alain-Gerbault, 41000 Blois, tel: 02 54 42 95 60.*

Public holidays

I Jan: New Year's Day
Mar/Apr: Easter Monday
I May: Labour Day
8 May: VE Day
May: Ascension
May/June: Pentecost (Whit Monday)
14 July: National Day
15 Aug: Assumption
I Nov: All Saints
11 Nov: Armistice Day
25 Dec: Christmas
When a national holiday falls on a Sunday, the next day is taken as a holiday instead.

Public transport

Town buses – called *bus* – are available in all cities from about 0700–2100.

Trains are useful for excursions, with stations at almost all towns.

Taxis are available in all towns; these are licensed private cars, which usually have to be called by phone.

Safety and security

All towns and rural areas included here are generally very safe. However, it is wise to take certain precautions: do not wear ostentatious jewellery, openly handle large sums of cash, or leave anything of value on view in cars. To call the police, dial 17.

Telephones

With few exceptions, public phones in France require a pre-paid phone (*une télécarte*), available from newsagents, tabacs and other shops.
Directory Enquiries: 12.
Operator: 13.
Police: 17.
To call the UK from France, the international dialling code is 00 44. The code for Australia is 00 61, USA and Canada 00 1, New Zealand 00 64. Calling from the UK or any other country, the code for France is 00 33.

Time

France uses Central European Standard Time and Central European Daylight Saving Time. These are one hour ahead of UK time and five hours ahead of US Eastern Standard Time. Central European Daylight

Tipping

Restaurants – included, not necessary.
Bars – included, not necessary, but you could leave a few cents.
Taxis – up to 1€.
Hotels, room service – included, not necessary.
Tour guides – 1–2€
Toilet attendants – a few cents.

Toilets

Usually called WC (pronounced *veh-seh*) or *toilettes*. Free or small charge in bars. Small charge for attended public toilets, no charge if not attended. Many are automatic self-cleaning (these can be unsafe for children).

Saving Time ('Summer Time') starts at 0200 on the last Sunday in March and ends at 0300 on the last Sunday in October.

Travellers with disabilities

For parking, the orange card scheme applies in France. For the removal of any doubt, replace your orange card with the new Europe-wide blue card. Vehicles modified for a disabled driver and showing 'disabled' on the registration document are entitled to lower autoroute tolls.

Accessibility information for tourists available from:

Association des Paralysés de France *17 blvd Auguste Blanqui, 75013 Paris, tel: 01 40 78 69 00.*

CNFLRH *236bis r. de Tolbiac, 75013 Paris, tel: 01 53 80 66 66.*

RADAR *12 City Forum, 250 City Rd, London EC1V 8AF, tel: 020 7250 3222.*

World Heritage Site

The Loire Valley was declared a World Heritage Site in the year 2000.

Driver's guide

Breakdowns

Hazard warning lights or a warning triangle are compulsory (most motoring organisations recommend you have both). On *autoroutes* (motorways), use the red emergency phones provided every 2km. Approved recovery vehicles will be sent and a fixed fee charged (around 35€; more at night, weekends and during holidays). On other roads, members of motoring organisations with European cover should contact their emergency phone number. Those without European cover should simply make contact with a local garage.

Accidents

If you are involved in a road accident you must stop the vehicle immediately, with minimum obstruction to traffic. If anyone has been injured, or either party is under the influence of alcohol, the police must be called. French motorists will probably complete a *constat* (an insurance form verifying the facts) and all parties must sign to show that it is an accurate account. Non-French motorists should simply exchange details with the other parties.

It is worth knowing that a pedestrian under 16 or over 70, or a severely disabled person, cannot be held responsible for an accident. The *Ponts et Chaussées* (bridges and roads) authority may be liable for an accident due to poor road surface or faulty traffic light. A hitch-hiker may claim against his driver even if not responsible for the accident.

Caravans and camper vans

On hills, watch out for signs applying a lower speed limit for caravans. Before setting out, check that brake and other cables to the caravan are firmly in place and correctly adjusted, and that caravan tyres are of the same size and type and in sound condition. The make and serial number of a caravan must be clearly displayed. When making stops, remember that stopping overnight in a caravan or camper van is only permitted on campsites or at other authorised locations.

Driving conditions

Motorways are called *autoroutes* in French – they are of high standard, with frequent service stations where food and sometimes accommodation is available. Main roads (N or RN) are called *routes nationales*. Secondary roads (D) are called *routes départementales*. The extensive network of clearly marked, straight, well-maintained D roads in France makes it easy to avoid busy main highways.

Main highways are generally well maintained and of high standard and are kept clear in snowy weather. Roads in town may be of poor standard, and are often cobbled. While locals may drive normally over cobbles, it would be wiser to protect your car's suspension by driving gently on these streets. Some country lanes may be of a poor standard, too.

Autoroutes in the Loire Valley

Most of the Loire Valley region is served by *autoroutes*. The A10 (Paris–Bordeaux) runs between Orléans and Tours. The A11 (Paris–Nantes) gives access to Chartres and Angers and the western part of the region. The A71 runs from Orléans to Bourges. A short stretch of the valley west of Tours has no autoroute access; the A85 then starts and continues to Angers and Nantes. Website www.autoroutes.fr gives information on autoroutes, including tolls.

Car hire

Car hire is very widely available all over France from both major international and local firms. Prices are generally higher than in other countries.

Driving rules

It's important to understand the *Priorité à Droite* rule, the main cause of accidents involving foreign drivers in France. The rule is this: drive on the right and always give way to anything approaching from the right, except where signs indicate to the contrary. There is one other exception: vehicles emerging from private property don't have priority over traffic on the public highway.

Be especially careful in the following situations:
- where two major highways merge - watch for priority signs;
- in towns, where traffic coming from side roads on your right may drive out as if on a 'green light', even if you are on the main road;
- at roundabouts. Most roundabouts give priority to vehicles already on the roundabout (as in the UK). If you see signs reading *Vous n'avez pas la priorité* and/or *Cédez le passage* ('You don't have priority' or 'Give way'), this is the case. If there are no such signs, the usual priority rule applies, so traffic already on the roundabout has to give way to traffic entering it. Remember to go round the roundabout in an anticlockwise direction!

Also, take extra care when overtaking – driving on the right in a right-hand-drive car makes it difficult to see oncoming traffic.

Documents

Insurance and car registration papers and a full driving licence must always be carried when driving. A full UK or other western European or US driving licence is accepted. The minimum driving age for a car or motorcycle is 18.

Drink-driving laws

In France, the maximum legal level of alcohol in the blood is 0.05 per cent. Depending on the amount of excess, penalties range from on-the-spot fines, impounding of the vehicle, confiscation of driving licence, and so on, up to a jail sentence.

Fuel

Regular unleaded (*essence sans plomb*), high-octane unleaded (*super sans plomb*) and diesel (*gasoil or diesel*) are all widely available. Leaded petrol is almost impossible to find. Petrol prices are a little higher than

Road Signs

Visual signs:
rectangular yellow sign –
your road has priority

yellow rectangle crossed
out – you no longer have
priority

Text signs:
Chaussée déformée –
uneven surface

Gravillons – loose chippings

Nids de Poules – not 'hens'
nests' but potholes

Passage protégé – you have
priority

Rappel – literally
'reminder' – a restriction
already indicated is still in
force (such as a reduced
speed limit)

in the UK except for diesel, which is much cheaper. Credit cards are widely accepted at petrol stations, but not universally; be sure to know your PIN number as customers are sometimes required to 'verify' the card by tapping in their PIN on a keypad. Travellers' cheques cannot usually be used to pay for petrol.

Information

The *Bison Futé* organisation provides traffic information and organises alternative routes (*Routes Bis*) to avoid congestion. They publish an annual map, available free from tourist offices and some gas stations. For comprehensive up-to-the-minute traffic information, visit their website: *www.bison-fute.equipement.gouv.fr/* or, for AA Road and traffic conditions in Europe: *www.aaroadwatch.ie/driving_europe.asp*

Insurance

Third-party insurance is compulsory. Comprehensive insurance issued by UK insurers is valid in the EU (a Green Card is no longer required, though a few insurers still wish to be informed that you are going abroad).

Seat belts

Seat belts must be worn at all times in both the front and back of the car, except in older vehicles which have no seat belts fitted. Children under ten are not allowed to travel in front seats (except babies up to nine months weighing under 9kg and seated in a rear-facing baby seat). Even in rear seats, children must use seat belts. Although children over ten may travel in the front of a car, remember that airbags can kill a child or small adult.

Lights

Dipped lights and main beam must be adjusted using headlight deflectors to avoid dazzling oncoming drivers when driving on the right. Dipped lights must be used in rain and poor visibility as well as after dark. Motorcycles over 125cc must use a dipped headlight at all times.

Parking

The Loire Valley region is predominantly rural, with few busy urban areas other than along the river Loire itself. Parking is not usually a problem outside large towns. However, in town centres, especially Tours, Amboise, Blois and Orléans, cars left in no-parking zones are generally quickly towed away without warning – often within ten minutes of parking. Kerbside signs always make it clear what the parking regulations are in each street.

Police

Law enforcement in France is perfunctory and severe. French police (*gendarmes*) have generally not been to charm school and have considerable powers. Many offences, including speeding, not stopping at a Stop sign, overtaking where forbidden, driving with worn tyres, and not wearing a seat belt (or a helmet, for motorcyclists), are punishable by an on-the-spot fine of as much as 60€. Issuing a receipt is part of the on-the-spot procedure – always be sure to get one, and keep it carefully. More serious motoring offences such as drink-driving are liable to impounding of the car, heavy fines, or imprisonment. Drink-driving enforcement has recently been tightened up.

Safety and security

Ensure tyres are in good condition and properly inflated – worn tyres can incur on-the-spot fines. Motorcyclists must wear a helmet. Glasses wearers should carry a spare set. It is wise to carry spare bulbs for the lights.

Crime is not a problem in the Loire Valley, but it's a wise precaution everywhere to put all valuables out of sight when leaving your car parked.

Speed limits

Speed limits reflect road conditions, and variable limits are used on some busy roads so watch for signs. In normal conditions, limits are generally 50kph (31mph) in town, 90kph (55mph) out of town. The limit is generally 110kph (68mph) on dual carriageways, and 130kph (80mph) on motorways (sometimes lower on toll-free motorways). Motorways often also have a minimum fast lane speed of 80kph (49mph). Signs indicate lower speed limits for wet weather or fog. New drivers (first two years) must also keep to limits about 10kph lower than indicated.

Getting to the Loire Valley

From the UK

Option one: just get in your car and go

France's impressive and ever-increasing network of *autoroutes* (motorways) makes driving to the area straightforward. The shortest route from the UK is via St-Malo, from where Angers is only a three-hour drive.

For those travelling from the north or west of the UK, any of the western Channel crossings to Caen, Cherbourg, Le Havre or St-Malo from Portsmouth, Poole or Plymouth have the advantage of avoiding London and Paris, although they involve a longer crossing by day or overnight.

On the shorter sea route from England, the French ferry ports at the eastern end of the Channel – Boulogne, Calais and Dunkerque – all have easy links to the *autoroute* network.

Eurotunnel's car-carrying rail service through the Channel Tunnel from Folkestone takes 35 minutes and operates 24 hours a day with up to four departures an hour at peak times (when booking is recommended). Its terminal near Calais is directly linked with the *autoroute* network.

Calais-Paris is 290km. From Paris, the A83 *autoroute* goes to Chartres (85km) and Le Mans (206km), both on the northern borders of the area. The A10 (off the A83) goes to Orléans (130km) and then southwest through Blois to Tours (236km).

Option two: rail and drive

Eurostar passenger trains run through the Channel Tunnel from London Waterloo (some stopping at Ashford in Kent) to Lille (2 hours) and to Paris (3 hours), where they link with SNCF's high-speed TGV trains.

- Paris to Le Mans about 1 hour, Lille to Le Mans about 2 hours
- Paris to Angers 1.5 hours, Lille to Angers 3 hours
- Paris to Nantes 2.5 hours, Lille to Nantes 3 hours
- Paris to St Pierre des Corps (1 hour) for Tours (10-minute shuttle).

Reservations must be made in advance with Rail Europe (*tel: 08705 848 848; www.raileurope.co.uk*) or, in France, with SNCF (*tel: 0892 35 35 35; www.sncf.com*). Other express services go from Paris to Chartres (about 1 hour), Orléans (1 hour), Blois (2 hours), Amboise (2.5 hours) and Tours (2.5 hours). Local services go to Bourges, Chartres and Saumur.

Cross-Channel services

Brittany Ferries *tel: 08705 360 360; www.brittany-ferries.com*

Condor Ferries *tel: 0845 345 2000; www.condorferries.co.uk*

Eurostar *tel: 08705 186 186.*

Hoverspeed *tel: 08705 240 241; www.hoverspeed.co.uk*

P&O Portsmouth *tel: 0870 2424 999; www.poportsmouth.com*

P&O Stena (Dover) *tel: 0870 600 600; www.posl.com*

Rail Europe *tel: 08705 848 848; www.raileurope.co.uk*; or in person at Rail Europe's Travel Shop, 179 Piccadilly, London W1.

SeaFrance *tel: 08705 711 711; www.seafrance.com*

Option three: fly and drive

Nantes International Airport is served by direct flights from Paris, and also from Gatwick in the UK and elsewhere in Europe. Though west of the region, it is less than an hour from Angers by road or rail. Also worth considering are flights to Angers from Clermont-Ferrand, which connects with London City airport and elsewhere in Europe. Airlines offer fly-drive arrangements and airports have car-hire desks. Car hire is relatively expensive in France, and do-it-yourself car hire is usually more expensive than taking it as part of a package.

Option four: a package holiday

Several British tour operators offer holidays in the Loire area, including travel and accommodation. Eurocamp features pre-erected tents or mobile homes (*tel: 01606 787 033; www.eurocamp.co.uk*). Holidays by rail are offered by French Travel Service (*tel: 08702 414 243*). A selection of Gîtes de France, Chambres d'Hôtes and other accommodation is bookable through Brittany Ferries (*tel: 0990 360 360; www.brittanyferries.com*). Other operators featuring villas, apartments and houses include VFB (*tel: 01242 240 310; www.vfbholidays.co.uk*) and Vacances en Campagne (*tel: 01798 869 461*). For walking or riding holidays, and also short breaks at small hotels (often Logis de France), try Inntravel (*tel: 01653 628 811; www.inntravel.co.uk*). A full list of British tour operators to France is available from the Association of British Tour Operators to France (*tel: 01989 769 140; abtof@aol.com*), or get the free *Traveller in France* brochure from the French Government Tourist Office, 178 Piccadilly, London W1V 0AL (*tel: 09068 244 123 – premium line; www.franceguide.com; e-mail info@mdlf.co.uk*).

From other regions of France

Autoroutes and *routes nationales* link the Loire Valley with other regions of France, although most routes from the north are via Paris (*see above*). From other directions:

- A11 from Nantes to Angers, Le Mans and Chartres
- A10 from Bordeaux to Tours
- A20 then A71 from the Dordogne to Orléans
- A71 from Clermont-Ferrand to Orléans
- N7 then N76 from Lyons to Tours
- A40, N79 then N76 to Bourges and Tours
- A35, A36, A6 then N60 from Strasbourg to Orléans

From outside Europe

There are frequent direct scheduled flights to Paris from over 30 North American cities, and from Australia and New Zealand. On arrival there are fast and simple TGV rail connections, as well as car hire and road links, as described above.

Maps

Maps of the *autoroute* network, also showing service stations and their facilities, are available free from the Association des Sociétés Françaises d'Autoroutes, *3 r. Edmond Valentin, 75007 Paris (tel: 01 47 05 90 01; e-mail: asfa@autoroutes.fr)*. Three of Michelin's Regional Maps (1:200,000) cover the area, numbers 232, 237 and 238. Michelin's Departmental Maps, which are smaller but have the same scale and information, are numbers 60 (Le Mans area), 63 (west of Angers), 64 (Angers to Orléans) and 65 (east of Orléans). Michelin also offers an internet route-planning service: *www.michelin-travel.com*

Setting the scene

The Loire – Valley of the Kings

The 'Valley of the Kings' merits its epithet, for on its banks and along its tributaries are many reminders of the region's significant role in the regal history of France. Early invaders tried their luck in this fertile land before the crown established its authority in the 16th century. When the kings of France chose to bring their courts to the banks of the Loire, they built castles and lodges without parallel and invited the best artists to decorate their domains. Even the great Leonardo da Vinci lived out his last years here. It was in the Loire Valley that the French Renaissance flowered, and its artistic importance was to continue until the Revolution – even, in the case of its literary exponents, into the 20th century.

Spanning eight *départements*, and extending over one-fifth of the country, the Loire Valley is one of France's best-loved and most-visited regions. Within the area covered by this guide there are hundreds of medieval villages, scores of old towns and a handful of cities. Le Mans is the largest, with 145,000 inhabitants, closely followed by Angers with some 142,000, Tours with 130,000 citizens and Orléans with 105,000. Most famous for its glorious châteaux, the Loire Valley has much more besides to lure its visitors, to keep them entranced, and to have them return time and again.

Hills, valleys and plains

Little of the area covered by the scope of this book rises to any great height. By definition the Loire Valley is an area of lower lands, undulating through the central plains of France. It rises in the south to the Central Massif, in which the Loire itself has its source, and again slightly in the eastern parts of the Berry, where the Sancerrois hills rise to around 250m. Westward from the city of Tours, the land slopes gently all the way to the sea. Either side of the valley cut by the river, there are gentle hills which, in the Touraine area, are particularly noted for viticulture.

The River Loire runs for 1 020km flowing northwards from the foot of Mont Gerbier-de-Jonc, in the Ardèche, turning westwards at Orléans and continuing west right into the Atlantic Sea at Saint-Nazaire, beyond the port of Nantes. Its waters are composed of run-off from other rivers, the most important of which are the Nièvre, Allier, Beuvron, Cher, Indre, Vienne, Maine, Layon, Esure, Sèvre, Nantaise and the Erde, but the Loire also transports meltwater from the Central Massif, and carries a large quantity of sand and other fluvial material. To prevent the risk of flooding where the Loire has low banks, levees were constructed to contain the river – great for viewing the river and its wildlife. As another measure against the risks of rising water, and to join the various rivers within this vast basin, a number of parallel and transversal canals were built beginning in the early-17th century, and proved a boon to transport. Of these, the Canal Latéral à la Loire, Canal de Briare, Canal d'Orléans and the smaller Canal de la Dive are the most important.

Because of the rich alluvial deposits laid down by the mighty river's course, the area around the Loire has developed as prime agricultural land. And, with the successful cultivation of cereals, root vegetables, seeds, medicinal plants (yes, those poppy-like flowers in some parts really are opium), asparagus, strawberries, mushrooms, rape and sunflower seeds, apples and pears, the region has earned another sobriquet as the 'Garden of France'.

Who goes?

One of this region's greatest assets is that it is a year-round destination. Its appeal knows no seasons, and the breadth of its sights and attractions enables the first-time visitor to sample many quintessential elements of the country while holidaying here, while travellers who comes to explore France's culture or history will find more than enough to satisfy their quest for knowledge. Nature-lovers will adore its watery and wooded delights, while gourmets can take pleasure in fine cuisine and good wines, often served in a delightful setting. And it's good to know that children are more than welcome and often particularly well catered-to: water activities, zoos and animal breeding centres, and themed amusement parks ensure there is much to entertain the Loire's younger visitors.

When to come

A land-locked area of forests and agricultural land, where the hills rarely breach the 300m limit, the climate of the Loire basin is

generally mild. Its winters are tempered in the west by the proximity to the Atlantic, from where the rainfall comes, and the summers are warm but rarely too hot. It can rain at any time of the year although there is less precipitation in July and August, sometimes only falling as brief thunderstorms. In the southeastern part of the Berry, around Bourges and Sancerre, the climate is slightly more extreme. Temperatures in the hills around Sancerre will drop on cold winter nights to less than 4°C. Tours seems to have the warmest summers, averaging 19.1°C in July, and only receiving 690mm of annual rainfall. Summer months are inevitably the most popular (French school holidays, from the first week in July to the end of August, mean that all those child-friendly sights are saturated) though late April to early June, when the leaves unfurl and fields of brilliant yellow mustard and rapeseed splash the countryside with colour, are delightful. So, too, are the mellow months of early autumn. Late September and October are often warm and dry, and the gentle tones of a countryside closing down for winter can be magical. Plus, of course, the annual wine harvest enlivens the region and is cause for celebration. Although winters can be dull, weather-wise, the lack of crowds visiting monuments and dining out makes this also an appealing time to visit.

History

The Loire Valley, the geographical and cultural dividing line between north and south, has played a central, turbulent role in French history. For many centuries the power of the local nobility rivalled that of the throne, and the region was the scene of bloody and repeated territorial conflict.

Early times

Imposing prehistoric tombs and sacred sites testify to a thriving Neolithic culture in the Loire Valley as early as the third millennium BC. Celtic tribes founded settlements at Blois, Orléans and Chartres around 800BC, and came under the umbrella of the Roman empire in 51BC when France (known as Gaul) was conquered by Julius Caesar. Under the *pax romana* the region experienced 300 years of peace and prosperity. Latin speech and Roman law prevailed and a distinct Gallo-Roman civilisation developed.

The spread of Christianity coincided with Rome's decline and successive waves of barbarian invasions. Franks and Visigoths fought for domination until the Frankish king Clovis won the day in 507. His successors' endless fratricidal quarrels caused economic, social and political fragmentation. In a rare episode of national unity, Charles Martel repulsed the Moors in a battle south of Tours in 732, but the French soon took a battering from repeated Viking raids and this period was characterised by the weakness of central authority.

Barons and battles

The decline of royal authority was a major reason for the development of feudalism, a service-and-protection social system that enabled local warlords to establish enormous power bases staffed by their own private armies. From the ninth century onwards the Loire Valley was dominated by factious feudal magnates, of whom the most famous was Foulques Nerra of Anjou. His inheritance passed to the Plantagenets, rulers of territory from Normandy to Aquitaine, who also gained control of England when Henri of Anjou inherited the English crown in 1154.

The fact that the English kings were also French nobles, holding or claiming vast fiefs in France, brought the two nations into centuries of conflict, culminating in the period known as the Hundred Years' War. This flared intermittently between 1337 and 1453, and major battles between France and England were fought in the Loire region. At one point the English held most of France, including Paris, but their decision to besiege the key city of Orléans in 1428 was thwarted by the teenage Joan of Arc, who helped relieve the city and inspired a French recovery.

During the 16th century, the region became the playground of kings and dukes. Prolonged wars with Italy gave successive French kings, particularly François I, a taste for Italian art and architecture, and the Loire Valley became a great Renaissance building site. Amboise, Blois and Chambord were transformed into dazzling centres of culture and court life. But artistic and intellectual renewal was followed by nearly 40 years of ferocious religious war (1562–98) between Catholics and the Protestant Huguenots, which brought the French state close to disintegration.

The French court moved to Paris at the end of the 16th century and a strong, centralised monarchy, epitomised by Louis XIV, developed. The Loire ceased to be at the centre of French politics and turned into a quiet backwater. But political and religious peace permitted slow, steady economic growth. Market gardens and the wine trade expanded, and textile manufacturing prospered. Canals were dug to connect the wealthy port of Nantes and the Loire river directly with Paris, with the Loire remaining a key transportation route until the advent of the railway in the 19th century.

However, the Loire Valley remained essentially conservative and agricultural and, during the French Revolution, the Vendée became the centre of a violent popular uprising against the Republicans. The Grand Royal and Catholic Army (the Whites) used guerrilla tactics to gain control of nearly all the Vendée and won several battles against Republican forces (the Blues) until defeated at Cholet on 17 October 1793. Republican reprisals decimated the Vendée and, in all, more than 250,000 locals died.

Modern times

After the Revolution the region once more took a back seat but, during World War II, the Loire Valley was the demarcation line between occupied and unoccupied France and became a centre of French resistance. Many of the Loire's cities came under German control and were also bombed. Post-war, the region has traded on its rich architectural legacy, as well as its climate, its beautiful landscapes and its varied wildlife, to become one of the most important tourist destinations in France. The inauguration in 1989 of high-speed train services brought the region within fast commuting distance of Paris, and in 2000 a large zone was designated a *Patrimoine mondial*, a national heritage area, by UNESCO.

Navigating the river

The Loire's importance was acknowledged by the Romans. As a source of transport it was invaluable, for its waters were navigable from as far up as Saint-Thibault right down to the coast – a distance of over 500km. During the Middle Ages, its staging points grew into villages, gradually becoming small towns where crafts and trades were closely linked to the river. A number of interesting museums outline riverine life along its course. As we see through many of the following chapters, the Loire, its man-made canals and its major tributaries – the Cher, Loir, Sarthe and Vienne – still play an important role in transport. Working barges and boats may have reduced in numbers but, instead of cargo, the river now carries an increasing quantity of visitors and locals in leisure cruisers of all kinds.

The wines of the Loire

What to bring home

Wines head the shopping list but other bargains should include the myriad styles of porcelain, the unusual sweets, and dried fruits.

Thanks to the River Loire, the climate of the surrounding hills is tempered, providing an even range of temperatures – ideal for viticulture. Chenin noir (also known as pineau d'aunis) has been growing in the valley for over 11 centuries. Some 60 per cent of wine produced is white: the muscadet et folle blanche cultivars from around Nantes; chenin blanc (sometimes called pineau de la loire) around Anjou and Touraine; sauvignon around Sancerre and Pouilly. Thirty per cent is made up of the reds: cabernet franc, cabernet sauvignon and a lesser proportion of gamay are all grown around Touraine, while pinot noir is used around Sancerre. Some 10 per cent of red cultivars are used for rosé wines. A smaller still percentage of vines is used to create sparkling wines, of which the AOC Saumur is the undisputed king.

Wines to look out for include Chinon, Rosé d'Anjou, Sancerre (possibly the finest of the Loire's white wines), Saumur, Vouvray, Muscadet de Sèvres-et-Maine, Reuilly, Quincy and Pouilly. Some châteaux, such as Cheverny and Valençay, have their own appellations. A wine guide is an invaluable companion to the better wine estates.

If you've a taste for adventure...

...lookout for the next signpost.

You're likely to discover good local wines with a gourmet meal, but visitors are usually welcome to visit local wine estates; tourist offices in each area can provide addresses. Various wine routes are marked, notable in Touraine and around Sancerre, and visitors are welcome to stop wherever they see the sign *dégustation* (tasting). Although there is no obligation to buy, *politesse* dictates that you should perhaps purchase a bottle as goodwill. If you come across some real finds, the wine estates will be happy to ship your wines home. Note, too, that the northern part of this area is known for its cider, a powerful brew when produced in its *artisanale* form but toned down when mass-produced. Lastly, that much-loved liqueur, Cointreau, is produced in Angers.

Gastronomic temptations

It is far from easy to characterise the gastronomy of an area as vast, and as varied, as the Loire basin. Although it is not best known for its cuisine, the area does have plenty of interesting specialities to offer, and the marriage of wine sauces and fresh local produce invariably creates some culinary distinction.

Touraine is known for its *charcuterie* (pork cookery): pork *rillons* (*rilles* means little snips of pork) and *rillettes* from Tours and Vouvray are made from practically any and all parts of a pig, stewed for hours with herbs and sometimes vegetables, then poured into little pots and sealed with pork dripping. Touraine is also noted for *andouillettes* (sausages made with tripe). Anjou is known for its *rillauds* (similar to *rillettes*) and *pâtés de prunes*, while Pithiviers has a reputation for a *pâté de alouette* (lark's liver pâté) usually padded out with other livers. Elsewhere, especially in the Sologne and Berry, *terrine de gibier* (game pâté) is a firm winter favourite.

Vegetables in this area are plentiful – it is one of the country's prime areas of cultivation – but are rarely used for more than soups (lentil and pumpkin in particular) or for dressing a main dish. A little *salade composée* (mixed salad) is usually the French answer to eating vegetables, although seasonally new potatoes, beetroot and asparagus are particularly delicious. Mushroom cultivation is also important,

Truffles

Diamants noirs, or black diamonds, are the recipe for success in Marigny-Marmande. This town has styled itself as the capital of the truffle trade, and the lucrative business of growing these black diamonds has been filling the town coffers for over a century. There are more than 30ha of truffle beds and the cultivation is celebrated each 21 December with a truffle market of national importance.

especially in those chalky caves along the river banks. *Champignons de Paris* (round white mushrooms), *girolles* (chanterelles) and *morilles* (morels) are all favourites, while the popular but difficult-to-translate *bolets rude*, *shiitakes* and *cèpes* all appear on the dining table often accompanying game and frequently served lightly fried in butter and garlic with a sprinkling of parsley.

Inevitably, the rivers provide many a main course. Carp, perch, eel and salmon are all fished and served with sauces such as the *beurre blanc* of Nantes, or rich reductions made from local wines. Locally-reared meat includes beef, though probably the area is best known for its *gibier* or game: *chevreuil* (young buck) or *venaison* (venison), *sanglier* (wild boar) or *faisan* (pheasant) are usually roasted or stewed slowly. *Lapin farci* (stuffed rabbit) and *lièvre* (hare) can also be found on winter menus. Other main courses include *chapons* or capons and fattened chickens from La Flèche. *Poulet George Sand*, named for the author, is a Berry speciality in which chicken or young capons are served with a sauce made from freshwater crayfish.

The Loire produces a number of cheeses, predominantly from goat's milk. The whiter the exterior, the younger and usually milder the cheese. Yellowing crusts denote a drier cheese and a far more pungent taste. Some cheeses have been elevated to AOC (*appellation d'origine contrôlée*) status, ensuring a continuing quality. Look out for the *Crottin de Chavignol*, a small round cheese from near Sancerre; the pyramids from Selles-sur-Cher, Saint-Aignan and Valençay; the *pavé de Sologne* and ash-covered goat's cheeses from Vendôme.

On a sweet note, the area is known for its pears, strawberries, and Golden Delicious apples. Locally collected honey is an important ingredient in many desserts and *pâtisseries*. Favourite dishes include *tarte Tatin* (*see page 220*), an upside-down apple tart, *prunes de Tours* (plums steeped in red wine), *fromentée* (a wheat cake with almond milk), almond biscuits, *pruneaux de Tours* (dried prunes), *les sanciaux* (honey-filled doughnuts from the Berry) or *cotingnac* (a quince compôte), sold in a little box. Dried prunes are also a Berry speciality.

Markets

Part of the French experience is to stroll through her *marchés* (markets). Market day has traditionally been one of the week's highlights, a chance to purchase freshly picked fruit and vegetables, fill up with locally-produced cheeses, sample wines or pâtés and cold cuts, replace the chicken or rabbit stock, buy saucepans and exchange gossip. In days gone by, market folk were often the heralds of news and, although the media now fulfills this role, market day is still an excuse to get out and meet people. Today's markets tend to bring household appliances and cheap clothing into the sales place but there is also a growing demand for locally-produced breads, cheeses, jams and handicrafts. That enticing tag, *artisanale*, may not mean quality but it does mean hand-made and should invite consideration.

Snacks, treats, self-catering – and where to buy a picnic

On non-market days, head for a popular *boulangerie*, where bread will be freshly baked. A stick-like *baguette* is the usual request, though you might like to try *pain au seigle* (rye bread) or *pain complet*, a rather pale wholemeal bread. A *boulangerie* may also function as a *pâtisserie* selling delicious *friandises*: croissants, *pain au raisins* (raisin-filled pastry wheels), *pain au chocolat* or *chocolatines*. However, for the best pastries and tarts, head for a dedicated *pâtissier* – he's a professional pastry chef. If you're stuck for bread but see a sign for a *depôt de pain*, that means the shop sells bread and pastries, but they aren't baked on the premises. For those little extra goodies, you can spend hours in a *confiserie* where an amazing array of sweet confections and imaginative chocolates are often hand-created.

A *supermarché* or *hypermarché* will have all you require, and more, though it's not quite as much fun as buying in small shops. However, their range of cheeses, cold cuts and wines is usually excellent. Bread, by contrast, is not such a good buy here. If you are after a bottle of wine, don't waste time looking for an off-licence or liquor store: away from the largest cities, they hardly exist. Everyone heads for the supermarket where the choice is good and the prices are fair.

Chances are that you will not want a *boucherie* (butcher's) if all you are buying is picnic food. But French meat is excellent in quality, and often the *bouchier* will also sell cold meats, pre-cooked cold dishes, and some canned foods. For a wider range of cooked meats and other prepared dishes, visit a *charcuterie* (a pork butcher) or a *traiteur*. Watch out though for the *boucherie hippophragique* or *boucherie chevaline*: these butchers deal only in horse meat.

Tourist offices

Tourist offices have a confusing number of names in France. They are usually known as:
- Office de (or du) Tourisme;
- Bureau de (or du) Tourisme;
- Syndicat d'Initiative;
- OTSI (standing for Office du Tourisme/Syndicat d'Initiative).

In this book we have called them all 'Tourist Office'. As a general rule, they are open Mon–Sat 0900–1200, 1400–1800, but with longer hours in July and August. Note that the departmental tourism offices, listed as the *Comité départemental de tourisme*, are not open to public visitors, but are happy to answer queries by phone, letter or e-mail.

Highlights

Best cathedrals
- Cathédrale de St-Etienne, Bourges (*see page 263*)
- Cathédrale Ste-Croix, Orléans (*see page 244*)
- Cathédrale St-Gatien, Tours (*see page 46*)
- Cathédrale St-Julien, Le Mans (*see page 166*)
- Cathédrale Notre-Dame, Chartres (*see page 186*)

Best churches
- Cunault (*see page 107*)
- St-Benoît, St-Benoît-sur-Loire (*see page 246*)

Best châteaux
- Château d'Angers (*see page 140*)
- Château d'Azay-le-Rideau (*see page 70*)
- Château de Brézé (*see page 107*)
- Château de Chambord (*see page 234*)
- Château de Chenonceau (*see page 59*)
- Château de Grand-Lucé (*see page 177*)
- Château de Saumur (*see page 120*)
- Château de Serrant, St Georges-sur-Loire (*see page 135*)
- Château de Villandry (*see page 78*)
- Château du Lude (*see page 152*)
- Château d'Ussé (*see page 77*)
- Château Royal de Blois (*see page 206*)
- Château Royal, Amboise (*see page 54*)
- Château Sully-sur-Loire (*see page 258*)

Best museums
- Musée Bertrand, Châteauroux (*see page 273*)
- Musée de l'Automobile de la Sarthe (*see page 178*)
- Musée Jean Lurçat et de la Tapisserie Comtemporaine, Angers (*see page 145*)
- Musée Maurice Dufresne, Marnay (*see page 74*)

Best towns
- Briare (*see page 250*)
- Le Mans old town (*see page 164*)
- Loches (*see page 98*)
- Romorantin-Lanthenay (*see page 220*)

Best villages
- Asnières-sur-Vègre (*see page 173*)
- Crissay-sur-Manse (*see page 80*)
- Montrésor (*see page 100*)

Best for wine-tasting
- Angers (*see page 138*)
- Grand Châteaux: Tours–Blois route (*see page 54*)
- Saumur (*see page 118*)
- Upper Reaches route (*see page 250*)

Best for caves
- Grand Châteaux: Chinon–Saumur route (*see page 70*)
- Le Loir: Vendôme–La Flèche route (*see page 148*)

Best for children
- Château d'Ussé (*see page 77*)
- Doué-la-Fontaine zoo (*see page 109*)
- Grottes Pétrifiantes, Savonnières (*see page 76*)
- Musée Maurice Dufresne, Marnay (*see page 74*)
- Musée du Masque, St-Hilaire-St-Florent (*see page 113*)
- Saint-Aignan zoo (*see page 221*)

Best son-et-lumière
- Bourges (*see page 264*)
- Château d'Azay-le-Rideau (*see page 70*)
- Château de Chenonceau (*see page 59*)
- Château de Montsoreau (*see page 112*)

Tours

Ratings

Architecture	●●●●●
History	●●●●●
Restaurants	●●●●●
Street life	●●●●○
Entertainment	●●●●○
Museums	●●●○○
Shopping	●●●○○
Children	●●●○○

The city of Tours, capital of the Loire Valley region, has no great Renaissance château of its own. Yet, to the French mind, Tours is the very essence of what these palatial, aristocratic Renaissance homes are all about. The city has a long reputation for civilisation, culture and refinement. Great restaurants, chic shopping, style and flair the city possesses in plenty and, even in today's France, the Tours accent is considered the 'best' in the land. The old quarters down by the riverside, with a grid of streets laid out by the Romans, remain attractive and atmospheric. Even its appearance (apart from some hasty building to repair wartime damage) seems elegant, a black and white city, smart in tufa and slate. The more modern quarter has benefited in recent years from some stylish, attention-grabbing new architecture. There's a cheerful, bright quality to the light, and Tours is still, as Balzac described it, 'a smiling city'.

Getting there and getting around

ⓘ Tours Tourist Office 78–82
r. Bernard Palissy (opposite railway station); tel: 02 47 70 37 37, fax: 02 47 61 14 22, e-mail: info@ligeris.com; open 16 Oct–15 Apr 0900–1230, 1330–1800 Mon–Sat, 1000–1300 Sun and hols, rest of year 0830–1900 Mon–Sat; 1000–1230, 1430–1700 Sun and hols.
The tourist office provides information, maps, and bookings for events, hotels, excursions, etc.

By road
Autoroute A10 (Paris–Bordeaux) and major roads N152 (Loire Valley), N10 (from Chartres) and N138 (from Le Mans) enter into the city. The city centre lies on the south bank of the Loire between the Mirabeau and Napoléon bridges.

By rail
TGV direct from Paris or Lille (same-station connection with Eurostar from London) stops at St-Pierre-des-Corps station, 3km from the city centre. A shuttle train into the central station runs every few minutes.

Parking
There are car parks on the perimeter of the old central quarter, close to pl. Jean-Jaurès, pl. des Halles, pl. de la Préfecture, and near the main station at pl. Général de Gaulle.

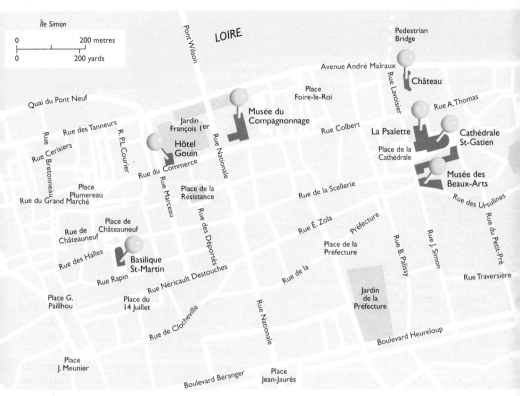

Île Simon

| 0 | 200 metres |
| 0 | 200 yards |

LOIRE

Pont Wilson

Pedestrian Bridge

Avenue André Malraux

Château

Rue A. Thomas

Rue Lavoisier

Quai du Pont Neuf

Rue des Tanneurs

Rue Cerisiers

Rue Bretonneau

R. P.L.Courier

Rue du Commerce

Jardin François 1er

Hôtel Gouin

Rue Marceau

Place Foire-le-Roi

Musée du Compagnonnage

Rue Colbert

La Psalette

Place de la Cathédrale

Cathédrale St-Gatien

Place Plumereau

Rue du Grand Marché

Place de la Résistance

Rue Nationale

Rue des Déportés

Rue de la Scellerie

Musée des Beaux-Arts

Rue des Ursulines

Rue du Petit-Pré

Rue de Châteauneuf

Place de Châteauneuf

Rue É. Zola

Préfecture

Place de la Préfecture

Rue B. Palissy

Rue J. Simon

Rue des Halles

Basilique St-Martin

Rue Rapin

Rue Néricault Destouches

Rue de la

Rue Traversière

Place G. Paillhou

Place du 14 Juillet

Rue de Clocheville

Rue Nationale

Jardin de la Préfecture

Boulevard Heureloup

Place J. Meunier

Boulevard Béranger

Place Jean-Jaurès

W www.ligeris.com (the tourist office site, in French and English. Informative and useful); www.ville-tours.fr/ (the town's official site, mainly in French, some English); www.tours-business.org/ (a local site with an economic perspective); www.jeanbardet.com/touraine/francais/tours.htm (a tourism site presented by top restaurateur Jean Bardet).

Carte Multi-Visites

The Carte Multi-Visites from the tourist office gives entry to all major monuments and sights, and a lecture tour. It is valid for one year.

Guided tours

The tourist office organises, or can book, a choice of guided tours of the city and surrounding area. A small 'tourist train' gives a 45-min tour of the city centre, leaving from the tourist office every 40–50 min throughout the day in summer.

Sights

Basilique St-Martin*

The present church, built in the early 20th century in a mock Romanesque-Byzantine style, replaces a vast basilica, famed throughout Christendom, erected in 1175 and destroyed in 1802. For centuries St Martin was revered in Tours. A Roman legionnaire, Martin was noted for the decisive moment of his life when he saw a shivering pauper by the road. Taking out his sword, he cut his cloak in two and gave one half to the poor man. The act caused Martin to become convinced of the rightness of Christianity, and he devoted the rest of his life to spreading its teaching, converting much of France, demolishing pagan shrines and building churches. In Poitou he founded the first monastery in Gaul, and became the symbol of French Christianity. Although Martin had little connection with Tours

Basilique St-Martin
€ Pl. de Châteauneuf
(off r. des Halles); open daily.

– he was from Hungary, and the cloak incident occurred at Amiens, in northern France – his relics were stolen from his Poitou monastery and brought here to encourage pilgrims to visit the city, which they did in great numbers. The importance of Tours goes back to the St-Martin pilgrimage, and his relics can still be seen in the crypt. The street outside the church, r. des Halles, roughly follows the huge nave of the original building. Lighter-coloured cobbles pick out the position of the capitals.

Cathédrale St-Gatien♦♦♦

Cathedral Pl. de la
Cathédrale, on
r. Lavoisier; tel: 02 47 47 05
19; open approx.
0830–1230, 1400–2000.

Cloître de la Psalette €
Pl. de la Cathédrale, on
r. Lavoisier; tel: 02 47 47 05
19; open daily (except Mon
and Tue Dec–Mar, and
some hols) approx.
0930–1230, 1400–1800
(1700 in winter). Not open
for visits during services.

The 19th-century architect and restorer Viollet-le-Duc described the cathedral at Tours as 'a book of architecture'. It is especially a book about French Gothic, tracing the style through all its stages from the lovely 13th-century choir through the 14th-century nave to the amazingly elaborate 15th-century Flamboyant west façade, with its three doorways, crowned with Gothic-Renaissance lantern towers which mark the first move into the next architectural style. The two towers rise from Romanesque bases standing on Gallo-Roman foundations.

Inside, the building is white, with a very narrow nave giving an illusion of height. Despite the evolving style, the building creates an impressive sense of unity. Although much of the glass was blown out in World War II, several exceptional stained-glass windows of the 13th, 14th and 15th centuries around the choir managed to survive. Note especially the superb 14th-century rose windows in the transept. Most of the original statuary destroyed during the Revolution has been replaced with 19th-century replicas. There is a good Renaissance organ.

The cathedral gives access to the **Cloître de la Psalette♦♦♦**, an exquisite 15th- to 16th-century Gothic-Renaissance structure with three galleries, including an open Renaissance staircase. La Psalette was originally for the use of the cathedral choir. Up the stairs are a former scriptorium and a vaulted library. The round stone tower beside the building is a restored remnant of the city's Roman wall.

Since 1996, the cathedral is beautifully floodlit every night; the lighting is by Bideau (a native of Tours), who designed the acclaimed Year 2000 lighting for the Eiffel Tower.

St Martin

The pious, ascetic ex-soldier is the most popular saint in France, with more than 450 towns and villages bearing his name. Fittingly for a man who turned away from war, his feast day is 11th November, Armistice Day.

Opposite
Stained glass, Tours Cathedral

Château*

Little survives of Henri II's fortress at Tours, apart from the 12th-century Tour de Guise (altered in the 15th century) and the Pavillon de Mars, added in the 18th century. The Guise connection comes from the tower's most famous prisoner, the son of the Duke de Guise, who had been assassinated in Blois. Today the château is home to two tourist attractions, the **Historial de Touraine Musée Grévin** (a waxworks museum on the theme of local history), which takes up most of the building, and a tropical **Aquarium**, which can be found on the ground floor. Look out, too, for temporary art exhibitions that are sometimes held here.

Hôtel Gouin / Musée Archéologique*

A Gothic house with rich Renaissance decoration, the Gouin mansion is set back within its courtyard on Tours' historic main street. Although much-damaged by wartime bombing, this is a good example of a prosperous 15th-century private home transformed in the Renaissance by the addition of a lavishly carved south façade and a staircase tower on the north side. Inside, the museum displays a wide variety of local relics illustrating the whole period of human habitation in the Tours area. The Gallo-Roman, medieval and Renaissance periods are well represented, and a special attraction is Jean-Jacques Rousseau's physics laboratory (18th century), brought from Chenonceau. Interesting temporary exhibitions are also held here.

Aquarium €€
Château; tel: 02 47 64 29 52; open Apr–Nov 0930–1200, 1400–1800, Closed Sun am (Jul–Aug no lunchtime closing, stays open until 1900), rest of year 1400–1800.

Historial de Touraine Musée Grévin €€
Château; tel: 02 47 61 02 95; open Mar–Oct 0900–1200, 1400–1800 (Jul–Aug no lunchtime closing, stays open until 1830), rest of year 1400–1730.

Hôtel Gouin / Musée Archéologique € 25 r. du Commerce; tel: 02 47 66 22 32; open 0930–1230, 1400–1730 (longer afternoon hours Apr–Sept).

Above
Cathedral cloisters, Tours

Musée des Beaux-Arts**

ⓘ Musée des Beaux-Arts €€ *18 pl. F. Sicard; tel: 02 47 05 68 73; open Wed–Mon 0900–1245, 1400–1800. Closed hols.*

Beside the cathedral, in the 17th- to 18th-century former Archbishops' Palace, the works of the Fine Arts Museum are displayed in a grand setting of wood-panelled walls, fine silks, tapestries and furnishings of the period. The round tower on the street side of the building is a remnant of the town's Gallo-Roman fortifications. In the centre of the courtyard stands a vast cedar of Lebanon, planted in 1809. Also in the courtyard, under shelter to one side, is the remarkable stuffed circus elephant Fritz, which had to be killed here in 1904. (Part of the Barnum & Bailey touring circus, he had turned 'rogue' and dangerous.) The treasures of the museum are mainly 17th- to 19th-century paintings and sculpture, with works by Rubens, Rembrandt, Degas and Delacroix. Striking is Louis Boulanger's portrait of Balzac in his dressing gown. Older works represented are some Italian Primitives and Mantegna's *Christ in the Garden of Olives* and *The Resurrection*.

Musée du Compagnonnage**

ⓘ Musée du Compagnonnage €€ *Cloître St-Julien, 8 r. Nationale; tel: 02 47 61 07 93; open daily 0900–1200, 1400–1800 (mid June–mid Sept: open until 0030), Sept–June closed Tue. The other sights have the same address, phone number and entry times.*

Compagnonnage means craft guilds, the historic brotherhoods of artisans qualified in a trade. An early form of trade union, a guild defended the rights, status, interests and wage levels of its members. This intriguing and unusual museum gathers together a variety of documents, tools and finished work to illustrate the guilds of such ancient trades as roofers, ropemakers, clogmakers and woodturners.

The museum is housed within the 15th- to 16th-century guestroom and dormitory of the monks of St-Julien abbey. The 13th-century Gothic **St-Julien abbey church** (founded as long ago as the 5th century) has older, Romanesque sections, including the west tower, as well as being lit through modern stained-glass windows by Max Ingrand. Another of the abbey buildings, the superbly vaulted 12th-century Celliers St-Julien in the chapter house, contains a fascinating **Touraine museum of wine**, dealing with the history, cultivation and tradition of wine. Exhibits include an original Gallo-Roman wine press from near Azay-le-Rideau.

Right
Hôtel Gouin, Tours

Accommodation and food in Tours

Jean Bardet €€€ *57 r. Goison; tel: 02 47 41 41 11, fax 02 47 51 68 72, e-mail: sophie@jeanbardet.com, www.jeanbardet.com/* For people all over France, especially celebrities, politicians and the rich, the relaxed, friendly and informal restaurant and hotel run by Jean and Sophie Bardet is reason enough to visit Tours. This imaginative establishment brings together Jean's genius as a chef, Sophie's flair as a host and hotelier, and the elegance of their white Napoleon III villa with balustrades and columns and pink flowers on the balconies. It has lovely waterside gardens, in part of which Jean Bardet cultivates his own vegetables, including rare varieties, for his kitchen – one of his 7-course set menus consists entirely of vegetable dishes. Famous wine list, very strong on Vouvray. Brilliant desserts. Upstairs, bedrooms in the Bardet villa (also called Château Belmont) are luxurious and each has its own character. Book well ahead. On the north bank, Bardet's is a ten-minute drive from the city centre.

Charles Barrier €€–€€€ *101 av. Tranchée; tel: 02 47 54 20 39, fax: 02 47 41 80 95.* A great classic gastronomic restaurant, pleasantly located overlooking a garden, Barrier and his team offer traditional dishes perfectly prepared with imaginative touches. Seafood is a speciality, with an interesting use of spices in some dishes. Excellent local wines, superb desserts. The restaurant is on the Loire's north bank, about ten minutes' drive from the city centre.

Hôtel des Châteaux de la Loire €€ *12 r. Gambetta; tel: 02 47 05 10 05, fax: 02 47 20 20 14, e-mail: hoteldeschateaux. tours@wanadoo.fr* Not far from the sights of the old town, this unpretentious mid-range hotel has adequate, well-kept rooms with TV and bath, plus private parking, at a modest price. There's a breakfast buffet, but no restaurant.

Le Petit Patrimoine € *58 r. Colbert; tel: 02 47 66 05 81.* There are several informal and inexpensive eating places along r. Colbert, in the old quarter. This is one of the very best of them. Enjoy good, low-priced eating here, with simple, classic menus well prepared. Local specialities are strongly featured, such as *Tourte Tourangelle*, pastry with pork.

Les Tuffeaux €€ *19 r. Lavoisier; tel: 02 47 47 19 89. Tuffeau* is the French name for tufa, the Loire's white stone, and this small, appealing restaurant has bare walls of it as well as a fireplace in the middle, and a friendly atmosphere. Excellent food and good wine are served, with fish dishes skilfully prepared.

Hôtel Univers (and Restaurant La Touraine) €€€ *5 blvd Heurteloup; tel: 02 47 05 37 12, fax: 02 47 61 51 80, e-mail: hotel-univers-sa@wanadoo.fr, www.hotel-univers-loirevalley.com* Around the corner from the railway station, adjacent to the central pl. Jean-Jaurès, with its flowers and fountains and wonderfully florid neo-Baroque town hall, this is the best hotel in the town centre. Quiet, comfortable and professional, the hotel is also known for an impressive frieze in the large reception area depicting all the illustrious guests who have stayed here since 1846 (including several heads of state). Good breakfasts. The long-established restaurant serves classic French gastronomic dishes expertly prepared. Expensive.

Shopping

The main shopping street is r. Nationale. For a wide selection of high-quality local specialities try Les Douceurs Tourangelles, 104 r. du Commerce. Antiques-lovers should browse r. de la Scellerie.

Markets

There are street markets every day of the week in different parts of the city centre.
- **Daily produce market** (covered market) – *Les Halles, r. des Halles; all day (am only on Sun).*
- **Evening produce market** – *pl. de la Résistance; 1800–2000 on the first Fri of every month.* An unusual, atmospheric market.
- **Flower market** – *blvd Béranger; twice weekly.*
- **Antiquarian books** – *blvd Heurteloup; Sat.*
- **Antiques** – about three markets are held each month.

Entertainment

The city enjoys a full programme of concerts, exhibitions and shows. Ask the tourist office for Tours Spectacles, detailing current and forthcoming events. Several city-centre bars have live music in the evening.

Suggested walk

Total distance: About 2km.

Time: About half a day.

Links: Tours is the starting point for two driving tours: The Grand Châteaux: Tours–Blois (*see page 54*) and The Grand Châteaux: Tours–Chinon (*see page 70*).

Route: Start at the **CATHEDRAL ❶**. Beside it is the **MUSÉE DES BEAUX-ARTS ❷**. Round the back of the cathedral in r. de la Psalette is the house of the priest as described by Balzac in *Curé de Tours*. Walk the few paces down r. Lavoisier to r. Colbert.

Detour: Continue on r. Lavoisier across r. Colbert to the **CHÂTEAU ❸**, beside the main through road on the riverbank. A pedestrian suspension bridge, the Vieux Pont or the Pont de Fil, crosses the river just here, and there is a waterside walkway.

Walk west along r. Colbert, the main street of Tours in medieval times. Mainly pedestrianised, it is a pleasant thoroughfare with many restaurants. Architecturally, every period from the 15th century to the present day is represented, including several very old half-timbered houses, as well as some ugly post-war houses. Some of the older doorposts or lintels – for example, at Nos 25–27 – have interesting carvings. Joan of Arc had her armour made at 39 r. Colbert.

At the intersection with r. Nationale turn right for the **MUSÉE DU COMPAGNONNAGE ❹**, in the old St-Julien abbey church. R. Nationale is the modern main street of Tours, which was largely rebuilt after the

Below
Place Plumereau

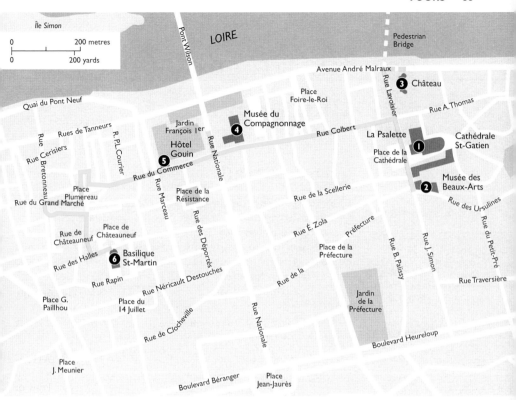

war, connecting pl. Jean-Jaurès to pont Wilson, the main Loire bridge. Balzac was born at No 39, but the house has disappeared. Return to r. Colbert.

Further along, r. Colbert becomes r. du Commerce, where the **HÔTEL GOUIN / MUSÉE ARCHÉOLOGIQUE** ❺ stands within its courtyard. R. Colbert enters the old quarter, known as Quartier Vieux Tours or Quartier St-Martin, and arrives at **pl. Plumereau**, a popular focal point, filled with café tables and enclosed by historic buildings, mainly 15th century. The mulberry tree in the centre is a reminder that Tours (with Lyon, its rival) was the capital of the medieval silk industry. Explore the lanes off the square, in which several medieval houses have external staircases and other interesting features. One of the more striking old streets is r. du Grand-Marché. Off the north side of the square, in picturesque little pl. St-Pierre le Puellier, remnants of Roman homes have been uncovered.

A few paces away is **BASILIQUE ST-MARTIN** ❻. The old tower that you will pass on the way is the Tour Charlemagne, a remnant of the original St-Martin basilica that was destroyed in 1802. As you are walking in r. des Halles on the approach to the basilica, notice that differently coloured cobbles pick out the position of the capitals of the nave of the original building.

The Grand Châteaux: Tours–Blois

Ratings

Châteaux	●●●●●
History	●●●●●
Winetasting	●●●●●
Museums	●●●●○
Entertainment	●●●●○
Children	●●●●○
Caves	●●●●○
Restaurants	●●●●○

For some 30km, the capricious Loire and gentle Cher flow alongside each other, almost parallel, gradually coming to a meeting point west of Tours. The old heart of Tours itself stands on a narrow spit of land between the two rivers, which both run through the city. The countryside to the east, as far as Chaumont on the Loire and Montrichard on the Cher, forms a narrow peninsula that feels enclosed by these majestic waterways. The area is exceptionally rich in European history, art and civilisation. An unhurried journey from Tours to Blois, with a detour along the valley of the river Cher, captures among the best that the Loire Valley region can offer. Not only the loveliest château of them all, at Chenonceau, but the finest wines, from Vouvray, and one of the most agreeable and interesting towns, at Amboise, are here together with an abundance of other châteaux, sights and attractions.

AMBOISE✦✦✦

ⓦ www.amboise-valdeloire.com/ (the town's tourism site, in several languages).

⇄ The main road into (and through) Amboise is the D751, running along the waterfront. The heart of town lies south and west of the Loire bridge.

The **Château Royal**✦✦✦ of Amboise, standing firmly on its riverside rock facing the Loire, was home to every king or queen of France for 160 years, up to the end of the 16th century. Charles VIII – who was born and died in the castle – added the first Renaissance decoration to the old Gothic fortress that Louis XI had already greatly enlarged and improved. It was here that the first Italian influence was seen in French art and architecture, when Charles returned from Italy in 1495. Louis XII continued the work with a new wing. Although François I is so closely linked with the vast château he constructed at Chambord, he lived at Amboise from the age of 7 to 27 (he became king at 24). The early years of his reign were associated with constant parties and dances and complete immersion in art and luxury, to the point of employing a team of prostitutes to service the young men of the court. In those days, the castle area was six times larger than now, and a second river ran behind it, along present-day r. Victor Hugo and pl.

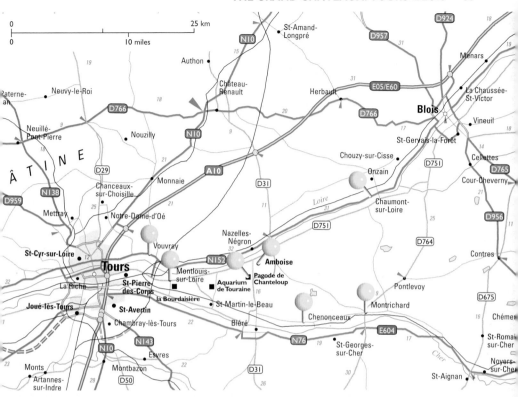

P Difficult in high season. There are small pay-and-display car parks beside and opposite the tourist office and beside the château. There is a much larger, free car park signposted Parking du Château a few minutes' walk beyond the château.

ⓘ Amboise Tourist Office *Quai Général de Gaulle; tel: 02 47 57 09 28, fax: 02 47 57 14 35, e-mail: tourisme.amboise@ wanadoo.fr; open low season Mon–Sat 0930–1230, 1400–1830, Sun, hols and eve of hols, morning only; intermediate season Mon–Sat 0930–1230, 1330–1900; Sun, hols and eve of hols, 0930–1230, 1500–1800; high season Mon–Sat 0900–2000, Sun*

Debré (where the visitors' entrance is now). Inherited by Gaston d'Orléans (Louis XIII's brother), who involved himself in conspiracies against the crown, the huge château was largely demolished in 1631, with further damage done after the Revolution. But what remains of the château still dominates this lively, popular town, and makes an impressive view from the Loire bridge.

From the château entrance, a steep ramp turns up to reach the high terrace overlooking the Loire. The little white Flamboyant chapel here is dedicated to St Hubert, patron saint of huntsmen – note the antlers on the spire, and the extraordinary carved animal frieze above the entrance. Extending away from the terrace are the attractive park and gardens, with a memorial to Leonardo da Vinci. On his death in 1519, Leonardo was buried in the château grounds. Despite claims that his grave is in the chapel, the exact location of his body is not known.

The château interior feels bare and spacious inside, and has almost no furniture or decoration; a few 15th-century pieces survive, some brought from other locations. The lovely Salle du Conseil has a white fireplace, red brick walls and a white vaulted ceiling, supported by four slender columns decorated with the ermine tail emblem of Anne of Brittany, twice queen of France. From its balcony ironwork, hundreds of Huguenots were hanged in 1560. In the Salle de l'Echanson – a kind of dining room – fine medieval tapestries depict Biblical scenes. Climb

and hols 1000–1800. Closed 25 Dec and 1 Jan.

🅠 Guided tours are organised by the tourist office, including (weekends only) a young guide in period costume who acts out the story of Amboise. A guided tour by Little Train runs Apr–Oct from beside the tourist office and from the château, 1000–1900.

🌓 **Son-et-Lumière:** For the 1-hr *son-et-lumière* at the Château, called *A La Cour du Roy François*, 250 actors illustrate the world of François I and Leonardo da Vinci. *Tel.* 02 47 57 14 47, *www.renaissance-amboise.com/; performances Wed and Sat at 2230 in June–July, 2200 in Aug–Sept.*

🅷 **Château Royal €€** *Entrance in pl. Debré; tel: 02 47 57 00 98; open Jan, Dec 0900–1200, 1400–1700 (closed 25 Dec and 1 Jan), Nov, Feb–Mar 0900–1200, 1400–1730, Apr–June 0900–1830, Jul–Aug 0900–2000, Sept–Oct 0900–1800.*

Aquarium de Touraine *€€€ On D283, near Lussault-sur-Loire; tel: 08 36 68 69 37 / 02 47 23 44 44; open Apr–June, Sept–Oct: 0900–1900, July–Aug: 0900–2000 (2300 on Sat and Sun), rest of year shorter hours, closes 1700. Closed Dec–Jan and part of Nov, Feb.*

Le Clos Lucé €€ *Av. du Clos-Lucé; tel: 02 47 57 62 88; open Jan 1000–1700, Nov–Dec, Feb–22 Mar*

Above
Amboise, view from château

to the roof of the Tour des Minimes for a view across the bridges, sandy banks and wooded islands of the Loire. The tower has a spiral ramp allowing horsemen to ride to the top, as does Tour Hurtault, on the other side of the terrace.

From the château, a 400-m walk leads to **Le Clos Lucé✦✦✦**, the grandly elegant red brick and white stone mansion in extensive gardens that was Leonardo da Vinci's home for the last four years of his life. On the way there, notice several houses on the left carved into the rock face, although they have modern façades. Leonardo moved to Amboise from Florence in 1516 at the invitation of François I, and was

0900–1800, Sept–Oct, 23 Mar–June 0900–1900, July–Aug 0900–2000.

La Maison Enchantée
€€ 7 r. Général Foy; tel: 02 47 23 24 50; open Nov–Mar 1400–1700 (closed Mon), Apr–June, Sept–Oct 1000–1200, 1400–1800 (closed Mon in Sept–Oct), July–Aug: 1000–1900.

Parc Mini-Châteaux €€€
Route de Chenonceaux; tel: 08 25 08 25 22, www.alize-parc.fr; open Apr–June, Sept–Oct 0900–1900, July–Aug 0900–2000 (2300 on Sat and Sun), rest of year shorter hours, closes 1700. Closed Dec–Jan and part of Nov, Feb.

Parc le Fou de l'Ane €€
Route de Chenonceaux; tel: 08 36 68 69 37; open Apr–June, Sept–Oct 1000–1900, July–Aug 0900–2000, rest of year 1000–1700.

given a pension as well as lodgings in this royal possession. Leonardo brought with him four of his most treasured paintings, one of them the *Mona Lisa*. It appears that he did no painting in France, instead working on his scientific ideas, which are emphasised in the displays within the house. Especially interesting are IBM's computer-engineered working models of Leonardo's 'machines'. Also worth seeing are the historic kitchens and Renaissance gardens.

Near the château, **La Maison Enchantée**✢ is an amusing miniaturised world of 25 scenes from fact and fiction – a Wild West bar room, Leonardo painting the *Mona Lisa*, a carousel – peopled by tiny working models. On a similar theme of miniaturisation, on the outskirts of town, the children's attraction **Parc Mini-Châteaux**✢✢ entertains and educates visitors of all ages. The 2-ha park contains accurate scale models of every one of the great Loire châteaux and their parks, at 4 per cent of their actual size. Amusing touches are figures in 15th-century dress, miniaturised trees and working-model TGVs and other trains. At night the châteaux are illuminated and have mini-firework displays to scale. Close by, on the same road, and run by the same company, **Parc le Fou de l'Ane**✢ gives a chance to admire donkeys from Egypt, Ireland and France. Ten kilometres west of Amboise, the **Aquarium de Touraine**✢ is a large sea-life park with 10,000 fish, a glass tunnel passing through a shark tank, a crocodile area and a 3D film show.

Accommodation and food in and around Amboise

Hôtel-Restaurant Le Blason €–€€ *11 pl. de Richelieu; tel: 02 47 23 22 41, fax: 02 47 57 56 18, e-mail: leblason@wanadoo.fr* Excellent value for good, classic cuisine with local wines. The hotel, too, in a half-timbered house in the heart of town, is plain and simple but good value for money.

Right
Leonardo's 'car', Clos Lucé

Château de Pray €€€ *Route de Chargé, off D751, 2km east of Amboise; tel: 02 47 57 23 67, fax: 02 47 57 32 50, e-mail: chateau.depray@ wanadoo.fr, http://praycastel.online.fr/.* An interesting, well-preserved Gothic and Renaissance mansion of the 13th and 16th centuries, with round corner turrets topped with black spires, de Pray was among the first family-home châteaux to open its doors to paying guests. The public rooms are filled with historical furnishings, decorations, and memorabilia, but the house is no museum – it has been altered and modernised in every century. The bedrooms are adequately comfortable, with many period touches. Attractive gardens include a large vegetable plot and a swimming pool, and have a view down to the Loire. The cosy main dining room, done up in medieval style, has wooden beams, framed portraits, a big old tapestry and crossed swords over the fireplace. The food is elegant, tasty and well-prepared. An excellent breakfast is served in the château's curious orangerie, a 'room' carved out of the tufa rock (concerts are also held here).

CHAUMONT-SUR-LOIRE❖❖

ℹ Chaumont Tourist Office *24 r. du Maréchal Leclerc; tel: 02 54 20 91 73, fax: 02 54 20 90 34; open daily all year.*

❂ Festivals: Last weekend in June – Solstice Bonfire, and market. Jun–Oct – Festival International des Parcs et Jardins; details from *Conservatoire International des Parcs et Jardins, Chaumont-sur-Loire, tel: 02 54 20 99 22, www.chaumont-jardins.com/*

🏰 Château de Chaumont €€ *Chaumont-sur-Loire; tel: 02 54 51 26 26, fax: 02 54 20 91 16, e-mail: chaumontsurloire@chateaux country.com; open 15 Mar–22 Oct 0930–1800, rest of year 1000–1630. Closed some hols.*

From the small, pretty village of Chaumont, beside the south bank of the Loire, a path leads steeply up through extensive château parkland to the impressive clifftop castle. With massive round towers in white tufa, under pointed black slate roofs, and with a working drawbridge, the château stands picture-perfect on its table of flat green turf. It commands a magnificent view of the river. Chaumont is an excellent example of a feudal Gothic fortress, with Renaissance decoration inside and out. Catherine de Medicis, Henri II's queen, acquired Chaumont after the king died, and was able to force Diane de Poitiers, who had been the king's mistress, to accept Chaumont in exchange for her beloved Chenonceau. Although a royal castle, Chaumont eventually came into the hands of Mademoiselle Say, heiress to a huge fortune made in the sugar trade. She married the Prince de Broglie, and became Princess. The last private individual to own the château, her legacy is the rich decoration of the residential apartments, including fine furniture, glazed tiles, and tapestries. Of particular note is the Council Room, in which hang some fine Flemish tapestries. It is floored with 17th-century majolica tiles taken from a Sicilian palace. The portrait medallions on display were made in the 18th century by the Italian engraver Nini, whose workshop was in the old stables. Preserved there today are the fine 19th-century stables fitted out by Princess de Broglie to the highest possible standard. These now house a riding centre. At a little distance is the château's farmhouse, today home to the Conservatoire International des Parcs et Jardins, a study and information centre on landscaping. The Conservatoire organises Chaumont's remarkable annual garden festival.

Accommodation and food in and around Chaumont

Restaurant La Chancelière €–€€ *1 r. de Bellevue; tel: 02 54 20 96 95, fax: 02 54 33 91 71.* Inevitably touristy, but this charming, simple, friendly place beside the Loire, at the foot of the château park, serves generous, tasty, classic French cooking at very modest prices.

Relais des Landes (and Restaurant La Closerie) €€–€€€ *N of Ouchamps on D7; tel: 02 54 44 40 40, fax: 02 54 44 03 89, e-mail: info@ relaisdeslandes.com* A 13-km drive from Chaumont, this pretty, flowery 17th-century farm estate is a perfect haven of unpretentious peace and comfort in tranquil open countryside 15km south of Blois. Swans swim in the lake, there are 10ha of grounds, a swimming pool, and comfortable rooms arranged around gardens. There's also an excellent restaurant.

The Chaumont International Garden Festival

Weeds, lawns, pests and flowerbeds are not the issue, beauty and charm are hardly the point, at Chaumont's astonishing annual festival of gardens. Indeed, keen gardeners may be horrified by what they see here. The Chaumont festival, held in the château's former farm, is more of an outdoor art exhibition, and treats the garden as a medium in which a full range of ideas and messages can be creatively conveyed. Most of the 'gardens' on display resemble modern art installations and may consist of ground-up tyres, smashed bricks, broken glass or rusted metal... as well as plants. Each year, artists around the world apply to be allocated one of the 27 festival plots – all are exactly 250 sq m and identically shaped – on which to deal imaginatively with the season's theme. A new theme is announced each year. At the end of the summer, the gardens are destroyed.

CHENONCEAUX✦✦✦

ℹ️ **Chenonceaux Tourist Office** *l r. Bretonneau; tel: 02 47 23 94 45; open daily May–Sept.*

Dramatic, romantic, beautiful – **Chenonceau✦✦✦** is arguably the greatest of the Loire châteaux. It is also the most popular, and the pretty village of Chenonceaux (the village has an x in its name, the château does not) is often uncomfortably overcrowded during the day. The château stands in the waters of the river Cher, a magnificent display of Renaissance architecture, with one long gallery spanning the river from bank to bank, stepping through the

Right
Gardens at Chenonceau

ⓘ Château de Chenonceau €€€ Off D176 about 1km E of Chenonceaux; tel: 02 47 23 90 07, fax: 02 47 23 80 88, e-mail: chateau.de.chenonceau@ wanadoo.fr, www.chenonceau.com/; open all year round from 0900 daily. Closing time depends on the month as follows: mid-Mar–mid-Sept 1900, 2nd half Sept 1830, 1st half Oct and 1st half Mar 1800, 2nd half Oct, and 2nd half Feb 1730, 1st half Nov, and 1st half Feb 1700, mid-Nov–end-Jan 1600. Guided tour available if required.

Waxworks Museum €€ At the château, same tel. and entry times.

☾ Son-et-Lumière: At the château, end-June to early Sept nightly at 2215.

water on arches. The château was built in 1521 and, for almost all of its history, has been owned or managed by women. Two of its proprietresses brought great festivity and society to Chenonceau: in the early 16th century, Catherine de Medicis held extravagant and ostentatious parties here, with naked nymphs, mock river battles, and fireworks, for Europe's aristocracy, and 200 years later, at Madame Dupin's huge parties for the most distinguished people of the day, Chenonceau's guests included Voltaire, Bolingbroke and Montesquieu, while Rousseau was hired as a live-in tutor.

The château is reached by an avenue of trees, or on an enjoyable meandering route through the wooded park. There are lovely gardens each side of the keep (Diane de Poitiers' garden upstream, Catherine de Medicis' downstream). The park, gardens, riverside paths and maze also make good places to relax after touring the château. To the right of the entrance, in the Orangerie and Bâtiment des Dômes, are places to eat and a **Waxworks Museum***. A drawbridge crosses to a terrace with the circular keep in the far corner. Called the Tour des Marques, this is a last remnant of a fortified manor house that originally occupied this part of the site: it bears the logo TBK (Thomas Bohier and Katherine), and Bohier's amusing motto – '*S'il vient à point me souviendra*' ('If it works out right I'll be remembered'), in memory of the Bohiers who originally constructed Chenonceau.

A bridge crosses to the main, square body of the château with corner turrets and corbels, standing on the underwater remnants of a watermill that once stood here. Inside, on both floors, four rooms open onto a central hall with curiously offset ribbed vaulting. On the ground floor, the Salle des Gardes (Guardroom) has a painted wooden ceiling and large Flemish tapestries. The Chapel has windows created by Max Ingrand in 1954 to replace those destroyed during the war. English inscriptions date from the time of Mary Stuart's stay here, when Scottish Guards accompanied her. Diane de Poitiers' room also has good 16th-century tapestries, as well as a distinctive fireplace. The modern portrait above is of Catherine de Medicis, not Diane. Among the decorations in the Cabinet Vert (Green Room), Catherine de Medicis' study, is a painting by Jordaens and a 16th-century tapestry in honour of the recent discovery of the Americas. It depicts flora and fauna previously unknown to the rest of the world. Off the study is Catherine's small Library, with a coffered ceiling dating from 1521, and a view onto the river. François I's room has some beautiful 16th-century furniture, a Renaissance fireplace, Van Loo's *Three Graces* and other paintings, and a cabinet with autographs of Diane de Poitiers, who

Below
Gallery at Chenonceau

The Ladies of Chenonceau

The château's *son-et-lumière* on summer evenings, tracing its history, is called *Les Dames de Chenonceau*. One of the most unusual features of Chenonceau is the pre-eminent role played by women in its construction, design and decoration. Although the château was built from 1513 to 1521 by Thomas Bohier, chief tax collector for Charles VIII, Louis XII and François I, he was away while in Italy while the work was in progress and left his wife **Katherine Briçonnet** to oversee the plans and construction. The basic design, style and positioning are thought to be due to her. In 1535 Chenonceau was taken by the crown in settlement of Bohier's debts and, in 1547, Henri II gave it to his mistress **Diane de Poitiers**. She added the gardens and a bridge. When Henri died in 1559, his widow **Catherine de Medicis** avenged herself on the mistress who had shamed her, forcing Diane to move out of Chenonceau (she gave her Chaumont in exchange). Catherine made a second garden, laid out the extensive château park, added the stables and other outbuildings, and turned the bridge into an elegant two-storey gallery. The next two owners were both women – Catherine de Medicis left the château to her daughter in law **Louise de Lorraine**, and she in turn bequeathed it to her niece **Françoise de Lorraine**. The next proprietor was the tax collector Dupin, but the château and estate were managed by his wife. **Madame Dupin** was so popular locally that Chenonceau remained uniquely unharmed during the Revolution. After the Revolution, the château was bought by a **Madame Pelouze**, who made several changes, removing some of Catherine de Medicis' constructions, and redecorating the interior.

At the château

- free parking
- waiter-service restaurant in the Orangerie
- cafeteria in the Bâtiment des Dômes former stables
- crêche
- play and games area
- boat rides on the Cher

we discover wrote her name as Dianne de Poytié. Several interesting paintings hang in the Grand Salon (or Louis XIV room), including a Rubens, and a portrait of Madame Dupin. The upholstery on the chairs is Aubusson tapestry. That the two flights of Italianate stairs to the first floor are straight was considered an innovation when first installed by Madame Bohier. The landing between the two flights has a balustrade with a good river view. The first-floor hall and the beautifully restored rooms on that floor are hung with remarkable 16th- and 17th-century tapestries.

The 60m-long gallery across the Cher, so beautiful when seen from outside, is less remarkable inside. Its bow windows look out onto the water, and at each end is a fine Renaissance fireplace. Stairs lead down to the interesting Renaissance kitchens. The upper floor of the gallery serves as a modern art showplace and opens onto the south bank with a drawbridge. During World War I, the gallery became a hospital. In World War II, it played a vital secret role for the Resistance because its main entrance on the north bank was in the occupied, German-ruled zone, while on the south bank it was in the so-called Free Zone ruled by the collaborationist Vichy government.

The Château de Chenonceau remains privately owned, property since 1913 of the Menier family, famous chocolate manufacturers.

Overleaf
Chenonceau

Accommodation and food in and around Chenonceaux

Hôtel-restaurant Le Bon Laboureur €€–€€€ *6 r. Dr Bretonneaux; tel: 02 47 23 90 02.* 'The Good Workman' may sound plain and simple, but here is an outstanding and long-established restaurant (in the same family for three generations) dedicated to skilful preparation of refined dishes using the best local products. The hotel, a former coaching inn, is exquisite with flowers and greenery. Book well ahead.

Hôtel-restaurant Le Cheval Blanc €€ *Pl. Église, Bléré; tel: 02 47 30 30 14, fax: 02 47 23 52 80.* Much less touristy than Chenonceaux, yet only 8km away, Bléré is a civilised little town by the Cher. This delightful family-run small hotel offers a friendly welcome and comfortable rooms with beamed ceilings. The restaurant is stylish and serves superb Michelin-rosetted food. Prices are very reasonable.

MONTLOUIS-SUR-LOIRE❖❖

ℹ Montlouis Tourist Office *Pl. F Mitterand; tel: 02 47 45 00 16, fax: 02 47 45 10 87, www.ville-montlouis-loire.fr/; open Mon–Sat 0900–1230, 1400–1830, Sun 1000–1300.*

◉ Wine-producers co-operative: *Cave des Producteurs 2 route de Saint-Aignan; tel: 02 47 50 80 98, fax: 02 47 50 81 34, e-mail: cave-montlouis @france-vin.com; opening times vary seasonally – phone for details. Free tastings.*

ⓘⓘ Château de la Bourdaisière €€ *Open May or June–Sept: daily 1000–1900, Oct–mid-Nov: 1000–1200, 1400–1800, rest of year may be closed.*

La Maison de la Loire € *60 quai Albert Baillet; tel: 02 47 50 97 52, fax: 02 47 50 81 93, e-mail: maison.loire@wanadoo.fr; open Mon–Sat 1400–1800.*

This unremarkable but pleasant little town climbs the south bank of the Loire, facing Vouvray on the other side. It gives its name to one of the region's highly reputed white wines. The Montlouis *appellation* covers just 350ha extending from the Loire to the Cher, and only one grape variety is grown, chenin blanc (known locally as pineau de la loire). The wines can be sampled in and around town at the **Cave Co-opérative** or a number of private wineries. Several have cellars cut into the tufa cliff along the main road. **La Maison de la Loire❖** has permanent and temporary exhibitions on the region's wildlife and vegetation. Montlouis was built by the influential Babou family, whose home was **Château de la Bourdaisière❖❖❖**, a short journey away. An imposing, restored Renaissance mansion in 55ha of parkland, it was constructed in 1520 for Philibert Babou, royal silversmith, and his wife, a royal mistress, the first of several to reside at the château. As well as the extensive park (restored since 1998), it has a famous 19th-century 2-ha vegetable garden where some 500 varieties of tomatoes are grown, with an amazing range of shapes and colours, among many other historic vegetable varieties. Tastings may be possible as part of the visit, according to the season.

Accommodation and food around Montlouis

Château de la Bourdaisière €€€ *Follow signs from Montlouis-sur-Loire; tel: 02 47 45 16 31, fax: 02 47 45 09 11, e-mail: labourd@club-internet.fr, www.chateaux-france.com/-bourdaisiere* The charming Renaissance château in its own parkland offers several comfortable rooms done out in grand, quasi-aristocratic style reminiscent of former residents. Good breakfasts.

MONTRICHARD❖❖

❶ **Montrichard Tourist Office** / r. du Pont; tel: 02 54 32 05 10, fax: 02 54 32 28 80; open in season 0900–1200, 1400–1800 (answering machine out of season).

❶ **Donjon (castle keep) and museum** €€ Tel: 02 54 32 05 10; open from about Easter to mid-Sept, 0930–1200, 1430–1800.

❶ **Birds of prey flight demonstrations** €€ At the keep; tel: 02 54 32 01 16; twice daily (1530, 1700) from about Easter to mid-Sept.

Spectacles Médiévales in summer daily at 1430, 1600, 1715.

❶ **Bourré caves** €€ 40 route des Roches; tel: 02 54 32 95 33, fax: 02 54 32 42 99, e-mail: andredelalande@aol.com; open Mar–Nov. The Caves Champignonnières and Ville Souterraine each have a 50-min guided tour. Tours depart at 1000, 1100, 1400, 1500, 1600, 1700, 1800 (the 1000, 1700 and 1800 tours do not run in Oct or Nov). Combined tickets available for the two tours, or to include Caves Monmousseau.

Rare mushrooms for sale before or after tour, including some new varieties being developed here.

Caves Monmousseau €€ Tel: 02 54 32 15 15, fax: 02 54 71 66 64, e-mail: monmousseau@monmousseau.com, www.monmousseau.com; open Apr–Nov daily 1000–1900 (last tour 1800), rest of year 1000–1200, 1400–1700.

Right
Donjon, Montrichard

This lively, picturesque little town rises from the Cher riverside up steep steps and narrow lanes lined with tiny white tufa houses. At the top of the town, the imposing ruins of its massive square **Donjon (castle keep)**❖ are still enclosed by remnants of once-daunting fortifications. As well as giving a wonderful view along the Cher, the keep houses a local archaeological museum and a bird of prey centre, which puts on impressive flight demonstrations. The *donjon* is also the setting for 'Spectacles Médiévales' on summer afternoons. Just below stands the Romanesque castle chapel, now the local parish church, where Jeanne de France, the disabled 12-year-old daughter of Louis XI, was married to an unwilling Louis d'Orléans. He abandoned her later to marry Anne of Brittany and be crowned Louis XII. Fine 15th- and 16th-century Gothic and Renaissance houses cluster near the church, and in r. Porte-au-Roi and other streets. Take the stairway called Petits-Degrés Ste-Croix to reach cave dwellings carved into the tufa cliff. The **Caves Monmousseau**❖ wine cellars, making a traditional local sparkling wine, have 15km of underground storage tunnels in the cliff. Tufa, or *tuffeau*, the stone used for constructing the Loire châteaux, used also to be called Pierre de Bourré, because so much of it was quarried around **Bourré**❖❖, 3km east of Montrichard. The roadside cliff between the two villages is riddled with dwellings, a silk farm, and storage areas carved out of the soft rock (some can be visited – ask at the tourist office). Impressive tours can be made in the darkness of the **Bourré caves**, labyrinthine underground tufa quarries now used for growing various varieties of mushrooms (*Caves Champignonnières*), with another section (called the *Ville Souterraine*, or 'Underground City') where cut and carved quarry walls eerily resemble real châteaux.

Accommodation and food in Montrichard

Hôtel de la Tête Noire €€ 24 r. de Tours; tel: 02 54 32 05 55, fax: 02 54 32 78 37. Unpretentious family-run hotel with simple, comfortable rooms. Ask for a room away from the road; it is prettier and quieter at the back, with a shaded terrace facing the Cher. Pleasant, reliable restaurant with modestly priced set menus.

PAGODE DE CHANTELOUP✢

Pagode de Chanteloup €€ *On the outskirts of Amboise on the Bléré road (D31); tel: 02 47 57 20 97, email: tourisme.amboise@wanadoo.fr; open May 1000–1800. June, Sept 1000–1900, July–Aug 0930–2000, rest of year 1000–1200, 1400–1700 (afternoons only in Feb; open until 1800 in Apr and Oct).*

Festival: Easter Egg Festival at the Pagoda on Easter Monday.

The Château de Chanteloup was demolished in 1830, but its curious pagoda remains. Built in 1778, inspired by the similar structure at Kew Gardens in London, the exquisitely elegant 44m-tall tower stands in a lovely lakeside setting close to the Forêt d'Amboise woodland. There is a superb view from the top. Picnic baskets are available on the site, as well as a variety of traditional games and boat rides.

Right
Pagode de Chanteloup

Above
Vouvray produce

VOUVRAY*

ⓘ **Vouvray Tourist Office** *Mairie; tel: 02 47 52 68 73; open approx. Apr–Oct 0900–1300, 1400–1830 (on Sun, am only), rest of year Tue, Wed, Fri, Sat 0900–1300 (on Fri, also 1400–1700).*

Times may vary. When closed, tel: 02 47 52 70 48 (Mairie).

Markets: Tue and Fri ams.

Festivals: Wine Fairs are held at Whitsun, in mid-Aug, mid-Nov, and at the end of Jan.

🏛 **Ecomusée du Pays de Vouvray** *€ 30 r. Victor Hugo; tel: 02 47 52 76 00; open Wed–Mon 1030–1800.*

The small, rustic village lies off the busy main road beside the north bank of the Loire, hugged by its famous vineyards. On the edges are several cave dwellings or wine cellars cut out of tufa escarpments. Among the most highly regarded of French wines, with great character and finesse, the Vouvray appellations are all produced from chenin blanc (called pineau de la loire locally). Nevertheless, Vouvray comes in several different styles, from crisply dry to richly sweet wines, still or sparkling. All should be drunk chilled. They are made by small growers in and around the village; several offer tastings. The **Ecomusée du Pays de Vouvray*** explores local history, folk culture and winemaking.

Accommodation and food in Vouvray

Le Grand Vatel €–€€ 8 av. *Brûlé; tel: 02 47 52 70 32, fax: 02 4752 74 52.* This modest but comfortable family-run hotel has a popular restaurant with excellent set menus at moderate prices. River fish is the speciality, though meat is expertly prepared too, and wines, of course, are Vouvray – the wine list features about 200 of them. Dine indoors, or on an attractive terrace with pink and white tables and chairs.

Suggested tour

www.tourism-touraine.com/ (Indre-et-Loire *département*); *www.chambordcountry.com/* (Loir-et-Cher *département*). Both in English and French.

Autoroute A10 (Paris-Bordeaux) and the N152 on the north bank, and the quieter D951 on the south bank, go to Tours and Blois. TGVs run direct to Tours from Paris and Lille (with Eurostar connection to London). There is a frequent rail service along the Loire valley between Tours and Blois.

Total distance: 95km, or 100km with the detour.

Time: The driving takes only 2hrs, but allow 2 days to visit the sights.

Links: At Tours (*see page 44*) this route connects with the Grand Chateaux: Tours–Chinon tour (*see page 70*), while at Blois (*see page 204*) it links up with that of the Cher and Sologne (*see page 214*).

Route: From **Tours**, leave town on N152, the main road (direction Orléans) on the north bank of the Loire. The road passes **Parc de Loisirs Rochecorbon**, a 3-ha family leisure park and play area, with masses of entertainment (daily 1000–2200). It takes just a few minutes to reach **VOUVRAY** ❶.

Right
Vineyards at Vouvray

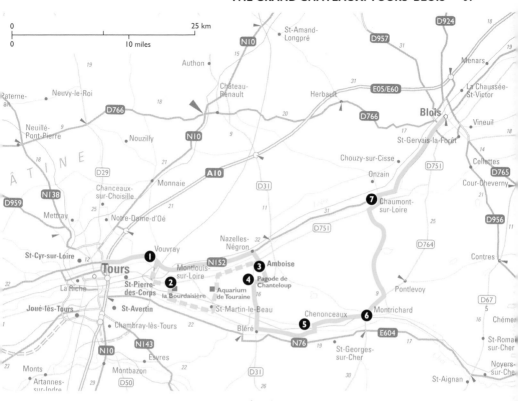

Detour: Cross the Loire here and follow signs carefully on complicated road junctions to reach **MONTLOUIS-SUR-LOIRE ❷**. Leave the village centre, again following signs carefully, to **Château de la Bourdaisière**. Using either the D751 along the Loire's south bank via Lussault-sur-Loire, or taking the cross-country route via St-Martin-le-Beau, continue towards Amboise. The **Aquarium de Touraine** lies just off D283, the road between Lussault-sur-Loire and St Martin-le-Beau. Continue into **Amboise**.

From Vouvray, continue on the Loire's north bank road into **AMBOISE ❸**. When leaving the town, the **Parc des Mini-Châteaux** and **PAGODE DE CHANTELOUP ❹** are both easily reached from D31 as it circles Amboise on the south side. From the Pagoda, take D31 to the attractive and appealing old market town of **Bléré**, turning there for **CHENONCEAUX ❺** (or travel straight from Amboise to Chenonceaux on D81 through the Amboise Forest). Follow either bank of the river Cher upriver to **MONTRICHARD ❻**. Take D764 out of Montrichard (direction Blois), and turn off onto D62 for **CHAUMONT-SUR-LOIRE ❼**. From Chaumont, take the Loire's south bank riverside road into Blois.

The Grand Châteaux: Tours–Chinon

Ratings

Châteaux	●●●●●
Architecture	●●●●
Gardens	●●●
Food and drink	●●
Museums	●●
Villages	●●
Children	●
Geology	●

This route, west of Tours, takes in a further selection of distinguished châteaux as well as offering a good variety of scenery and sights. The Loire is never far away, and vineyards, pear orchards and willow plantations flourish on its great flood plain. Each of the castles along the way has its own very different speciality – the great medieval fortress at Langeais, atmospheric *son-et-lumière* at Azay, immaculate gardens at Villandry and the 'Sleeping Beauty' legend at Ussé. In between, there are fascinating villages to discover, such as Villaines where wickerwork is made, and Quinçay, home of the ancient craft of pear-drying. A highlight, even for those not normally interested in old vehicles, is the extraordinary array of them, from a horse-drawn guillotine to children's scooters and fire engines, at the Musée Maurice Dufresne at Marnay. Meanwhile the countryside, though never spectacular, is always pleasantly rural and quiet.

Right
Azay-le-Rideau Château

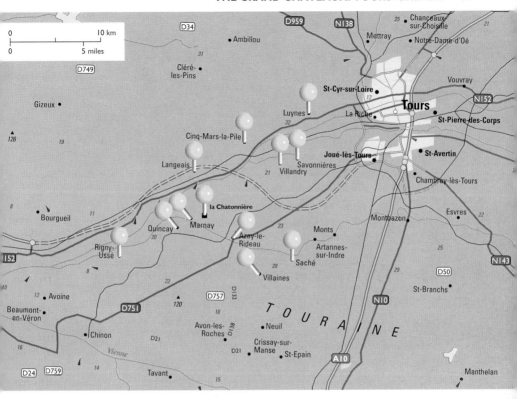

AZAY-LE-RIDEAU ❖❖❖

ℹ Azay-le-Rideau Tourist Office *r. Nationale (opposite town hall); tel: 02 47 45 44 40, e-mail: otsi.azay.le.rideau @wanadoo.fr.*

🛒 Market: Wed.

🏛 Château d'Azay-le-Rideau *Open daily except some bank hols. Son-et-Lumière Les Imaginaires d'Azay in the castle grounds daily mid-May–Sept, usually from 2230.*

🏛 Musée du Jouet € *31 r. Nationale; tel: 02 47 26 81 64; open Jun–Sept pm, then by arrangement.*

This pleasant little town is worth a visit in its own right, though the attraction for most visitors is its charming **château❖❖❖**. It has an 11th-century church, a small toy museum the **Musée du Jouet❖** which displays the lifetime collection, particularly trains, of Michel le Tenaff, a speciality delicatessen and a *salon de thé*.

The elegant Renaissance château, built by Gilles Berthelot, Treasurer to François I, is one of the Loire's most visited, thanks in part to its lovely riverside setting and extensive park. Work on it started in 1518 but after nine years, before it was completed, the king confiscated it, accusing Berthelot of embezzlement.

Slender turrets crown each corner, while the centre is notable for the ornately carved exterior of its square staircase. This is an unusual feature because most grand buildings up to that time had spiral ones. The fine rooms have impressive stone or marble fireplaces but are only sparsely furnished, mainly with portraits and tapestries. Even the kitchen is impressive, having rib vaulting and a huge fireplace. The château's *son-et-lumière* show, **Les Imaginaires d'Azay❖❖❖**, is outstanding. Spectators wander around the grounds, through trees and beside the lake, to the accompaniment of music and lighting effects which

J P Esclasse *delicatessen 22 r. Nationale specialises in home-made conserves.*

imaginatively evoke the château's heyday during the Renaissance.

Accommodation and food at Azay-le-Rideau

Le Grand Monarque €€ *3 pl. de la République, Azay-le-Rideau; tel: 02 47 45 40 08, www.legrandmonarque.com* This 200-year-old coaching inn (with later additions) has an inner courtyard shaded by trees where guests can dine during the summer months. Menus are limited but inventive.

LA CHATONNIÈRE✣

 **La Chatonnière €** *Open Apr–Nov daily.*

When the owner of this small castle decided in 1992 to replace the orchards around it with a themed garden, he enlisted the help of a gardener who had been working in the famous château grounds at Villandry. Already it is fascinating to see how the garden, divided into six themes, is gradually maturing. The *Jardin des Romances* has bowers of white roses, the *Jardin de l'Exubérance* is full of colour, and the *Jardin de l'Abondance* grows many varieties of vegetables and fruit. Further developments are planned.

CINQ-MARS-LA-PILE✣

Château de Cinq-Mars € *Open Mar–Oct weekends, July–Sept Wed–Mon.*

This small village, now virtually a continuation of Langeais, owes the last part of its curious name to the square red-brick tower, over 30m high and dating back to Gallo-Roman times in the 2nd century, that stands on a wooded ridge above its eastern approach. No-one knows why it was built. All that remains of the Château de Cinq-Mars, originally a classic feudal castle with a moat, is two fine round towers, each with beautifully vaulted rooms and lovely views over the Loire. The rest of it was demolished in the 1640s by Louis XIII's ruthless minister, Cardinal Richelieu (*see page 101*), after its flamboyant owner, the 22-year-old Marquis de Cinq-Mars, made the mistake of plotting against him. The Marquis' exploits subsequently become well known when local writer Alfred de Vigny made them into an heroic story. The gardens are informally romantic with sweet-smelling bushes, topiary and many trees.

Above
Bridge at Langeais

LANGEAIS✢✢

ⓘ Langeais and Castelvalérie Tourist Office Pl. du 14 Juillet; tel: 02 47 96 58 22; open daily except Sun pm.

ⓘ Château de Langeais € Open daily May–mid-Sept.

◖ Market: Sun am; renowned for local melons. Good selection of small shops selling local food specialities and crafts.

This pleasant little riverside town is dominated by its castle-like château✢✢, built by King Louis XI in the 1460s to establish his authority on the north bank of the Loire. Looking extremely forbidding with high, sturdy walls, three round towers and a heavily machicolated drawbridge that still works, it broods over the short main street. However, viewed from the interior courtyard, the mullioned windows and delicately pointed dormers make it seem much more like a manor house. Originally four wings were planned, but only two were built. They form a right angle and, remarkably, have been altered very little since. In 1491 Anne of Brittany and Charles VIII of France married here in secret. A tableau of lavishly costumed figures in the room where the ceremony took place depicts the event, and Anne's wedding chest is among the items on show. At the end of the 19th century, the château was owned by Jacques Siegfried, a rich businessman and art lover, who devoted many years to refurnishing it in the authentic style of the 15th century, complete with fine French and Flemish tapestries. The terraced gardens lead up to the ruins of a keep. The oldest still extant in France, it was built in the 11th century by Foulques Nerra, Count of Anjou. The suspension bridge over the Loire at Langeais, opened in 1849, has had a rather chequered history, having had to be closed three times for repairs totalling nine years.

Accommodation and food in Langeais

Errard Hosten €€ *2 r. Gambetta; tel: 02 47 96 82 12.* Only 200m from the castle, this small ivy-clad inn is family-run. The owner-chef, Yannick Errard, specialises in seasonal country produce and local wines.

LUYNES✣

Château de Luynes
Open Apr–Sept daily.

The sturdy grey stone towers of Château de Luynes, high on the hillside above the little terraced town, make it look like a real fortress. In fact it was transformed from a castle to a home 600 years ago and is now occupied by the 12th Duke. The main rooms, overlooking a charming courtyard, are sumptuously furnished with antiques and tapestries. Neatly laid-out gardens spread down the hillside. Over the years it has hosted many royal visitors, from King Louis XI of France in the 15th century to Britain's Prince Charles in the 20th.

MUSÉE MAURICE DUFRESNE✣✣✣

Musée Maurice Dufresne € *Off the D120 in Marnay; open daily; www.musee-dufresne.com*

This wide-ranging and still growing collection of over 3000 vehicles, engines and machines has been gathered over a lifetime by Maurice Dufresne, a local businessman who built up a thriving business repairing and renovating second-hand machinery. He opened the museum to the public in 1992, having rebuilt an old mill to house it. Everything on show has been lovingly restored and smartly painted. The variety is amazing, ranging from a macabre horse-drawn guillotine to a British double-decker bus. There are children's scooters, a 150-year-old hearse, a 1930s fire engine, traction engines, a World War II American tank, a 1959 shiny grey Buick, and antique farm vehicles galore. Something for everyone, in fact! Adding to their interest, a notice by each exhibit says where it was found - often abandoned and rusting in a barn.

QUINÇAY✢

Poires Tapées à l'Ancienne *Quinçay, near Rivarennes; open daily.* Pears also on sale as jam or pâtés, or in pots with wine.

The traditional way of preserving the pears grown in this area for centuries was to dry and crush them, producing *la poire tapée*. Christine and Yves Herin still use this *ancienne* method in a troglodyte cave at their home, where visitors are welcome to watch them. The whole pears are first dried very slowly in a wood-fired oven. Then they are squashed flat in a simple wooden press which expels any remaining air. The result is a delicious speciality for eating on its own or with a variety of dishes.

CHÂTEAU DE SACHÉ✢

Château de Saché *in Saché village; open Feb–Nov daily.*

This is a place of pilgrimage for devotees of the 19th-century writer, Honoré de Balzac. He was a frequent visitor as it was owned by one of his friends, and he wrote many of his famous novels while staying here. It is a large country house rather than a castle, surrounded by open parkland running down to the River Indre. Now impressively restored and furnished as Balzac would have known it in the 1830s, including reproduction wallpaper, it contains many of his personal possessions. Most of his manuscripts are covered in corrections - he was a consummate perfectionist. One room is devoted to caricatures of some of the contemporaries featured in his books; another contains the old printing presses and equipment he used while trying to earn a living in publishing.

Accomodation and Food in Saché

Auberge du XIIe Siécle €€ *tel: 02 47 26 88 77.* Balzac liked to frequent this ancient hostelry close to the château. To dine under its 900-year-old beams today, you need to book ahead; its gourmet menus have a high reputation.

Balzac

Born and educated in Tours, Honoré de Balzac (1799-1850) spent most of his working life in Paris. However, he was a frequent visitor to the Loire Valley and often set his novels here. His first attempts at writing were unsuccessful so he went into publishing instead, but fared no better. At the age of 30 he tried again, spurred on by the need to pay off his debts, and went on to produce over 90 books. They reflected contemporary society in extraordinary detail through a wide variety of vividly portrayed characters.

SAVONNIÈRES✣

Les Grottes Pétrifiantes de Savonnières € *situated left of D7 just west of Savonnières. 60-min guided tours of the caves Feb–Dec daily. Small museum, shop and wine on sale.*

The main reason to head for this riverside village is **Les Grottes Pétrifiantes de Savonnières**, two extraordinary caves, where *tuffeau* stone was quarried out of the hillside as early as Gallo-Roman times. One was discovered around 500 years ago but the other remained hidden until 1947. Over the centuries water has seeped into them from springs, creating shallow pools and forming stalactites and other curious patterns in their extensive galleries. Both can now be visited and are exciting for all ages, although children will particularly like the models of dinosaurs and other animals displayed in alcoves. Everything has been petrified by the dripping water, leaving it coated in creamy white calcium. The museum shop at the entrance sells a range of small items such as vases, dishes and carvings that have been petrified through being left in the caves for at least six months. Visits end with a glass of local wine served in a large grotto that has been transformed into a bar, at the far end of one of the caves.

Below
Fishing on the Indre

Above
Château d'Ussé

USSÉ✦✦✦

Château d'Ussé €€
for guided (obligatory)
visits of the interior; € for
grounds, chapel and
'Sleeping Beauty' tower only.
Open mid-Feb–mid-Nov daily.
A Boutique Gastronomique
next to the castle has a
selection of local
specialities including wines,
jams, biscuits and sweets.

Set against a wooded hillside overlooking the River Indre, **Château d'Ussé✦✦✦** looks as much like Sleeping Beauty's castle as one could wish. Covered with pointed turrets and mysterious little windows, it inspired the French writer Charles Perrault to use it as the setting for his version of the famous fairytale, after he was invited to stay there by his friend, the Count of Blacas, an ancestor of the present owner who is an international lawyer. Today's visitors can climb 84 steps up a spiral staircase in one of the towers to see life-size tableaux depicting the story. Occupying the site of a medieval fortress, the building dates from 1642 but was extended during the following two centuries to create an elegant family home to which formal gardens and an orangery were added. The main part of the castle is furnished with original pieces and many of the walls are covered in Flemish tapestries. The grounds also contain a 16th-century chapel in pure Renaissance style with fine stone carving and wood panelling.

Accommodation and food at Ussé

Le Clos d'Ussé € *Rigny-Ussé, tel: 02 47 95 55 47.* An intimate eight-room hotel with a terrace restaurant in the long street below Ussé castle.

VILLANDRY❖❖❖

Château de Villandry *Open mid-Feb–mid-Nov daily. Details of all the plants are displayed on boards.*

Above
Villandry, château and gardens

The Château de Villandry's chief attraction is its outstanding gardens, but it would be a mistake to underrate the building itself which has elegant classical façades and an ornamental moat. When Joachim de Carvallo, a Spanish doctor, bought the estate in 1906, he and his family devoted themselves to restoring the extensive gardens to their original formal Renaissance style. The best way to appreciate their scale and precise detail is to look down on them from the top of the château's keep. There are three large terraces to walk around, as well as a maze. The top terrace has a small lake and water garden, the middle one is a flower garden where neat box hedges form geometric shapes, and the bottom level has seasonal fruit and vegetables including melons (a speciality of the area), artichokes and asparagus, growing in precise patterns bordered by box and yew hedges.

Accommodation and food at Villandry

Auberge Le Colombieu € *2 r. de la Mairie, Villandry; tel: 02 47 50 07 27.* A short walk from Villandry castle, this charming family-run hotel and restaurant in the centre of the village occupies three converted cottages set around a small courtyard.

L'Etape Gourmande € *Domaine de la Giraudière, ask in Villandry for directions; tel: 02 47 50 08 60.* A lovely farmhouse restaurant a few kilometres from Villandry is well-worth seeking out for delicious and simple meals featuring their own goat's cheese, complemented by excellent local wines. Visit the dairy and buy more cheeses if you like.

VILLAINES-LES-ROCHERS*

Villaines-les-Rochers Co-opérative de Vannerie de Villaines; *admission free. Large shop open mid-Oct–Mar daily, except Sun morning (no production to watch at weekends).*

Museé de la Vannerie *22 r. des Caves-Fortes; open May–Sept, Tue–Sun pm.*

Over 150 years ago, one of France's earliest co-operatives was set up in this straggling village where wickerwork has been the main source of income since the Middle Ages. Baskets and furniture made by local craftsmen – who grow and gather the canes from the riverside willows – are on sale in workshops throughout the village and also at the workers' co-operative, where visitors can watch the different products being made. In the village's small museum, old basket-making implements are on show, together with a variety of antique wickerwork items.

Right
Basket-maker, Villaines

Suggested tour

L'Auberge à
Crissay € tel: 02 47
58 58 11, e-mail:
CrissayAuberge@wanadoo.fr
All four rooms in this
recently-converted village
inn open onto a terrace
garden beneath the ruins
of a castle and have
glorious views over the
quiet Manse valley. It also
serves simple meals. A
truly rural retreat.

Total distance: 104km. The detour to Crissay adds 22km.

Time: 2 hours' driving time, but allow two days for the full route. Those with limited time should concentrate on Villandry, Azay-le-Rideau and Ussé.

Links: At Tours the route links with the Grand Châteaux: Tours–Blois tour (*see page 54*) and the two routes could easily be combined into one longer tour, starting from Blois and driving the first tour in reverse order. Likewise, at Chinon, the route links with the circular South Touraine tour (*see page 92*), and these (or indeed all three) could be linked into a major tour of this part of the region.

Route: Leave **Tours** (*see page 44*) along the north bank of the Loire on the N152 to see **LUYNES ❶** and its magnificent castle. Then, after a further 10km, turn right to **CINQ-MARS ❷** and then **LANGEAIS ❸**. Leave Langeais across its handsome suspension bridge over the Loire, turning immediately left onto the D16 which goes northeast following the river closely to **VILLANDRY ❹**. On this pleasant country road, just before **SAVONNIÈRES ❺**, you see **Les Grottes Pétrifiantes** beside the road at the foot of the wooded hillside. Then, passing through the village itself, animal-lovers should look out for the unusual doorway of the church on the left as it is carved with doves and other animals, though now eroded by time. After the church, turn right past the *Mairie* and shortly fork right following the signs to **Druye**. Here the road climbs up to large expanses of open fields, crossing the railway and the new A85 motorway to continue along the D751 to **SACHÉ ❻**. Leave Saché on the D17 signed for Azay-le-Rideau, turning left onto the D217 to go to **VILLAINES-LES-ROCHERS ❼**.

Detour: Continue on the D217 for a detour to **Crissay-sur-Manse**. Crissay has been designated one of France's *Plus Beaux Villages* (most beautiful villages). Nestling below the ruins of its medieval castle are an old church with a spire, a handful of 15th-century houses with small turrets, and two tiny shops. One sells antiquarian books, the

Right
Crissay village

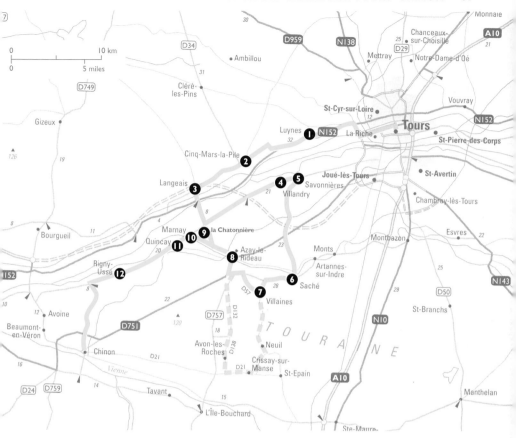

other delicious home-made honey. Leaving the D21 shortly after Crissay, a narrow country road leads past cornfields to another tiny village, **Avon-les-Roches**. Its small 12th-century church is one of the route's real gems, particularly the porch which has delicately carved pillars and arches. Visitors who want to see inside can borrow the key from the *Mairie* round the corner. Next, turn right onto the long straight D132 which leads directly to Azay-le-Rideau. On the way it crosses a military training area where you pass a small memorial on the right to members of the French Resistance who were executed at the nearby Ruchard barracks in 1944.

From **Villaines** take the D57 for 6km to **AZAY-LE-RIDEAU** ❽ . Leave Azay on the D57 to visit **LA CHATONNIÈRE** ❾ gardens and then return to the junction with the D120 which leads to **Musée Maurice Dufresne** at **MARNAY** ❿ . From there the D7 continues to **QUINÇAY** ⓫ and on to **USSÉ** ⓬. Leave the village on the D7 beside the Chinon forest, turning left onto the D16 at **Huismes** to continue to Chinon (*see page 82*).

Chinon

Ratings

Restaurants	●●●●●
Châteaux	●●●●○
History	●●●●○
Architecture	●●●○○
Historical sights	●●●○○
Walking	●●●○○
Winetasting	●●●○○
Museums	●●○○○

Wine is Chinon's primary concern, which may explain why this small, pretty town has never become swamped with visitors, despite its attractive riverside setting and 2000 years of history. You sense that its inhabitants are too deeply steeped in the trade to want to get involved in anything as frivolous as tourism. And yet Chinon has much to offer the interested visitor – after all, it was here that Joan of Arc first stepped into the pages of history and Richard the Lionheart lay in state – without the trappings of tourist exploitation that sometimes accompany such an illustrious heritage. Built in creamy *tuffeau* stone with grey rooftops, Chinon nestles between a wooded ridge, topped by the ruins of its once-formidable castle, and the serene River Vienne. All the sights are easily manageable on foot and could be covered in a single day, although this would prevent you from doing justice to the outstanding choice of restaurants. From their calibre it's clear that the people of Chinon take their food as seriously as they do their wine.

Getting there and getting around

ⓘ **Chinon Tourist Office** *Pl. d'Hofheim; tel: 02 47 93 17 85, www.chinon.com; also at the castle, r. François Mitterrand Jul–Aug.*

🛒 **Market:** Thur, pl. Jeanne d'Arc; produce morning only, clothes, etc all day. A recent Chinon speciality is wine jam.

By road
Leaving the A85 at exit 5 (where it currently ends), the town centre is a 14-km journey south along the D749. From Tours the shortest route is on the D751.

By rail
Trains operate between Chinon and Tours. There are also steam excursions in summer departing from Richelieu (35km southeast).

Parking
In the town centre, parking is allowed beside the River Vienne and on other streets, except in the old town. Meters operate 0900–1200 and 1400–1800 on the central streets (maximum 1hr 20min), or you can stay in the town's car parks for up to 3hrs. Free parking Sun and Mon and near the castle or streets further afield. Several central streets are

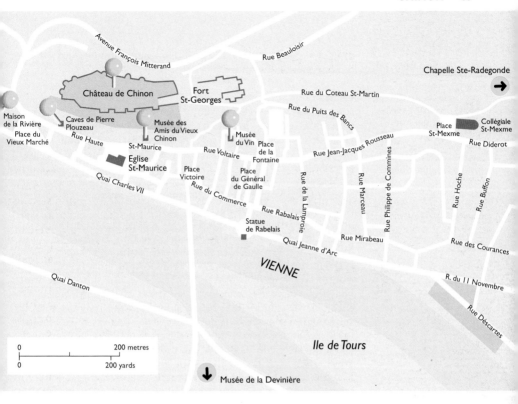

The Plouzeau wine cellars stretch for 100m into the hillside under

**Marché à
l'Ancienne** 3rd Sun
in Aug when Chinon turns
the clock back to the
1900s, celebrating with
costumed stallholders,
local products and folk
music.

pedestrianised: r. Voltaire and its continuations (r. St-Maurice and r.
Jean-Jacques Rousseau) and also r. du Commerce/r. Rabelais.

Getting around
Bicycles, including children's cycles and tandems, can be hired from
the Hôtel Agnès Sorel, *4 quai Pasteur; tel: 02 47 93 04 37.*
Guided walking tours of the old town are run June–Sept. A 45-min
'road train' tour with English commentary runs Easter–Sept weekends,
Jul–Aug daily.

Sights

**Caves de Pierre
Plouzeau** *94bis r.
Voltaire; open Apr–Sept
Tue–Sat.*

Caves de Pierre Plouzeau **
The Plouzeau wine cellars stretch for 100m into the hillside under
Chinon castle and are wide enough for a car to drive through. They
result from the quarrying carried out in the 12th century for stone to
build the castle above. The shaft through which it was hauled up can
still be seen. Today they make perfect wine cellars, being at a constant
12°C. However, the 150,000 bottles stored here take up only a fraction

of the space available and the caves are a sight in themselves, whether or not you intend to invest in a bottle or two of the excellent wine.

Château de Chinon
€ *Open daily.* The best views of the castle are from quai Danton across the River Vienne, especially when it is floodlit at night.

Château de Chinon**

Chinon's castle has seen 2 000 years of history, though its most glorious time was the second half of the 12th century when it was the favourite residence of the Plantagenet kings. Henry II (Count of Anjou and King of England) built most of it, intending to make it the hub of his vast empire. After he died of a fever there in 1189, it was completed by his son, Richard the Lionheart.

Spread along a hillside above the town, the massive fortress is now largely in ruins. Nevertheless its three main sections, separated by dry moats, can still be detected. Fort St-Georges, built by Henry II to protect the eastern end, is now a complete ruin. From it, you cross a bridge over a dry moat leading into the unusually shaped Tour de l'Horloge (clock tower), which is tall and thin. This houses a small exhibition about Joan of Arc, the Musée Jeanne d'Arc. The sturdy ramparts around the main part, called the Château du Milieu, now enclose lawns and the remains of various towers whose slit holes and steep interior steps, leading down as well as up, make them intriguing to explore and particular fun for children. From the walls you get good views down to the river over the rooftops of the town. Inside the Royal Apartments, now a stone shell, a large model shows the castle as it was 500 years ago, and a ten-minute audio-visual presentation in their Guard Room provides a useful introduction to its history. Next

Below
View of Château de Chinon and bridge

comes the Great Hall, empty except for a huge fireplace, where Joan of Arc was received by the Dauphin, Charles VII. In an anteroom, a life-size tableau depicts the famous meeting at which the king hid in the crowd but was immediately recognised by Joan, convincing him that she was a divine messenger. Across another dry moat, the round Fort du Coudray keep is where four Templar knights were imprisoned in 1308 on their way to be tried. Their names, which they carved on the north wall, can still be seen.

Maison de la Rivière 12 quai Pasteur; open Apr–Nov Tue–Sun.

Maison de la Rivière⁕

A unique collection of scale models of the boats that once plied up and down the Loire is gathered in this airy 150-year-old building, formerly an abattoir. They show how the river's trade reached its height in the 18th century when cargo boats sailed up and down it for 400km, until the arrival of railways largely superseded them. Other models illustrate the role that ferries played until they were replaced by bridges. Altogether, the displays illustrate a fascinating variety of stories about the Loire's history. The museum's workshop shows how boats were built.

Water jousting

Until World War I, water jousting was a popular feature of the river festivals held each summer along the Loire and other rivers in the area. The last surviving example of one of the dunking horses used is on show in the Maison de la Rivière at Chinon. Attached to a rope, the 'horse' – hinged in the middle – was rolled down a sloping 8-m plank overhanging the river. When the rope abruptly stopped it, the rear half shot upwards catapulting the rider into the water. As he flew through the air he had to try to grab a flag placed alongside. The few who succeeded were acclaimed, but rewarded only with a few coins.

Chapelle Ste-Radegonde⁕

This tiny 11th-century frescoed chapel is built into a cave in the hillside where a 6th-century hermit had his cell and was buried.

Museé du Vin et de la Tonnellerie € 12 r. Voltaire; tel: 02 47 93 25 63. Open Apr–Sept daily.

Musée du Vin et de la Tonnellerie ⁕

Having descended into an ancient wine cellar, visitors pass a series of tableaux with full-size animated models illustrating how the commentator's 'grandfather' used to transform his grapes into wine in the days before mechanisation took over. The 19th-century equipment on show includes casks, grape-pickers and a huge wooden wine-press. Halfway round comes a welcome touch: you are invited to sample a glass of Chinon wine produced by today's methods. A selection is on sale in a small shop at the end of the tour.

Overleaf View from the Château

Musée de la Devinière 2 km southwest of Chinon in the village of Seuilly; open daily.

Musée de la Devinière*

La Devinière, the farmhouse where the writer François Rabelais was born in 1494, is a simple rectangular building. Its upper storey now houses some of his books and other memorabilia. A network of cellars runs under the house – you can go in one side and out the other.

Rabelais

Menus, streets and even restaurants are named after one of Chinon's best-known sons. François Rabelais, son of a local lawyer, was born here in 1494, became a monk, studied Ancient Greek and also became a doctor before making his name as a writer. His racy but erudite *Pantagruel*, published in 1532, and *Gargantua*, three years later, established his literary reputation throughout Europe.

Museé des Amis du Vieux Chinon et de la Batellerie 44 r. Haute St-Maurice; tel: 02 47 93 18 12; open Easter–Oct daily.

Museé des Amis du Vieux Chinon et de la Batellerie*

The Dauphin, Charles VII, summoned his supporters to a parliament in 1428 in this then newly-built mansion, la Maison des Etats-Généreaux, in order to raise support and funds to rid the country of the English. Today a fine collection of porcelain, furniture, paintings and other local treasures is on display in its beamed rooms.

Shopping

The town centre lacks any large stores, but there is a Leclerc hyper-market, *open daily until 1930 (2000 Fridays)*, just beyond the castle on the D751. Most of the small shops are gathered around pl. Victoire and the pedestrianised r. du Commerce that runs off it. Local specialities include wine jam and goat's cheese.

Accommodation and food in and around Chinon

Agnès Sorel € *4 quai Pasteur; tel: 02 47 93 04 37.* This small, unpretentious hotel, with ten smartly decorated new rooms, is well placed on the edge of the old town overlooking the River Vienne – though some rooms face a rear terrace. No restaurant, but picnic lunches are available; also bike-hire.

Hôtel de France €€ *47–49 pl. du Général de Gaulle; tel: 02 47 93 33 91.* Chinon's oldest hotel occupies a 16th-century residence in the centre of town. Some of its 30 rooms, each individually furnished, have views of the castle.

Le Manoir de la Giraudière € *Beaumont en Véron; tel: 02 47 58 40 36.* In peaceful countryside a short drive northwest from the town (follow the Savigny sign off the D749), this 17th-century farmhouse spreads around a courtyard shaded by lime trees. The 25 bedrooms are atmospherically furnished with antiques and period decor, but have modern bathrooms. After dining in the restaurant €€ guests can retire for a drink to the unusual square *pigeonnier* which has 901 holes in its white stone walls for the birds.

Camping de l'Ile Auger *Quai Danton; tel: 02 47 93 08 35; open mid-Mar–mid-Oct.* Facing Chinon castle and close to the River Vienne, the site has 300 emplacements set amongst trees and gardens.

Les Années 30 €€ *78 r. Voltaire; tel: 02 47 93 37 18.* Though located in the heart of old Chinon, the decor is 1930s and the menus anything but old-world. Instead they feature subtle modern combinations like shellfish with curry and pancakes with caramel sauce.

Le Crêperie € *30 r. de Grand Carroi; tel: 02 47 93 18 94.* A small, informal restaurant with a friendly style, serving an array of savoury and sweet pancakes and wholemeal Brittany *galettes*, along with huge salads to make them into a meal.

Restaurant l'Océanic €€ *13 r. Rabelais; tel: 02 47 93 44 55.* Chef Patrick Descoubes, owner of this highly-regarded restaurant, specialises in seafood – huge plates of oysters and choose-your-own lobsters from a tank – served by his wife Marie-Paule and a team of nimble waitresses. There are three small indoor sections and a terrace outside.

Suggested walk

Total distance: 2km; the detour to the Chapelle Ste-Radegonde adds 1km.

Time: One hour, but allow a day to see all the sights.

Start your walk at the town's highest spot – the **CHATEAU ❶**. Its ramparts provide a splendid panorama over the town – a tightly-packed jumble of cream buildings under steep grey roofs – down to the tree-lined River Vienne and its red sandbanks. Turn right outside the castle, where a rough stone path leads sharply downhill. The five-minute walk over large cobbles brings you to the old **r. Voltaire**, a narrow street which runs straight through the medieval part of the town. You join it at the **Grand Carroi**, the crossroads where Joan of Arc arrived in the town on 6 March 1649 and took her horse to drink at the well. It is said that this was the moment when she was transformed from mere peasant girl to the famous warrior who was to lead the French against the English. The Maison Bleu, now a craft shop, and the Maison Rouge restaurant both occupy carefully-restored medieval houses there. Many other buildings along r. Voltaire date back to the 15th century, including the **Maison des Etats Généraux**, now the **MUSÉE DES AMIS DU VIEUX CHINON ET DE LA BATELLERIE ❷**, where in 1428 the Dauphin summoned his supporters. It stands on the spot where Richard the Lionheart died on 6 April 1199 from wounds he had received in Châlus. A map on the nearby wall indicates which buildings date from the Middle Ages and which from the Renaissance. Quiet courtyards, interesting gables, miniature towers, white shutters and colourful window boxes all add to the interest of a stroll along this attractive old street. The Gargantua Hotel at No 48 occupies the 15th-century **Palace du Baillage**.

On reaching **Église St-Maurice**, which was rebuilt by Henry II and has a fine square tower and spire, you leave the cobbles – thankfully – and soon come to the end of the street. There the subterranean **CAVES DE PIERRE PLOUZEAU ❸** wine cellar deep under the castle provides a welcome opportunity to sample and buy some of the excellent local vintages. On **Quai Pasteur** beside the river, a memorial to 271 prisoners massacred in the

Below
Statue of Rabelais, Chinon

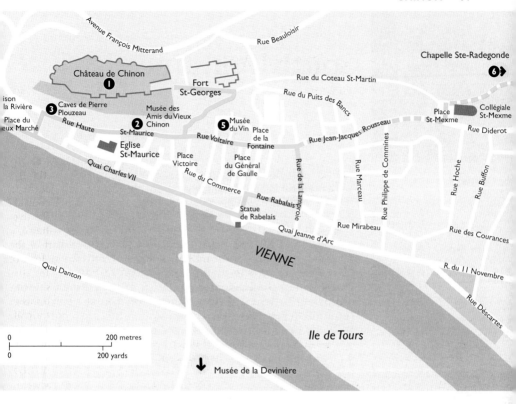

Avenue François Mitterand

Rue Beauloisir

Chapelle Ste-Radegonde

6

Château de Chinon
1

Fort
St-Georges

Rue du Coteau St-Martin

Rue du Puits des Bancs

ison
la Rivière
3 Caves de Pierre
Plouzeau

Musée des
Amis du Vieux
2 Chinon

Place du
eux Marché

Rue Haute

St-Maurice

Rue Jean-Jacques Rousseau

Place
St-Mexme

Collégiale
St-Mexme

Rue Diderot

5 Musée
du Vin   Place
de la
Fontaine

Rue Voltaire

Eglise
St-Maurice

Quai Charles VII

Place
Victoire

Rue du Commerce

Place
du Général
de Gaulle

Rue de la Lamproie

Rue Marceau

Rue Philippe de Commines

Rue Hoche

Rue Buffon

Rue Rabelais

Statue
de Rabelais

Quai Jeanne d'Arc

Rue Mirabeau

Rue des Courances

Quai Danton

VIENNE

R. du 11 Novembre

Rue Descartes

0   200 metres
0   200 yards

Ile de Tours

↓ Musée de la Devinière

Vendée wars in 1793 is a reminder of the town's often troubled past. The **MAISON DE LA RIVIÈRE** **4** is a little further along the riverside promenade. After visiting it, turn back and continue under the neat row of plane trees beside the river, past the arched bridge to the bronze statue of **François Rabelais**. He sits, book in hand, with his back to the water looking thoughtfully towards the busy **pl. du Général de Gaulle**.

The pedestrianised **r. Rabelais** (to the right off the square) has interesting shops and restaurants. A left turn along **r. de la Lamproie**, past its timbered houses, leads to the tourist information office on pl. d'Hofheim. Then it is a short way back across pl. Général de Gaulle to the **MUSÉE DU VIN ET DE LA TONNELLERIE** **5** for another glass or two of wine.

Detour: Before succumbing to the temptations in the wine museum, it is worth continuing along r. J-J Rousseau to the **Collégiale Saint-Mexme**, an impressive white-towered church. The road continues uphill to **Côteau Ste-Radegonde**, a quiet lane along a leafy ridge above the outskirts of the town which leads past troglodyte dwellings to the ruins of **CHAPELLE SAINTE-RADEGONDE** **6**. It is a delightfully peaceful spot.

South Touraine

Ratings

Churches	●●●●
Châteaux	●●● ○
History	●●● ○
Archaeology	●●●
Wines	●●● ○
Forests	●●●
Gardens	●● ○
Children	●● ○

South Touraine is one of the most battle-scarred parts of France. Long before written accounts recorded a succession of conquests, the area was inhabited by primitive tribes who have left us their Neolithic tools and dolmens. When the Romans came they ousted the Celtic tribes; later, the Moors tried to take the area but were turned back at Poitiers, and then the powerful counts of Anjou expanded their domain and built fortresses to protect it. Under the Plantagenets, the English made much of the area their own, ultimately to lose it to the French crown at the end of the Hundred Years' War. With growing stability, the gentle hills of South Touraine were to enjoy some prosperity and peace, while their geographical position – between Anjou and Bourges, Poitiers and Paris – ensured the constant passage of travellers and a continuing royal presence. Today, the fortified castles surmounting many towns are part of the area's great attraction, while its good wines and varied cuisine are an undeniable lure to the gourmet traveller.

AZAY-LE-FERRON✣✣

❶ Azay-le-Ferron Tourist Office 9 pl. de Verdun; tel: 02 54 39 21 91, fax: 02 54 39 22 88; open mid-June–mid-Sept 0900–1200, 1400–1700.

🏰 Château d'Azay-le-Ferron € Tel: 02 54 39 20 06; open Apr–Sept 1000–1200, 1400–1800 except Tue, Oct–Mar 1000–1200, 1400–1700 (Nov–Feb closes 1630), and closed Wed, weekend & hols in winter.

Like so many small towns in rural France, Azay-le-Ferron grew around its **château✣✣**. This stately 15th- to 18th-century building has four principal sections: the 15th-century tower Frottier, the 16th-century François I Pavilion, the 17th-century Brateuil Pavilion and 17th-century buildings for the domestic staff. Managed by the Musée des Beaux-Arts de Tours, it has been renovated and its 20-odd rooms redecorated with period furniture and paintings (including the well-known and rather risqué depiction of the beautiful Agnès Sorel, slightly under-dressed to reveal a naked breast) recreating the opulence of its original reception rooms. It was often used as a hunting lodge, and its 18th-century park is also open (free of charge) and boasts a neatly trimmed garden of geometric box hedges and an amusing topiary garden. Azay also boasts an interesting church dating from Romanesque times: the **Eglise Saint-Nazaire✣**. Of particular note in this church (hiding behind a 19th-century façade) is its nave, which

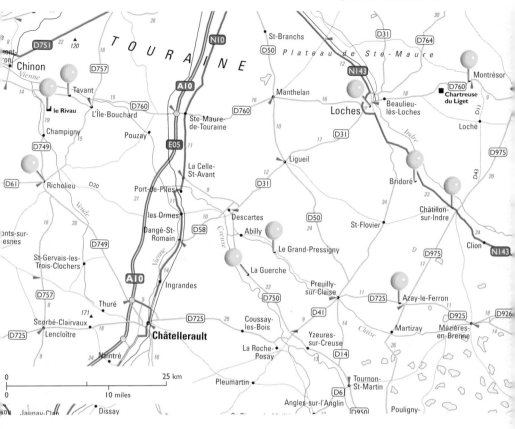

drew on the cathedral of Angers for its inspiration, and the various heads carved in the form of capitals and as keystones on the vaulting. The Romanesque portal on the south side of the church is also in a good state of repair.

BRIDORÉ❖❖

Château de Bridoré €–€€ Tel: 02 47 94 72 63; open June–Sept 1300–1900.

On the southern limits of this village, amid fertile agricultural country, rises the fortified **Château de Bridoré❖❖** with, between the servants' quarters and those of the seigneur, an impressive dungeon. Records mention it in the seventh century but most of what one sees today is 13th- to 15th-century. Amongst its guests were Joan of Arc, Charles VII and VIII, and François I. Imbert de Bastarnay was responsible for remodelling it in the 1400s. One of its curiosities is the steam bath on the ground floor, believed to have been brought back from the Crusades. The small and unfinished church of **Saint-Roch**

contains, in its crypt, the tomb of the family of Boursault de Vintais, one-time owners of the château. There's a fine 15th-century statue of St-Roch sporting an interesting floppy hat.

Accommodation and food around Bridoré

Hôtel Aux Dames de Touraine € *Oizay, RN143; tel: 02 47 94 72 67, fax: 02 47 94 88 55.* A simple, small hotel. Apart from traditional fare in the evenings, the restaurant menus also feature lighter meals for passing tourists.

CHÂTILLON-SUR-INDRE*

ℹ️ Châtillon Tourist Office Pl. du Champ-de-Foire; tel: 02 54 38 74 19; open summer 0900–1200, 1400–1800.

🛍️ Market: pl. du Marché, Fri am.

🏰 Tour de César € open daily 1030–1230, 1430–1830. Guided tour available.

Église Notre-Dame € Open daily 0800–2000.

The profile of this walled, hilltop town promises more than it offers. Its history dates back over a millennium but visitors have to content themselves with vestiges. The narrow lanes and flights of stairs in the old town, past its castle (built originally by Philippe III between 1274–78 as a royal residence but not open to the public), are not often trodden by tourists who prefer to visit the **Tour de César***, the town's dungeon, or spend time in the **Église Notre-Dame****, the former collegiate church of Sainte-Outrille. The church began its life under the influence of Romanesque art and was finished in Gothic style, and the visitor can see the gradual progression of its construction in moving from the earlier apse towards the later façade. Probably the most impressive element in this building is the fine work on its individual 11th-century carved capitals (one of which in the nave is, unusually, signed by its sculptor, Petrus Janitoris). The sculpture on the western portal is also remarkable and narrates events from the Old Testament starting with the *Temptation of Adam and Eve*.

Accommodation and food in Châtillon-sur-Indre

Auberge de la Tour €–€€ *2 route du Blanc; tel: 02 54 38 72 17, fax: 02 54 38 74 85.* A friendly, small hotel just on the edge of town. It also has a noted restaurant. The old city is within an easy walk.

LA GUERCHE*

🏰 Château de la Guerche € tel: 02 47 91 02 39; open July–mid-Sept daily 1000–1200, 1400–1900, Sun pm only.

Today La Guerche looks like a peaceful backwater, along the slow-moving Creuse valley, but in the Middle Ages it was a veritable hotspot. By the time the Renaissance took hold in France, La Guerche was a staunch Catholic settlement and during the Wars of Religion sheltered, amongst others, Catherine de Medicis. The most impressive

Below
La Guerche Château

views of the **Château de La Guerche**✣✣ are from the bridge crossing the River Creuse. The fortified town was surrounded by massive walls rising, in parts, 35m above its moats and the river. There is still a handful of ancient houses in its crooked streets which date from the Middle Ages, while the good-looking Romanesque church of **Saint-Marcellin**✣ was built in the 11th century and was under the control of the Benedictine Abbey at Preuilly-sur-Claise. Later restoration has unfortunately dealt a blow to its originality.

Le Grand-Pressigny✣

🛈 **Grand-Pressigny Tourist Office** *Hôtel de Ville; tel: 02 47 94 96 82, www.le-grand-pressigny.net; open June–Sept 0930–1230, 1400–1830, Oct–May 1000–1200, 1400–1730.*

🛑 **Market:** Thur am.

Far from the main roads that dissect France, Le Grand-Pressigny retains much of its old-world atmosphere. It was a strategic point between the battling Plantagenets and Capetians, so Guillaume de Pressigny, seigneur of Grand-Pressigny and a Philippe-Auguste faithful, decided to fortify his hilltop domain at the end of the 12th century. Ancient stone houses border the steep streets that mount the rocky hill on which the town's once-magnificent **château**✣✣ perches. Its most interesting features are the Renaissance gallery that was added in the mid-1500s by Honorat de Savoie, the 12th-century dungeon and the **Musée de Préhistoire**✣✣✣. This area of South Touraine has high-quality

Château du Grand-Pressigny (and Musée) €€ *tel: 02 47 94 90 20; open Feb–Mar & Oct–Dec 0930–1230, 1400–1700, rest of year 0930–1900, closed 25 Dec & Jan.*

flint which, millennia ago, was the ideal stone for fashioning tools. The deposits of flint attracted primitive man, who inevitably left his mark, and archaeologists are still discovering a rich heritage which charts the development of man between the Paleolithic era and the Bronze Age. The museum groups some of the finds and outlines the history of these early settlers. If you are coming to Grand-Pressigny in summer, check out the dates for the town's summer festivities, held in the château.

Accommodation and food in Le Grand-Pressigny

Auberge Savoie Villars €–€€ *pl. Savoie Villars; tel: 02 47 94 96 86, fax: 02 47 91 07 81, web: www.logis-de-france37.com; restaurant open year-round except Mon & Tue, Sept–June.* An attractive and very central hotel with a pleasant garden. Restaurant with local dishes and traditional French cuisine.

L'Espérance €€ *le Carroir des Robins; tel: 02 47 94 90 12, closed Mon and Jan.* A gourmet address with an interesting ambience. Much effort is given to preparation and presentation.

LE RIVAU✤✤

Château du Rivau € *tel: 02 47 95 77 47; open daily June–mid-Sept, 1300–1900, closed Tue.*

The impressive **château** sits amid arable land just near the small town of Le Coudray-Lémeré. Although not particularly fancy in style, it has all the ingredients of a fairytale castle and has been almost totally restored. With drawbridge, moat and a 13th-century feudal exterior (Joan of Arc passed through its portals), the castle has a Renaissance core built by the Beauvau family, who knew considerable fame some 500 years ago. In front of the residential building, the castle's stables, granary and domestic wings form an important part of the complex. Rabelais immortalised this mansion in his famous story of *Gargantua*. Gargantua's grandfather gave Le Rivau to Captain Tolmére, captain of the footsoldiers, as a reward for his victories in the Pirocholine War. The gardens are one of its highlights: a more recent addition, there are some 12 different themed plantings (including wild flowers, rose garden and secret garden) laid out to old documents and using paintings and tapestries as inspiration.

Accommodation and food near Le Rivau

Auberge du Val de Vienne €€ *30 route de Chinon, Sazilly (4.5km from Le Rivau); tel: 02 47 95 26 49, fax: 02 47 95 25 97.* A simple inn with a rustic ambience and a good restaurant with an excellent regional menu and large choice of wines.

LOCHES✦✦✦

Loches Tourist Office *Pl. de Marne; tel: 02 47 91 82 82, fax: 02 47 91 61 50, www.lochesentouraine.com & cg37.fr; open summer Mon–Sat 0930–1900, Sun 1000–1300, 1400–1900, winter daily 0930–1230, 1400–1730.*

How pleasant it is that Loches is a grossly under-publicised tourist destination, for it helps preserve the charm of this exceptional medieval town located on the banks of the Indre. Once through the 15th-century entrance gates, **La Porte des Cordeliers** or **La Porte Picois**, you'll soon decide that Loches merits a stay rather than a quick visit. Impregnable walls, impressive city gates and narrow cobblestone streets lead through the fortified walls to its **Cité Médiévale✦✦✦** crowned by the fine residence, **Logis Royal✦✦✦**. This Renaissance palace

Above
Le Rivau

Right
Rooftops of Loches

dominates Loches and was one of the favourite royal residences from the mid-13th century onwards. It is particularly associated with the beautiful Agnès Sorel, favourite mistress of Charles VII and mother to four of his children. On her death, she was brought back to Loches and her tomb is now in the Logis Royal. It features the 11th- to 13th-century Église St-Ours* (named for the fifth-century Lochois saint), an imposing rectangular **dungeon*** and towers built by Foulques Nerra. Logis residents, temporary or long-term, also included Anne of Brittany and Ludovic Sforza. Of humbler proportions than the Logis, the nearby **Maison Lansyer*** was the home of noted landscape painter Emmanuel Lansyer (1835–1893) who was arguably as good as, if not better than, his well-known friend, Gustave Courbet. On display in his house are some hundred or so of his fine works, an interesting collection of Japanese art and another of original engravings by notable 19th-century artists such as Corot, Canaletto and Gustave Doré.

The human cage

It was in Loches that the infamous human cage was used to house prisoners. Made from wood covered in metal it was, at its most spacious, 2m on each side enabling a prisoner to stand, though there was a reduced version which forced him to crouch. Stories tell how prisoners spent their sentences incarcerated in these cages, but documents suggest that they were for temporary, rather than permanent, use.

Markets: Wed 0700–1500, Sat 0700–1300; monthly market first Wed of the month.

Le Logis Royal and Dungeon €€ pl. Charles VII; tel: 02 47 59 01 32, fax: 02 47 59 27 45; open Oct–Mar 0930–1230, 1400–1700, Apr–Sept 0900–1900, closed 25 Dec & 1 Jan.

La Maison Lansyer € r. Lansyer; tel/fax: 02 47 59 05 45; open except Tue May–mid-June & Oct–5 Nov 1000–1200, 1330–1800, mid-June–Sept daily 1000–1900, closed Tue June & Sept.

During the summer months, the city of Loches mounts a number of interesting spectacles which include son-et-lumière performances, concerts, theatre and evening markets. It is also known for its Christmas market mid-December.

Foulques Nerra

Foulques Nerra, nicknamed the Black Falcon, crops up all over this area of France. It would seem he was responsible for the construction of almost all the Middle Age fortresses – and in many cases he actually was. But watch out: there were three Foulques. Our man is Foulques Nerra III (970–1040), Count of Anjou from 987 until his death. The great expansion of the house of Anjou at the beginning of the second millennium was due to Nerra. As expected of such a powerful character, he is said to have had an extreme character, given to periods of piety (including four trips to Jerusalem) and then of cruelty. He married three times and, with each marriage, increased his sphere of power.

Accommodation and food in Loches

Hôtel de France €–€€ 6 r. Picois; tel: 02 47 59 00 32, fax: 02 47 59 28 66; www.touraine.cci.fr; open daily in season, restaurant closed Sun pm & Mon Sept–June. A pretty, smallish hotel right in the centre of the old town with a good restaurant featuring traditional and modern cuisine.

Luccotel €€ 12 r. des Lézards; tel: 02 47 91 30 30, fax: 02 47 91 30 35; restaurant closed Sat lunch and from 18 Dec–second week Jan. A modern hotel, slightly away from the centre, with panoramic views over Loches. Comfortable rooms and a noteworthy restaurant.

Sforza €–€€ 3 pl. de l'Hôtel de Ville; tel: 02 47 94 06 19. In the heart of the Vieille Ville, this pizzeria and grill is a popular spot with locals.

MONTRÉSOR❖❖❖

ⓘ Montrésor Tourist Office *La Mairie; tel: 02 47 92 70 71, www.montresor-village.com; open 0900–1200, 1400–1700.*

ⓘ Château de Montrésor €€ *Open daily Apr–Oct 1000–1200, 1400–1800. Guided tours of the interior and free exploration of the garden.*

ⓐ Market: *Sat am.*

Montrésor justly earns its sobriquet as one of the *plus beaux villages de France*. This tiny medieval settlement, clustered on the hill around its château, sits above the shallow waters of the River Indroise. With its ancient stone houses, half-hidden gardens and the profusion of flowering plants, it is picture-postcard perfect and invites leisurely exploration. Foulques Nerra, Count of Anjou, built the original feudal fortress but it was Imbert de Bastarnay who improved the town's silhouette by constructing a Renaissance château. He also commissioned a collegiate church, consecrated in 1532, to shelter mortal remains of his family, and within its walls hangs a superb 17th-century *Annunciation* by Philippe de Champaigne. The family tombs are particularly moving, but it's a pity that the Revolution removed the heads of all the saints, mutilating otherwise fine statues. Interestingly, the château has been, and is still, owned by Polish nobility whose antecedents served with Napoleon III. Montrésor owes its medieval and Renaissance prosperity to the lucrative wool trade: in the 18th-century wooden building, the Halles des Cardeux, local wool was carded and woven for export.

Accommodation and food in and around Montrésor

Café Restaurant de la Ville € *29 Grande Rue; tel: 02 47 92 75 31; open Tue–Sun.* This family-run restaurant offers snacks and a full menu with local dishes. Although it's the only choice in Montrésor, it is still a pleasant, friendly place.

Auberge des Charmettes € *Beaumont Village, 3km from Montrésor; tel: 02 47 92 75 81, fax: 02 47 92 71 63.* A small, family-run hotel and restaurant near Montrésor. Attractive old inn with the usual regional fare.

RICHELIEU❖❖

ⓘ Richelieu Tourist Office *6 Grande Rue; tel: 02 47 58 13 62, fax: 02 47 58 29 86, www.cc-pays-de-richelieu.fr; open Apr–mid-May and mid-Sept–Oct Mon, Tue, Thur, Fri & Sat 0900–1230, 1400–1730, mid-May–mid-Sept Mon–Sat 0900–1230,*

Forerunner of our grid-plan towns, Richelieu was commissioned by Cardinal Richelieu (Armand du Plessis, bishop of Luçon) and designed by Jacques Lemercier who gave the execution of the work to his two brothers, Nicolas and Pierre. Overseen with interest by the Cardinal, and with the aid of 2000 workmen, it took some 11 years to complete and was largely finished on Richelieu's death in 1642. The wooden Halles, assembled out of chestnut and oak, were erected in 1638 and house exhibitions and markets. The rather dingy, Baroque Église de Notre-Dame-de-l'Assomption wasn't completed before the death of its architect, Pierre Lemercier, but the broad, 12m-wide Grande Rue,

*1400–1800, Nov–Mar Mon,
Tue, Thu, Fri & Sat
0900–1230.*

 Markets: *Mon all
day, Fri am.*

Hôtel de Ville € *1 pl.
du Marché; tel: 02 47
58 10 13, fax: 02 47 58 16
42; open Wed–Fri & Mon
1000–1200, 1400–1600 or
to 1800 in July & Aug.
Guided 15-min visits.*

Parc du Château € *open
Tue–Sun, 1000–1900, and
daily Apr–mid-Sept, closed 1
Jan.*

Right
Richelieu riverside

flanked by its 28 distinctive
mansions – the town's central
axis – was, and has lost little of
its original dignity and elegance.
The gracious buildings either side
are all designed to a similar plan,
with an interior courtyard and a
small garden. However, they
obviously didn't appeal to many
purchasers for it is related that
the illustrious Cardinal had to pressurise his wealthy friends and
associates into buying these and, after his death, there was a scramble
to sell them, with the result that few were ever actually finished on
the inside. Either end of the Grande Rue, the pl. du Marché and the pl.
des Religieuses bring space into the plan and function as social
gathering points. The **Hôtel de Ville**⁕ now houses a museum relating
to the Cardinal. The nearby **park**⁕ is also open and can be visited, in
tandem with the town, by a *petit train touristique.*

Accommodation and food in Richelieu

Hôtel Restaurant Le Puits Doré € *pl. du Marché; tel: 02 47 58 16 02,
fax: 02 47 58 24 39; restaurant closed Sun pm and Mon, Oct–Mar.* An
attractive small hotel on the main square with a good restaurant
offering traditional cuisine.

Train rides

For train buffs, a restored,
steam train runs along the
Veude valley between
Richelieu and Ligré (some
12km each way) during
the weekends in July and
August. Tickets **€€** and
information *La Gare,
Richelieu; tel: 02 47 58 12
97, fax: 02 47 58 28 72.*

Cardinal Richelieu

Armand du Plessis, better known as Cardinal Richelieu, was born in
Richelieu in 1585, his father being the seigneur of Richelieu. Forsaking a
military career, he entered the church and politics, became a cardinal in
1622 and, under King Louis XIII, rose to become his chief minister. To
thank him for his services, the Cardinal was given the title of duke and,
amassing a number of properties around Richelieu, created a duchy. He
decided to abandon the family mansion and commission the building of a
noble château (no longer extant) for himself and a town to house his
followers. He died as the new town neared completion.

TAVANT⁕

Église de Tavant €
*Tel: 02 47 58 58 06;
guided visit daily
1000–1200, 1430–1800,
except Tue.*

In the middle of this hamlet is a small **Romanesque church**⁕⁕⁕
dedicated to St-Nicolas with fine 12th-century frescoes in its low-
ceilinged crypt and somewhat restored paintings in the small apse. As
you enter, the mesmerising image of Christ in a mandorla gazes down

at you from behind the raised altar. The realism of the figure is uncommon amongst similar, contemporary works. The church was once part of the Abbey of Tavant.

Suggested tour

Comité Départemental du Tourisme de Touraine 9 r. Bouffon; tel: 02 47 31 47 48, fax: 02 47 31 42 76, www.tourism-touraine.com; open Mon–Fri 0900–1830.

www.tourainewines.com

La Sainte-Chapelle € Champigny-sur-Veude; open 1500–1800, closed Tue.

Musée René Descartes € 19 r. René Descartes, Descartes; tel: 02 47 59 79 19; open June–Sept 1400–1800, closed Tue.

Parc Zoologique de la Haute-Touche € Tel: 02 54 02 20 40; open daily 1000–1800 Easter –1 Nov.

Corroirie € Route de Loches à Montrésor, Chemillé-sur-Indrois; tel: 02 47 92 64 23; open July–Sept Tue–Sun 1000–1800.

Chartreuse du Liget € Tel: 02 47 92 60 02; open daily 0900–1200, 1400–1900.

Total distance: About 230km.

Time: Anything from 2 to 3 days.

Links: Chinon (*see page 82*), our starting point, also features as the starting point of the tour Chinon–Saumur (*see page 104*), and the end point of the Grand Châteaux: Tours–Chinon (*see page 70*). The N143 from Châtillon-sur-Indre leads to Buzançais, part of the tour of the Berry (*see page 270*).

Route: Leaving **Chinon** to the south, join the D751E and head eastwards in the direction of Loches. You'll drive around 4.5km before you see the N769 turning, on the right, towards Richelieu and Châtellerault. Don't miss the left turning in **Le Coudray-Lémeré** which leads off to the château, **LE RIVAU ❶**. To continue the route, backtrack to Le Coudray and pick up the same road again, to **Champigny-sur-Veude**, and stop here to admire the impressive glass windows in the 16th-century **La Sainte-Chapelle**, founded by the Bourbon Montpensier family, and once part of the château. The latter was destroyed by a jealous Cardinal Richelieu. This old village still has a number of 16th-century houses. It is only 6km along the wooded D749 till you reach **RICHELIEU ❷**.

Leave by the D757 which leads to the D20 in the direction of Marigny-Marmande, then **Les Ormes**, on the banks of the River Vienne. You turn left and first right, then via Alleux, on a well-marked road to **Descartes** named since 1967 for its most famous resident, philosopher René Descartes (1596–1650). His home is now a **museum** where, amongst other memorabilia, is an original edition of his opus magnum, *Principia Philosophiae*. The D42 southwards splits after 3km and you'll take the right fork, the D750, before you take a right turn and reach the largely medieval village of **LA GUERCHE ❸**, fanning out around its 15th-century fortified château. Backtrack onto the D750 and continue for 3km to Barrou. Here you turn left onto the D60 which comes in on the south side (stop to take in the views) of **LE GRAND-PRESSIGNY ❹**. The D42 leading out of Le Grand-Pressigny follows the Claise valley and enters the attractive town of **Preuilly-sur-Claise**, noted for its Benedictine

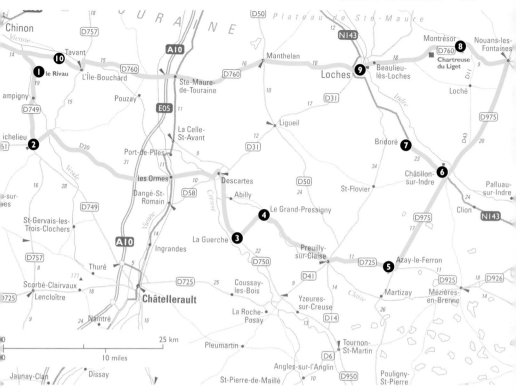

Opposite
Chartreuse du Liget

Auberge de l'Île €€
L'Île Bouchard (2km
from Tavant); tel: 02 47 58
51 07, fax: 02 47 58 51 07;
closed early Dec, hols Feb,
Tue pm & Wed. A pretty
location for this popular
and excellent restaurant.

Abbey. It's just 12km from here to **AZAY-LE-FERRON 5**. Taking the
D975 north, you'll pass a sign on the left to the breeding zoo, **Parc
Zoologique de la Haute Touche**. This is a good place to spend an
hour or so, if you have children with you.

Another 14km and you'll see the citadel at **CHÂTILLON-SUR-INDRE
6**. Leaving the town, follow the Indre valley northwards and, just
after the village of **Fléré-la-Rivière**, turn left on the D241 to **BRIDORÉ
7**. The easiest way to continue on the tour is to retrace your steps to
Châtillon and pick up the D675 to Blois, which passes by the little
town of **Nouans-les-Fontaines**, known for a beautiful rendition of the
Pietà by 15th-century painter, Jean Fouquet. The pretty D760 follows
the Indroise valley to **MONTRÉSOR 8**. The same road continues and
enters the important **Fôret de Loches** (there are plenty of pleasant
places to walk or cycle here). On the right, there's the ancient
Corroirie, a fortified refuge for the Carthusian monks from the nearby
12th-century **Chartreuse du Liget**. Founded by Henry II, King of
England, this chartreuse was a grandiose charterhouse. The cloisters
and remains of the church are open to visitors. The D760 continues to
meet the Indre and the city of **LOCHES 9** from which it continues
through **L'Île-Bouchard** westwards passing through **TAVANT 10**, a
tiny hamlet. The old church is just off to the left. It is a few minutes
run from here back to Chinon.

Chinon–Saumur

Ratings

Caves	●●●●●
Châteaux	●●●●●
Architecture	●●●●○
Churches	●●●●○
Food and wine	●●●○○
Historical sights	●●●○○
Villages	●●●○○
Museums	●●●○○

Though not as well-known as many of the Loire's grand châteaux, each of the castles dotted around the *tuffeau* (tufa) plain south of Saumur is a little gem. This region also offers a journey of discovery, as many other outstanding sights lie hidden underground in galleries left by centuries of quarrying the soft *tuffeau* stone to build the area's castles, towns and villages. At Brézé an underground stronghold is open to visitors, and at Rochemenier you can go round a *village troglodyte*. A quarry at Doué-la-Fontaine has been imaginatively transformed into a top-class zoo. Good use is being made of many of the other quarried-out caves too, as homes or for storing wine or growing mushrooms. While the scenery along the route is less spectacular than elsewhere in the region, an exception is the section where it runs beside the Loire – a glorious stretch!

BOURGUEIL✣

ⓘ Bourgueil Tourist Office 16 pl. de l'Église; tel: 02 47 97 9139; open daily except Sun pm and Mon am.

ⓘ Abbaye de St-Pierre Guided tours Apr–Oct.

Cave Touristique de la Dive Bouteille Open Apr–Sept Tue–Sun.

Markets: Stalls with local produce,

It can be hard to stay sober in this pleasant little white stone town, 19km north of Chinon, because of the constant opportunities to sample and buy its famous full-bodied red wine, produced from the Breton vines grown in the area. The Maison des Vins de Bourgueil, in pl. de l'Église, features a different producer's wines each week, and the **Cave Touristique de la Dive Bouteille** (Divine Bottle), a cellar hollowed out of the rock, has a collection of old presses on show. Two more wineries occupy the cloisters of **l'Abbaye de St-Pierre**, a large group of buildings dating back to the 10th century when it was one of the richest abbeys in Anjou and had vineyards stretching for miles around. Today only about 20 nuns live there. Its vaulted hall and staircase, built in 1730, are open to the public and a small folk museum occupies former monks' cells.

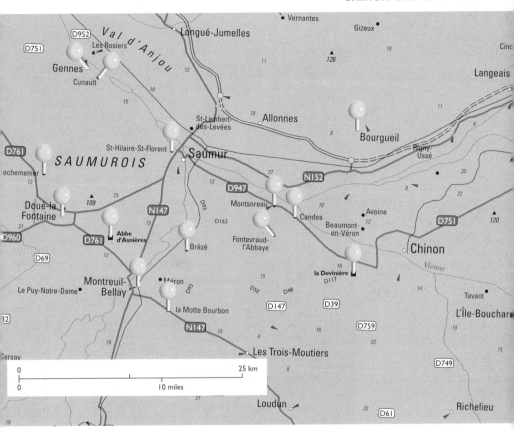

clothing and bric-à-brac take over the streets and market hall on Tues am; food only in the market hall on Sat am. Evening markets featuring local wines and specialities like wine jams and *rillettes* (potted meat) July–Aug.

La Galette Bourgueilloise

This *brioche* (sweet bread), filled with creamy vanilla custard, is the town's speciality. The recipe – top secret! – was created in the 1970s by Monsieur Ancelin, owner of the Bourgueilloise *pâtisserie* (beside the market hall), the only place where it can be bought.

Accommodation and food in and around Bourgueil

L'Ecu de France € *R. de Tours; tel: 02 47 97 70 18*. A small, family-run hotel in the centre of town, handy for the market and the abbey.

Restaurant l'Auberge La Lande €–€€ *D35, in direction of Cave Touristique de la Dive Bouteille; tel: 02 47 97 92 41*. In fine weather you can dine on the terrace of this charming restaurant. Good, regional cooking uses local produce, complemented by excellent Bourgueil wine.

Right
Bourgeuil street

CANDES-ST-MARTIN✦✦

This attractive riverside village, spread along the south bank of the Vienne at its confluence with the Loire, is named partly after St Martin, Bishop of Tours, who died here in 397. The splendid white 12th-century church, notable for its soaring pillars and rib vaulting, was erected to mark the spot. Three hundred years later a lavishly carved defensive porch supported by a central pillar was added. A series of steep cobbled paths, starting beside the church, climb to a hillside which provides a magnificent panoramic view of the two rivers (10-min walk). Opposite the church a short alley off the main street leads down to the river and its former slipways. These are a reminder that the Loire was once a busy waterway for transporting coal, slate, stone and grapes. An old notice lists the distances to the river's various ports.

CHÂTEAU DE BRÉZÉ❖❖❖

Château de Brézé
€€
www.chateaudebreze.com;
open May–Sept daily for
guided tours, castle (1 hour),
underground (90 min). Free
admission to grounds.

Though little-known compared with many of the Loire's châteaux, Brézé's is nevertheless one of the most extraordinary of all. On arrival you see a typical fortified *tuffeau* castle with two round towers surrounded by lawns from which there are wide views over the Loire Valley. The first surprise comes as you cross the moat, since it is 15m deep – the deepest in Europe – and has never been filled with water. The present building, consisting of three wings around a courtyard, dates from the 16th and 19th centuries and is elegantly furnished with antiques. One wing is occupied by the Count and Countess of Colbert, descendants of the family who built the original château in the 11th century. However the visible building is merely the 'modern' part of the castle. There is almost as much to see below ground where an extensive network of chambers, linked by low zigzagging passages, has only recently been discovered. They were hollowed out of the soft white *tuffeau* stone, probably around the 9th century, to provide a safe refuge. The torch-lit tour through them includes large kitchens, which were added later, complete with two big bread ovens, and wine cellars that had a direct shaft from the vineyards so that grapes could be dropped straight down for pressing. Today's vintages are on sale to visitors in the grounds near another remarkable feature, a tall circular *pigeonnier*.

Right
Moat at Brézé

CUNAULT❖❖❖

Cunault Music Festival during May.

Beneath a delicate stone figure of the Virgin, framed by semi-circular recessed arches, massive double doors lead into the village's huge cathedral-like abbey church, one of the most remarkable buildings in the whole of the Loire area. Built in the local creamy white *tuffeau* stone and dating back partly to the 11th century, it is a masterpiece of Romanesque art, pure in design yet richly decorated. Soaring pillars line its single nave, each with elaborately carved capitals at the top. The original bell-tower is topped by a spire added in the 15th century. Only fragments of the frescoes that decorated the interior at that time have survived, but other notable features include a rare carved and painted shrine and a 16th-century statue of the Virgin. The 3 074-pipe organ is in excellent condition thanks to President Georges Pompidou, who personally authorised its restoration after he visited the church in 1968.

Right
Fresco at Cunault

Accommodation and food near Cunault

Le Prieuré €€€ *Chênehutte-les-Tuffeaux, near Cunault; tel: 02 41 67 90 14, www.prieure.com* Looking down across the Loire from its commanding position on a wooded hillside, this gracious former priory is easily the most distinguished and luxurious place to stay in the area. The view at the front extends for 48km. All 20 bedrooms in the main building are a good size and furnished with antiques. Fifteen more are in modern villas in large wooded grounds that also include a heated outdoor pool and mini-golf; these rooms provide a less expensive option but lack the view across the river. The hotel's restaurant has large picture windows facing the river and serves gourmet dishes, notably local fish. Its waiters combine formality with friendliness and are particularly helpful over choosing wine. Breakfast and drinks can be taken on the terrace.

DOUÉ-LA-FONTAINE✦✦

Above
Chemins de la Rose, Doué

🛈 **Doué-la-Fontaine Tourist Office** *Pl. du Champ de Foire; tel: 02 41 59 20 49.*

🏠 **Doué Zoo** €€ *Route de Cholet; open Feb–mid-Nov daily. Programme of animal feeding events throughout the day.*

Les Chemins de la Rose €€ *Rte de Cholet; open May–Sept daily.*

Musée des Commerces Anciens € *Les Ecuries du Baron Foullon; open Feb–Dec daily.*

Though seemingly unremarkable when you drive into it, the town has three attractions which are definitely worth seeking out. Its **Zoo**✦✦✦ is unusual because it occupies former quarries and caves. Now overgrown with trees and foliage, they have been ingeniously converted into attractive enclosures with streams, waterfalls and grottoes where the animals and birds can largely roam free. There is even a large aviary in which visitors can mingle with 20 vultures though, even with keepers on hand for reassurance, this can be a rather unnerving experience! Other areas are home to a wide range of animals including lions, tigers, pigmy hippopotamuses and several kinds of monkey. Visitors observe them from a network of pathways which lead on two different levels through the almost jungle-like surroundings. Altogether, the zoo has about 500 animals representing 65 different species. At least half are involved in international breeding programmes for the conservation of endangered species, a major concern of the zoo's founder, Louis Gay, since he opened it in 1961. Subsequently he created **Les Chemins de la Rose**✦, a 6-ha rose garden a short walk away. Planted with over 6 000 bushes, it is truly a rose-lover's paradise. As you stroll around the beds, information boards provide a history lesson on the 950 varieties, ranging from the very latest to antique ones now rarely seen elsewhere. Every conceivable rose product is on sale in the shop, plus a small selection of plants. Nearby is the **Musée des Commerces Anciens**✦ where two 'streets' of old shops have been recreated inside the former stable block of a manor house. Although the French will be more familiar than foreign visitors with the old brand names, the objects on show, dating from 1850 to 1950, are highly nostalgic for all nationalities. The shops, each realistically laid out and fully stocked, include a grocer, ironmonger, clockmaker, seed supplier, parasol maker, and a pharmacy whose shelves are lined with large jars of potions and powders.

FONTEVRAUD-L'ABBAYE✦✦✦

Fontevraud-l'Abbaye L'Abbaye Royale € *open daily.*

Right
Tombs at Fontevraud

The village grew up beside L'Abbaye Royale✦✦✦, the largest group of monastic buildings in Europe and now the Centre Culturel de l'Ouest, a venue for concerts, exhibitions and conferences. Four recumbent effigies, lying in state in the abbey's huge 12th-century church, provide a vivid reminder that this part of France was under the same rule as England for many years. They are Henry II (King of England and Plantagenet Count of Anjou), his wife Eleanor of Aquitaine, their crusader son King Richard the Lionheart and Isabelle, wife of Richard's brother King John. The church itself has impressive stonework and is roofed with domes, a feature usually only found in southwest France. The abbey also has four 16th-century cloisters – including both the smallest and largest in France – together with its original refectory and chapterhouse. Particularly remarkable is the huge octagonal Romanesque kitchen and smokeroom which rises to a high pointed hood – the only surviving example from the period in France. It has several fireplaces so that, depending on the direction of the wind, the cooking could be done on which ever would work best. The original monastery, founded in 1099, consisted of four separate priories, all under the rule of an abbess. Each had a different vocation, such as caring for the sick or poor. Three were for nuns and one, prudently sited outside the main walls, for priests and brothers. During the Wars of Religion the buildings suffered considerable damage. More occurred in Napoleon's time when the abbey became a prison, which it remained until 1963. Fortunately, much survived in excellent condition and, thanks to the largest restoration programme in France outside Paris, its impressive white *tuffeau* buildings will continue to be improved.

Accommodation and food at Fontevraud-l'Abbaye

Prieuré Saint-Lazare €€ *Abbaye Royale de Fontevraud, Fontevraud-l'Abbaye; tel: 02 41 51 73 16; www.abbayehotelfontevraud.com; open Apr–Oct.* Fifty-two smart modern bedrooms now occupy a section of the abbey buildings that was transformed into a hotel in the early 1990s, creating a very special place to stay. The restaurant **€€** is located in serene white cloisters, now enclosed for comfort by large windows. Its various menus – des Moines, Abbesses or Plantagenets – feature local fish and other Anjou specialities. Afterwards, guests can retire to the lofty former refectory for drinks.

La Croix Blanche € *Fontevraud l'Abbaye; tel: 02 41 51 72 89.* For simple dishes – salads, pancakes and ice-cream sundaes – drop in at the *crêperie* of the family-run Croix Blanche hotel, a 400-year-old *auberge* with 21 rooms. It also has a more formal restaurant €€ *tel: 02 41 51 71 11.*

GENNES❖

ℹ️ **Gennes Tourist Office** *Square de l'Europe; tel: 02 41 51 84 14; open Mon–Sat and Jul–Aug Sun.*

🏛️ **Amphithéatre Gallo-Roman** *Open Apr–Sept Sun pm, Jul–Aug daily.*

Gallo-Roman remains have been discovered around this small riverside town which was on a major trading route between Tours and Rennes in the 2nd century. The most important is an **amphitheatre❖** that could have held up to 5 000 spectators, sitting on the grassy bowl of the hillside as there were no stone tiers.

MONTREUIL-BELLAY❖❖

ℹ️ **Montreuil-Bellay Tourist Office** *Pl. du Concorde; tel: 02 41 52 32 39, www.villemontreuil-bellay.fr*

🛒 **Markets:** *Tue, also Sun am mid-May–mid-Sept.*

🏛️ **Chateau de Montreuil-Bellay** €€ *Open Apr–Oct Wed–Mon (guided tours); € gardens only.*

La Soie Vivante € *Pl. des Petits Augustins; open mid-May–mid-Oct Tues–Sun.*

This lively little town, attractively situated beside the River Thouet, is the only one in Anjou still to have ancient ramparts dating back 1 000 years. Its impressive 15th-century **château❖**, itself largely surrounded by sturdy walls, stands guard over the river in terraced grounds which slope down towards the water. Entered over a moat and through a formidable gateway, it certainly looks like a fortress as it has battlements and turrets. In fact, much of it was built as a family residence, which it remains today. Seven beautifully furnished rooms and a medieval kitchen can be visited, together with the colourful terraced gardens. A stroll around the old part of the town takes you past several grand 15th- and 16th-century houses, each with a pretty courtyard, that have recently been refurbished. The grounds of a former convent, Des Petits Augustins, have been made into a small botanical garden. Next to it is **La Soie Vivante❖**, a silk museum displaying looms and old tools. Silkworms are bred here and visitors can observe how they develop and spin their cocoons.

Food in Montreuil-Bellay

Auberge des Iles €€ *Pl. des Vieux Ponts, Montreuil-Bellay; tel: 02 41 50 37 37.* Sandwiched between the castle and river, this looks like a snack bar but is actually an excellent restaurant. The Menu des Ducs and Menu des Plantagenets both include intriguing dishes.

MONTSOREAU✤✤

ℹ **Montsoreau
Tourist Office** *Just
west of castle on the D751;
tel: 02 41 51 70 22,
www.montsoreau.com; open
May–Sept.*

🏰 **Château de
Montsoreau** €€ *open
mid-Feb–mid-Nov daily.*

The impressive 15th-century **Château de Montsoreau**✤✤ – the only one whose grounds extend to the banks of the Loire – has recently undergone extensive renovations. Originally the home of the Chambes family, it was the setting of the Alexandre Dumas story, *La Dame de Montsoreau*, which he based on a true saga of infidelity and murder. Though the interior is unfurnished, it is brought to life by an innovative *son-et-lumière*-style presentation as you pass through the rooms. This explains the story of *La Dame de Montsoreau* and also covers the Anjou countryside, its traditions and people.

Accommodation and food in and around Montsoreau

Hôtel le Bussy € *4 r. Jehanne d'Arc; tel: 02 41 38 11 11.* A small, family-run hotel with Louis-Philippe-style furnishings and views of the castle and river.

Le Saut aux Loups € *Just west of castle on the D751; tel: 02 41 51 70 30, www.SautAuxLoups.fr.st; restaurant open lunch June and Sept Sun, July–Aug daily; caves open Mar–Nov.* A restaurant created inside part of a 2-km cave quarried out in the 15th century. Mushrooms have been cultivated here for around 100 years. Visitors see how they are grown in bags, and how new varieties are developed. A tasty speciality is *galipettes* (huge mushrooms up to 15cm across, baked with a variety of toppings).

Below
Château de Montsoreau

ROCHEMENIER**

Rochemenier Village Troglodyte
€ *Open Apr–Nov daily.*

Occupied until the 1930s by two farming families, Rochemenier's tiny **Village Troglodyte** consists of their homes, animal pens and a chapel, all built inside the caves of a medieval quarry around a central courtyard area. The method of construction was certainly very practical. When a family grew, they simply hollowed out the wall to make room for an extra bed! Photographs of the families and ancient farm tools are on display too. One dwelling is relatively modern, with electric light and simple furniture, as it was lived in by a caretaker until 1984. The tower of the underground chapel is visible

Right
Troglodyte houses, Rochemenier

above ground next to a tiny 13th-century chapel, **Ste-Emérance**, which has a beautiful apse and carved wooden ceiling. Elsewhere in the village, and around the area, there are modern troglodyte houses, as this style of accommodation has become rather fashionable.

ST-HILAIRE-ST-FLORENT**

Bouvet Ladubay Wine Cellars *Open daily but no production to watch at weekends or Aug.*

Centre d'Art Bouvet Ladubay *Open daily.*

Museé du Champignon € *Near St-Hilaire-St-Florent open Feb–Nov daily.*

Musée du Masque *R. de l'Abbaye; open Easter–mid-Oct daily.*

St-Hilaire-St-Florent, now very much a suburb of Saumur, is synonymous with wine. Several of the Loire's most famous wineries are to be found here, situated on both sides of the main street. This runs between the river Thouet, just as it joins the Loire, and the foot of the tufa cliffs. The most interesting to visit is the **Bouvet Ladubay Wine Cellars**. Founded in 1851, their cellars occupy miles of galleries in ancient *tuffeau* quarries. Visitors can see production in full swing, starting with the wine being piped from huge metal vats into bottles which are stored in special cubes of racks. These tilt automatically every three months to force the sediment up into the neck so it can be removed by freezing. Then they are stored for a second fermentation in the 8km-long cellars before emerging to be corked, wired and labelled. Visits end – of course – with a tasting of three wines including Saumur's unusual sparkling red.

Pierre et Lumière €
Near St-Hilaire-St-Florent open Feb–Nov daily.

Opposite the winery is the **Centre d'Art Bouvet Ladubay***. The gallery's nine exhibition halls are each devoted to the work of a different contemporary artist. There is also an architectural centre and a cinema where documentary films are premiered.

Also in St-Hilaire-St-Florent is the **Musée du Masque****. The César company, manufacturers of masks for a century, has set up an imaginative grotto-like museum to display some of its most famous creations, as well as others gathered from around the world. The exhibits show how the materials used have developed over the years, from the *papier-mâché* used for characters like Punch and Judy in the 19th century to synthetic materials like latex in which contemporary models are fashioned for television. There are tableaux in fairytale settings, as well as realistic scenes such as a baccarat table where heads of state, from Winston Churchill to Fidel Castro, are laying their bets. 2 000 masks, many inexpensive, are on sale in the shop and even more are available by mail order.

Just west of St-Hilaire-St-Florent are two more fascinating places to visit. The **Museé du Champignon*** explains all you ever wanted to know about mushrooms, in underground galleries created by quarrying for *tuffeau* stone. It shows how growing techniques have developed over the years, and you can see examples being cultivated in bags and trays of compost. Wild varieties are on show too, together with fossils found during the quarrying. At the end of the tour, *galipettes* (large mushrooms grilled or stuffed) can be sampled in a small restaurant.

Pierre et Lumière* (Stone and Light) is an appropriate name for this unusual *parc miniature* inside the caves of an old quarry hewn into the hillside west of St-Hilaire-St-Florent. It contains 17 large models of famous places in the area, each meticulously carved into the walls by sculptor Philippe Cormand and skilfully lit to show off the details. They include Fontevraud Abbey and the intricately decorated churches of Cunault and Candes. Most impressive of all is a large panorama of Saumur, complete with the Loire depicted by water flowing from a natural spring.

Right
Bouvet Ladubay Winery,
St-Hilaire

Suggested tour

Total distance: 86km. The detour to **Abbaye d'Asnières** adds 2km, the detour to **Les Rosiers** adds 3km, and the one to **Bourgeuil** adds 14km.

Time: 2 hours' driving time, but allow at least two days for the full route. Those with limited time should concentrate on Fontevraud l'Abbaye and Brézé.

Links: At Chinon (*see page 86*) this tour links with the South Touraine tour (*see page 92*). From Gennes it is a 10-km scenic drive along the river to link up with the Western Châteaux tour (*see page 128*).

Route: From **Chinon** set off west along the north bank of the **Vienne** on the D749. The road swings north to **Avoine** past the nuclear power station whose untidy mixture of enormous ugly buildings appears on the right, heralded by power lines sweeping over the road.

Detour: To visit **BOURGEUIL ①** continue on the D749 across the river and over the start of the A85 autoroute, straight into the town, before retracing your route. Immediately before the river (or immediately after, if you have visited Bourgeuil), turn left onto the D7 to **CANDES-ST-MARTIN ②**. This provides some good views of the lake-like river, though it is mostly just out of sight behind trees. Immediately after crossing the Vienne, turn right into Candes where you pass its church on the left.

Getting out of the car: In Candes, a short walk opposite the church leads down to the wide river and its old slipways. Better still, take the steeper series of paths (well signed) behind the church up to a hillside vantage point to enjoy a superb view of the confluence of the Loire and Vienne rivers.

Continue to **MONTSOREAU ③**. The château is on the left beside a paved section of road along the river bank. Originally this was the château's private terrace and all traffic had to go instead through the pretty but narrow village street at the back. Shortly beyond the château, **FONTEVRAUD L'ABBAYE ④** is signed to the left.

After visiting it, take the D162 signed St-Cyr-en-Bourg from the roundabout on its west side. On reaching the crossroads with the D93, turn left to **BRÉZÉ ⑤**. The château is 2km further on the left (but unsigned until you reach the turning to it). Next, continue on the same road to the village church, turn right beside it and follow signs to **MONTREUIL-BELLAY ⑥** and its château along the D178 and then D166.

Getting out of the car: A stroll around Montreuil-Bellay's 1000-year-old ramparts provides excellent views of the oldest part of the town and the surrounding countryside. They skirt the castle beside the

Mushroom growing

For over 300 years, mushrooms have been cultivated in the *tuffeau* caves which seam the hillsides along the Loire west of Saumur. Today, production is on a massive scale, accounting for around 70 per cent of France's total output. Most are *champignons de Paris* (button mushrooms). The caves provide perfect conditions for them to develop – darkness, unvarying 90 per cent humidity and a constant temperature of 15°C. The process begins with *mycelium* (seeds) being planted in trays or bags of compost. After six weeks these are transferred to the caves. Five weeks later a 'burst' of mushrooms appears over three days, followed at two-weekly intervals by four lesser ones. Picking is done early in the morning, and a skilled operator can collect up to 60 kilos a day.

River Thouet and pass three of the town's old fortified gateways. Leaving Montreuil-Bellay, follow the signs for Angers. After 5km on the D761, the **ABBAYE D'ASNIÈRES** ⑦ is signed off to the right.

Detour to the Abbaye d'Asnières: A short drive towards Cizay-la-Madeleine takes you to this ancient abbey which, except for the nave, has survived remarkably intact since the 13th century, including decorative glazed tiling (*open July–Aug Wed–Mon pms*).

The D761 continues to **DOUÉ-LA-FONTAINE** ⑧, a somewhat confusing town to find your way around due to poor signing. The **Zoo de Doué** is on its southwest side on the main D960 leading towards Cholet; the **Chemins de la Rose** are a little further along it. If you approach the D960 along the blvd du D Lionel, watch out for the **Maison Carolingienne** on the left. This fortified house, dating from the 9th century but still in good condition, looks like a castle keep. To visit the **Musée des Commerces Anciens**, return along the D960 to the Soulanger suburb where it is signposted to the left. The extraordinary troglodyte village of **ROCHEMENIER** ⑨ is shortly signed to the right off the busy D761 to Angers. Next, head north on the D69 through woods to **GENNES** ⑩. Just before Gennes, the ancient Dolmen de la Madeleine stands in splendid isolation in a field to the right, a few paces from the road. It is the most impressive of the many megaliths, dating from around 4000–2000BC, to be found in this area south of the Loire. Stepping inside, you realise how colossal the stones are – how did they get here, and why?

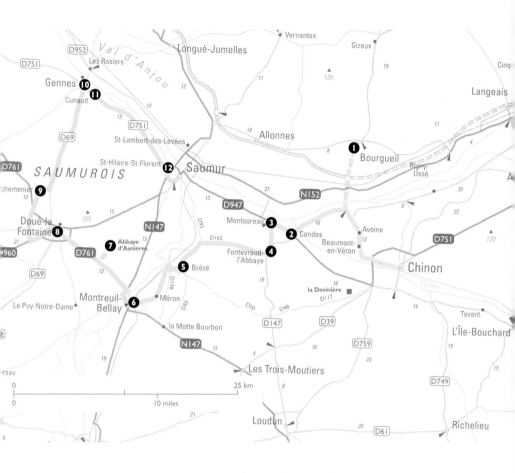

Detour: In Gennes, take a brief trip north across the pretty suspension bridge over the Loire to **Les Rosiers** to savour its serene views of the broad, gently-flowing water.

From Gennes, the D751 keeps close to the river as it passes through **CUNAULT** ⑪ and then the little hamlet of **Trèves**. There, just off the road, lurks a gleaming white crenellated tower, all that remains of a 15th-century castle, and a delightful little church. Then you pass another small Romanesque chapel with a handsome doorway beside the road in the village of **Chênhutte-les-Truffeaux** which nestles at the foot of a wooded hillside. Just before arriving at **ST-HILAIRE-ST-FLORENT** ⑫, home of Saumur's sparkling wine, both the **Pierre-et-Lumière** sculpture cave and the **Musée du Champignon** are beside the road. Then a short run takes you into **Saumur** itself, though the journey could take a long time if you succumb to the temptation of lingering at any of St Hilaire's wineries.

Saumur

Ratings

Castles	●●●●●
Winetasting	●●●●●
Gastronomy	●●●○○
Entertainment	●●○○○
Historical sights	●●○○○
Museums	●●○○○
Shopping	●●○○○
Outdoor activities	●○○○○

Saumur is the 'white city' of Anjou, built in the creamy local *tuffeau* stone from the limestone plain south of the Loire. People say it is a particularly agreeable place to live, and you soon realise why. Attractively situated beside a broad, dreamy stretch of the river, it is large enough to have an interesting selection of shops, restaurants and leisure facilities, yet also feels very laid-back. No doubt the fact that it is the home of some of France's best sparkling wines helps too! Most of the wineries are in the St-Hilaire-St-Florent suburb (*see page 113*), west of the town centre beside the River Thouet. The town's heyday was 400 years ago when it became a centre of Protestant scholarship. It was renowned for its tolerance, rather than getting involved in feudal power struggles. The huge castle – dating back to earlier times but still in good condition – is by far the most distinctive feature.

Getting there and getting around

ℹ Saumur Tourist Office Pl. de la Bilange; tel: 02 41 40 20 60; www.saumur-tourisme. com

◑ Markets: Thur and Sat.

◐ Summer Festival: Mid-July, with two weeks of concerts, street parades and fireworks, mostly free.

By road
Saumur is on the N147, 9km south of exit 3 on the A85.

By rail
There are frequent services from Angers (20 min), Nantes (1 hour) and Tours (40 min). The railway station is on the right (north) bank of the Loire, av. David d'Angers. Train enquiries *tel: 08 36 35 35 35.*

Parking
Parking is free 1200–1400, 1900–0900 and all day Sun. Meters operate in the town centre but many of the streets are no-parking zones. The most central car parks are the riverside pl. de la République, handy for the tourist office, and pl. St-Pierre. Elsewhere, car parks are free, including one next to the castle. A leaflet showing parking is available from the Tourist Information office.

Quai Carnot

Avenue de G. de Gau

Rue Paul Bert

Avenue de Verd

École Nationale d'Equitation

Pont Cessart

Quai Marine

Rue St-Nicolas

Place Bilange

Quai Lucien Gautier

LOIRE

Rue des Aulnes

Avenue Foch R. Beaurepaire

Rue St-Jean

Place République

Rue Gambetta

Rue d'Orléans

Ancienne Messagerie

Place St-Michel

Rue d'Alsace

Rue du Portail-Louis

Place St-Pierre

St-Pierre

Place St-Pierre

Rue du Temple

Grande Rue

Rue Dacier

Quai Mayaud

Place Maupassant

Rue Bodin

Avenue du Docteur Peton

Château

Rue du Maréchal Leclerc

RRue du Docteur Bouchard

Rue Seigneur

Rue Duruy

Place de Verdun

Jardin des Plantes

Rue des Mou

Boulevard Loius Renault

Rue Hoche

Rue du Nantilly

Place Nantilly

Notre-Dame de Nantilly

Rue Lamartine

Dolmen de Bagneux

Rue du Mouton

Rue Marceau

Rue Loucheur

Boulevard de la Marne

Rue Robert Amy

Rue Chemin Vert

Avenue Victor Boret

Rue Fricotelle

Rue de Fontevraud

Musée des Blindés

| 0 | | 200 metres |
| 0 | | 200 yards |

Equestrian events throughout the year, including the *Carrousel de Saumur*, a grand tattoo in July, featuring cavalry demonstrations by the horsemen of the Cadre Noir; tel: 02 41 67 36 37.

Getting around

The central area is easily manageable on foot. To go further afield there are local buses, including the B line to St-Hilaire. Bus station: *pl. St Nicolas; tel: 02 41 51 11 87*. There are tours of the town by tourist train and horse-drawn carriages Apr–Sept. Boat trips run from quai Lucien Gautier Jun–Sept Tue–Sun. Cycle hire: *Cycles Peugeot, 19 av. du Général de Gaulle; tel: 02 41 67 36 86*. Canoeing and sailing on the Loire from *Base de Loisirs de Millocheau, 1 r. des Tennis; tel: 02 41 51 17 65*.

Sights

Château de Saumur €
Castle/museums open Oct–May Wed–Mon, Jun–Sept daily. Floodlit tours July–Aug Wed & Sat 2030–2230.

Musée du Figurine-Jouet € *R. des Moulins; open mid-Jun–mid-Sept Wed–Mon pm.*

Dolmen de Bagneux € *56 r. du Dolmen, Bagneux; open daily.*

École Nationale d'Equitation *In suburb of Terrefort; open Mar–Nov for 45-min demonstrations, mostly Sat. Bookings tel: 02 41 53 50 60. Visitors can also have a guided tour of the stables and watch any classes taking place at the time €€ Apr–July & Sept Mon–Sat. Show jumping in May and Sept.*

Château de Saumur✧✧✧

Saumur's castle, topped by a forest of 'pencil' turrets, dominates the town from a mound once occupied by windmills. The views over the town and river from both the interior and the grassy ramparts are superb. Built in the 14th century as a residence for Louis I, Duke of Anjou, with spacious rooms and several spiral staircases, it became a Protestant stronghold 200 years later when a mighty outside wall was added to fortify it. Subsequently it was used as a prison and, later, as an army barracks. Now, still in a good state of repair, it houses two museums. The **Museé des Arts Décoratifs** displays a fine collection of tapestries, furniture and ceramics from the 13th to 19th centuries. The **Musée du Cheval** traces the history of the horse and the development of riding from prehistoric times to the present. An elaborately carved sleigh from Russia and a large collection of horseshoes and saddles from around the world are among the highlights. The castle's powdermill houses a third museum, **Musée du Figurine-Jouet**. This displays a collection of lead soldiers and models of the kings of France, together with 19th-century toys made from flour and plaster.

Dolmen de Bagneux✧

The dolmen, tucked away in the garden of a bar, is one of the biggest and most impressive Neolithic burial chambers in Europe. At 21m long and 7m wide, it is made of massive sandstone slabs standing 3m high. Astonishingly, they were transported, lifted and wedged together 5000 years ago. It's a shame that access to such an atmospheric place is through an uninteresting modern bar, although it does afford the opportunity to enjoy a drink in the garden as you contemplate this feat of ancient construction.

École Nationale d'Equitation✧

Saumur is home to France's prestigious riding academy, l'École Nationale d'Equitation, which has 400 horses, an Olympic-size indoor riding school, 50km of specially laid-out tracks and its own veterinary hospital. Leading riders come to it from all over the world to be taught by its famous instructors, the Cadre Noir, some of whom have a military background.

Opposite
Château de Saumur and Saumur vines

Église St-Pierre*

This fine old Plantagenet church which, in its time, has been used as a barn and gunpowder factory, is an architectural mixture of Romanesque, Gothic and Renaissance styles. The original façade was severely damaged when it was struck by lightning in 1674. Inside there is an outstanding set of intricately carved oak choir stalls depicting an entertaining array of characters. Unusually they are arranged in a horseshoe around the altar. Some of the stained glass is medieval, and the walls are hung with a particularly fine collection of 16th-century tapestries illustrating the lives of St Florent, a locally venerated hero, and St Peter.

Musée des Blindés**

Musée des Blindés € 1043 *rte de Fontevraud; open daily.*

This is the largest collection of tanks in Europe. All 200 are in working order, so they are much in demand as props for films. Now run by France's ministry of defence, the collection was started by Michel Aubry, an army officer, in 1964. Housed in a former cigarette factory, it ranges from examples of the earliest tanks, used in World War I, to modern ones which saw action in the Gulf. Sprucely painted and clearly labelled, they are grouped according to nationality in separate halls, and put into context by pictures and newspaper reports displayed around the walls. A small cinema shows archive film.

Notre-Dame de Nantilly*

Notre-Dame de Nantilly *Pl. Nantilly.*

Saumur's oldest church, dating back to the 12th century, is an austere-looking building with few windows, a small neat spire and interesting tapestries. A pillar on the nave's south side bears an epitaph that the 15th-century King René, the last Duke of Anjou and a scholar and poet, wrote to his nurse.

Right
Pl. St-Pierre

Shopping

Saumur is not a major shopping centre, though it has a branch of the **Printemps** department store in r. Franklin Roosevelt and three noteworthy specialist shops: **Gibardeau**, 51 r. St-Nicholas, stocks everything for the gourmet, particularly regional products such as mustards and *foie gras*; the **Lace Shop**, 7 La Dentellerie, sells whimsical-looking lace dresses, bonnets and even parasols; and **La Bôite à Pêche**, 7 pl. de la République, stocks everything for the angler from rods to bait. For fashionwear, r. Saint-Jean has several small boutiques. For antiques, r. St-Nicholas is the place to look. **La Maison des Vins de Saumur**, next to the tourist information office, offers advice about wines. You can sample and buy there too – or head for one of the cellars. **Caves de Grenelle**, r. Marceau, are the most central.

Entertainment

Live music comes onto the streets in July and August, particularly at pl. St-Pierre and pl. de la République, where groups play outside the bars and restaurants. Nightclubs with live music include **Blues Rock**, r. de la Petit Bilange, and **La Loco** on the north bank of the river on route de Rouen. Or head out to the suburb of St-Hilaire-St-Florent (*see page 113*), where several bars in *tuffeau* caves have music and dancing.

Boule de Fort

La Boule de Fort, a centuries-old game played indoors throughout Anjou, is bowls with a difference. The balls, 126cm in diameter, weigh 1.3–1.5kg and are made of wood or plastic with a metal strip around them. They are also weighted, making them *fort* – strong – on one side, giving the game its name. This makes them wobble when bowled towards the *maître*, or jack. The course is between 21 and 24m in length, 6m across, and slopes up on both sides like a boat. Indeed, one theory on the origins of the game is that it was devised by boatmen or prisoners on voyages along the Loire. To avoid damaging the plastic surface of the course, players wear slippers. Today there are about 400 *Boule de Fort* clubs, playing in the special halls devoted to it, so visitors should be able to find a game to watch. Women were not allowed to play until the mid-1980s, but many are now as addicted to it as their menfolk.

On the menu

Locally-caught fish is a feature of most menus, particularly pike, perch, sandre and eel. The area is also known for its *champignons de Paris*, mushrooms cultivated in the *tuffeau* caves. Asparagus, tomatoes, pears and apples are also grown locally. Several producers of Saumur Brut sparkling wine are based in and around the town, and all welcome visitors for tastings. The unusual red variety, which tastes of soft red fruits, makes a refreshing aperitif.

Accommodation and food in and around Saumur

Anne d'Anjou €€ *32–33 quai Mayaud; tel: 02 41 67 75 20*. Overlooking the Loire, this grand 18th-century building is an ideal place to stay for those with a sense of history. Some of the rooms are furnished in Louis XVI style and the façade and staircase are listed.

L'Auberge St-Pierre €€ *6 pl. St-Pierre; tel: 02 41 51 26 25*. Fifty metres from the Hotel Saint-Pierre, but a completely separate establishment, this is definitely the most interesting restaurant in the square at the front of the St-Pierre church, even if you get no further than admiring its distinctive 15th- to 17th-century façade of diagonal beams and red brick panels. The interior is spacious and heavily beamed. Excellent for snails and oysters as well as more homely fare like *coq-au-vin grandmère*.

Les Caves de Marson € *Marson, 5km west of Saumur; tel: 02 41 50 50 05; open lunchtime Sept–Jun weekends and July–Aug Tue–Sun*. Booking recommended. The restaurant occupies a series of large caves where you are served a meal of *fouace* – rounds of soft pitta-like bread baked in a troglodyte oven – which you spread with butter and fill with *rillettes* (potted meat), goat's cheese and white beans. Baked mixed fruit completes the unusual menu, which is best accompanied by a bottle of Saumur Rouge.

Cristal Hôtel €€ *10–12 pl. de la République; tel: 02 41 51 09 54*. This 300-year-old hotel, well-positioned facing the main square, bridge and river, has 23 rooms. Those at the front can be somewhat noisy but provide a good vantage point. No restaurant, but the ground floor is occupied by a lively bistro.

Hôtel Saint-Pierre €€ *8 r. Haute-Saint-Pierre; tel: 02 41 50 33 00*. A smart 15-room hotel tucked away handily in a narrow side street beside the St-Pierre church. Part of it dates back to the 15th century but the decor is modern and stylish throughout. Tiny bar and garden. Breakfast only.

Le Grand Bleu €€ *6 pl. du Marché; tel: 02 41 67 41 83*. Despite this restaurant's name, its decor is pale green, though the tables outside in summer are certainly blue. Big choice of fish, including a *Special Grand Bleu* for two which includes 16 oysters, 10 crayfish, two crabs and lots more.

La Mascotte €€ *60 r. St Nicholas; tel: 02 41 51 12 01*. One of several small restaurants in this street, it has pretty green decor and a conservatory-style extension jutting out onto the pavement. Plenty of interesting fish dishes such as salmon roasted in port and cream.

Les Ménestrels €€€ *11 r. Raspail; tel: 02 41 67 71 10*. Generally regarded as the best restaurant in town, it features regional cuisine that changes with the seasons. Distinguished list of Loire wines.

L'Orangerie € *cour du Château; tel: 02 41 67 12 88*. In the castle grounds, this is a handy spot for a pre- or post-visit meal or snack, though it also offers menus and local dishes in the evenings.

Restaurant le Pullman €€ *52 r. d'Orleans; tel: 02 41 51 31 79*. This small but smart eatery is fitted out like a pullman rail carriage, with bench seats in alcoves. Ideal for a quiet tryst.

Suggested walk

Total distance: 2km.

Time: 1 hour, but allow a day to see all the sights.

Below
Hotel de Ville, Saumur

Route: After a stroll along the river bank and admiring the impressive **town hall**, parts of which date back to the 1500s, at **pl. République**, take **r. Corneille** beside it to the pedestrianised **r. Saint-Jean**. A neglected-looking apartment above one of the shops, **Les Fleurs se Font Belles**, is where the fashion icon Coco Chanel (real name Gabrielle Bonheur) was born. **R. Saint-Jean** leads to **pl. St-Pierre**, the scenic heart of the old quarter where three half-timbered houses with gables and decorative red brick have survived since medieval times beside ÉGLISE ST-PIERRE ❶. Always a lively place, thanks to its pavement cafés, the square is at its busiest during the summer festival when street entertainers perform there. The narrow **r. de la Tonnelle** running off it was once a main road leading down to a wooden bridge across to the **Ile d'Offard** in the middle of the Loire.

As you begin to climb towards the castle along the short but steep **Monté du Fort**, you pass a house that fans of the 19th-century writer **Honoré de Balzac** will recognise as the home of Père Grandet, one of his most famous characters. Indeed, the whole area features in the novel named after him. Steps then lead up to the grassy grounds of the **CHÂTEAU ❷**, from which there are fine views over the red chimneys, grey slate roofs and white stone walls of the town and the river. The **Maison des Compagnons**, just below, is a school for apprentice stonemasons who can often be seen hewing lumps of white *tuffeau* stone in the courtyard. Considering the amount of restoration going on in and around Saumur, their skills are sure to be much in demand.

After leaving the ramparts, turn left into **r. Duruy** which leads to the **NOTRE-DAME DE NANTILLY ❸** church. Return along r. Duruy to **Grande Rue** which was the town's main street in the 17th century, when it had 25 bookshops and printers. At the time, Saumur was a centre of learning and tolerance, welcoming both Protestants and Catholics to its university, including William Penn who went on to found the city of Pennsylvania in the US. A 15th-century mansion with red gables and a delightful courtyard off **r. des Paiens** was a favourite hideaway with the poet-king Roi René – he preferred it to the castle. Later it was also used by Mary Queen of Scots for a two-night stay on her way to marry François II. The imposing **Maison des Abbesses** on the corner of **Ancienne Messagerie**, which leads back to **r. St-Jean**, is where abbey visitors once stayed; now it is the residence of the director of the École Nationale d'Equitation.

Tuffeau quarries

The limestone hillsides around Saumur are seamed with caves and tunnels left over from the quarrying, which has been going since Gallo-Roman times. Almost all the châteaux, as well as many other buildings in the area, are built in the chalky beige stone – called *tuffeau* or tufa – deposited here when the sea covered the area millions of years ago. Around 1500km are now used commercially, mostly for cultivating mushrooms. Others are occupied by wine cellars, restaurants and other businesses. Today *tuffeau* is extracted from only one quarry, in St Cyr-en-Bourg, and is used exclusively for restoration work.

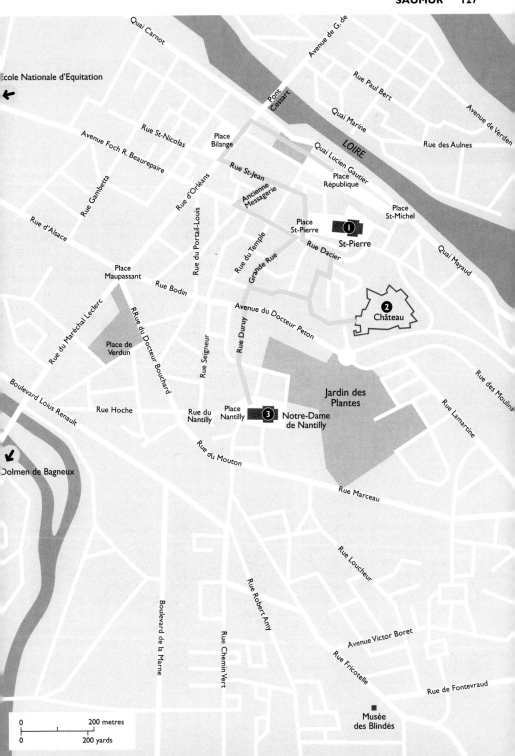

Quai Carnot

Avenue de G. de

Rue Paul Bert

École Nationale d'Equitation

Rue St-Nicolas

Place Bilange

Rue St-Jean

Pont Cessart

Quai Marine

Quai Lucien Gautier

LOIRE

Avenue Foch R. Beaurepaire

Rue Gambetta

Rue d'Orléans

Rue d'Alsace

Rue du Portail-Louis

Ancienne Messagerie

Place République

Rue des Aulnes

Avenue de Verden

Place St-Pierre

Place St-Michel

❶ St-Pierre

Rue Dacier

Quai Mayaud

Rue du Temple

Grande Rue

Place Maupassant

Rue Bodin

Avenue du Docteur Peton

❷ Château

Rue du Maréchal Leclerc

R. Rue du Docteur Bouchard

Place de Verdun

Rue Seigneur

Rue Duruy

Jardin des Plantes

Rue des Moulins

Rue Lamartine

Boulevard Loïus Renault

Rue Hoche

Rue du Nantilly

Place Nantilly

❸ Notre-Dame de Nantilly

Rue du Mouton

Dolmen de Bagneux

Rue Marceau

Rue Loucheur

Boulevard de la Marne

Rue Chemin Vert

Rue Robert Amy

Avenue Victor Boret

Rue Fricotelle

Rue de Fontevraud

Musée des Blindés

0   200 metres

0   200 yards

The Western Châteaux

Ratings

History	●●●●●
Châteaux	●●●○○
Activities	●●●○○
Restaurants	●●●○○
Winetasting	●●●○○
Museums	●●●○○
Scenery	●●●○○
Children	●●○○○

As the Loire nears Angers, there's a change in tone. This is the very heart of Anjou, land of the Plantagenets. For generations, Plantagenet counts sat on the English throne and spoke not English, nor French, but Angevin. That led to the Hundred Years' War, and eventually Anjou and the other Plantagenet possessions in France came under the control of the French king. Here the Loire expands on its right bank into a great watery plain, and several rivers converge from the north. The Loir, the Sarthe and the Mayenne join to become the Maine, which passes grandly through the city of Angers to reach the Loire. In every direction, Anjou's history, art and architecture, culture and civilisation enrich a gentle landscape. As well as its châteaux, the area has abundant fruit orchards, productive vegetable farms and famous vineyards.

BAUGÉ⁺

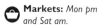

ℹ Baugé Tourist Office In the Château; tel: 02 41 89 18 07, fax: 02 41 89 04 43, www.tourisme-bauge.fr; open 15 Sept–15 June Mon–Sat 1130–1230, 1330–1800, rest of year Mon–Sat 1000–1230, 1330–1830.

🛒 Markets: Mon pm and Sat am.

💊 Apothecary R. Dr Zamenhof; tel: 02 41 89 18 07; open Wed–Mon, July–Aug daily (check with tourist office).

This appealing little market town on the Couasnon river, close to the extensive Chandelais forest, became illustrious as a medieval residence of the Anjou nobility, and was the preferred home of Good King René, Duke of Anjou, Count of Provence and King of Naples. That accounts for the many fine mansions along its old streets. René lived in the old **Château**⁺⁺⁺, which he greatly enlarged and improved, turning it into a handsome castle. A lovely tower staircase is its finest feature. Today the château houses the tourist office and the town's modest **Musée d'Art et d'Histoire**⁺. One of the town's retirement homes, Hospice St-Joseph, retains a 17th-century **apothecary**⁺, with panelled walls, beautiful wooden flooring and 16th-century *faïence* containers. In another former hospice chapel, the Chapelle des Fille-du-Coeur-de-Marie, is a venerated religious treasure, the **Croix d'Anjou (Cross of Anjou)**⁺⁺⁺. A striking double-armed cross brought back from Palestine in 1241 by a Crusader, it has been worshipped by some as Christ's

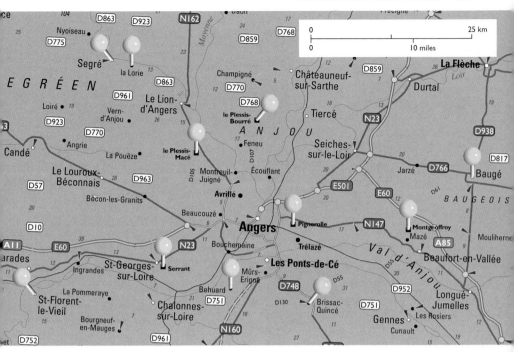

Château de Baugé €
Open 15 June–15 Sept daily
1100–1300, 1530–1730
(for more information call
tourist office).

Croix d'Anjou (Cross of
Anjou) *Chapelle des Fille-*
du-Coeur-de-Marie, r. de la
Girouardière; tel: 02 41 89
12 20. Open for guided visits
Wed–Mon 1430–1630,
closed Pentecost weekend
and preceding three days,
1st Sun in July, 24–26 July,
11–12 Dec, 25 Dec.

cross. It was reconstructed and exquisitely decorated with jewels and gold in the 14th century, and was especially revered by King René. Christ is depicted on both sides. Just out of town is another remarkable – and more ancient – religious relic, the **Dolmen de la Pierre Couverte**✢✢. It stands off the road in a forest clearing.

Accommodation and food in Baugé

La Boule d'Or €€ *4 r. Cygne; tel: 02 41 89 82 12, fax: 02 41 89 06 07.* An appealing, family-run little hotel-restaurant offering decent board and lodging at a moderate price.

BÉHUARD✢

ⓘ Béhuard Tourist
Office *In the village;*
tel: 02 41 70 20 17.

The long, narrow Loire island of Béhuard was formed millennia ago – and is still being formed – by the gradual build-up of river silt around a strange dark pinnacle of rock in mid-river. If you find something magical about this curious, serene place, you are not the only one: the island and its rock have been a place of worship and spirituality since

time immemorial. Before the Christian era, a river goddess was venerated here. Her shrine became a sailor's chapel in the 5th century. In the 15th century, Louis XI constructed the present unusual church on the site, dedicated to Our Lady of Béhuard. The narrow, concentric lanes of the island's attractive village keep many of their 15th- and 16th-century houses. Periodic floods, reaching about 7m, add to the island's unique character. There's a beach and picnic area, and a waterside footpath around the island.

Accommodation and food in Béhuard

Les Tonnelles €€ *Tel: 02 41 72 21 50; closed Sun pm, Mon (except lunchtime in summer), Tue in winter, and Wed*. For a true taste of the Loire in mid-stream, this excellent restaurant brings perfectly prepared fish or game dishes together with the best of local wines.

Above
Béhuard village

BRISSAC-QUINCÉ✤✤

Surrounded by vineyards, the sleepy little town of Brissac-Quincé was, until 1964, two separate parishes divided by the narrow Aubance river. Though the castle is its main attraction, a recently discovered curiosity exists under the market square. It's an **underground chapel**✤ with secret passages. No one knows why or when it was built, but possibly it was a hiding place.

Seat of the Dukes of Brissac for 500 years, the massive **Château de Brissac**✤✤✤ towers grandly up for nine storeys in its leafy park beside the River Aubance. Guided tours of a handful of its 203 rooms include Louis XIII's plush red bedroom and its large bathroom, a small 17th-century-style theatre (still occasionally used for performances), a chapel with fine wood carvings and the opulent *Salles des Gardes* where Aubusson tapestries hang beneath a gilded ceiling. All the rooms have intricately painted ceilings and are lavishly furnished with Renaissance pieces. The current duke's son now administers the castle, and recent family photographs stand on the grand piano in the Grand Salon. Visits end with a wine tasting in the 900-year-old cellars – and an opportunity to buy.

ⓘ **Brissac-Quincé Tourist Office** *8 pl. de la République; tel: 02 41 91 21 50, fax: 02 41 91 28 12, e-mail: Brissac. Tourisme49@wanadoo.fr; open daily May–Sept, rest of year Wed and Thur am only, but phone messages may be left on other days.*

Ⓦ *www.brissac-tourisme.asso.fr*

Ⓖ *The tourist office organises free walking tours of the town in June–July with English-speaking guides; also guided walks and tours to local villages and vineyards.*

Market: Thur am.

Chateau de Brissac €€
Tel: 02 41 91 22 21, fax:
02 41 91 25 60, e-mail:
charles-andre@chateau-
brissac.fr; www.chateau-
brissac.fr; open Apr–Oct
Wed–Mon, except first 2
weeks of Sept; July–Aug
daily, Apr–June, Sep–14 Oct
daily 1000–1200,
1415–1715, Jul–Aug
1000–1800 daily, 15–31
Oct 1000–1200,
1415–1615 closed Tue.

Underground chapel €
To visit, and for information,
call at the tourist office.

Accommodation and food in Brissac-Quincé

Hôtel le Castel €€ *1 r. Louis-Moron; tel: 02 41 91 24 74.* Handily placed opposite the castle, and all the rooms have recently been refurbished to a high standard, including a spa bath in the 'honeymoon suite'. No restaurant.

Le Clemenceau € *21 r. de la Marne; tel: 02 41 91 22 01.* A simple restaurant in a beamed room behind a bar. Menus feature country fare like rabbit and perch. Popular with locals.

CHÂTEAU DE LA LORIE❖

**Segré Tourist
Office** (2km) 5 rue
David d'Angers; tel: 02 41
92 86 83, fax: 02 41 61 05
73, email:
OTSI.SEGRE@wanadoo.fr;
open Mon-Fri 0900–1230,
1430–1800, Sat
1000–1200, 1500–1700.
Guided tours are available.

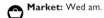 Market: Wed am.

Château de la Lorie
€€ 2km from Segré off
D863; tel: 02 41 92 10 04;
open for guided tours,
1500–1800, Easter–Sept
closed Tue.

The château stands just outside Segré, a striking and attractive little country town of dark houses stepping down a hillside to an old bridge and river quays on the bank of the Oudon. Built in the 17th century, altered in the 18th, La Lorie represents a last fling of aristocratic extravagance before the Revolution. Its glittering ballroom in particular, the highlight of the visit, has an unabashed opulence and was the last of its kind to be built. It forms part of the two wings added in the 1770s. It has a musicians' gallery in a rotunda, and fine marble-work created by Italian craftsmen brought here specially. The whole château has a light, elegant, almost frivolous formality, with French-style gardens, and pale tufa window surrounds and corners contrasting with the rest of the stonework.

CHÂTEAU DE MONTGEOFFROY❖❖

Standing with elegant dignity within its spacious parkland, Montgeoffroy is one of the best examples in this area of the later style of château, more stately home than castle. It was built for the

ⓘ Mazé Tourist Office *In nearby village, 94 r. Principale, Mazé; tel: 02 41 80 26 32.*

ⓘ Château de Montgeoffroy €€€ *Just outside Mazé on D74; tel: 02 41 80 60 02, fax: 02 41 80 62 66, email: montgeoffroy@wanadoo.fr; open for 1-hr guided tours 15 June–15 Sept 0930–1830, rest of year 0930–1200, 1430–1830, closed 1 Nov–15 Mar.*

Right
Montgeoffroy Château

Maréchal de Contades, governor of Strasbourg, during the 1770s and has been treasured and well-maintained by his descendants. Everything is still in place, nothing modernised. Furniture and tapestries specially made for the house remain in the rooms, which are light and airy thanks to rows of tall windows. The kitchen has kept its impressive collection of copperware and pewter. The house has its own chapel (part of an earlier structure on the site), stables displaying antique carriages, and elegant 18th-century gardens.

CHÂTEAU DE PIGNEROLLE✢

ⓘ Château de Pignerolle Musée Européen de la Communication €€ *5km E of Angers on D61; tel/fax: 02 41 93 38 38, www.museecommunication. org/; open daily all year 1000–1230, 1430–1800.*

A delightful 18th-century château, built as an exact copy of the Petit Trianon at Versailles, Pignerolle finds itself only just beyond the expanding suburbs of Angers, and its 70ha of grounds have become a public park. In World War II the château was, in turn, the seat of the exiled Polish government, a German HQ, and then an American base under General Patton. Today the château houses the imaginative **Musée Européen de la Communication**, popular with families, with fascinating displays illustrating the development of human communications from the cry of the newborn baby, via tom-tom drums and the invention of printing, right up to satellite broadcasting.

CHÂTEAU DU PLESSIS-BOURRÉ✦

Château du Plessis-Bourré €€€ *Ecuillé; tel: 02 41 32 06 72, fax: 02 41 32 06 01; open for 1-hr guided visits Jul–Aug daily 1000–1800, Apr, May, Jun, Sept daily except Wed and Thu mornings 1000–1200, 1400–1800, Feb, Mar, Oct, Nov Thu–Tue 1400–1800, rest of year closed.*

Le Plessis-Bourré is a splendid white château, rising dreamlike from a wide moat crossed by a long low bridge of many arches. Four graceful towers stand guard to protect this palatial country house where kings and queens have stayed. It's lavish inside – and the slightly vulgar and sometimes amusing scenes painted on the wooden ceiling of the *Salles des Gardes* (guardroom) have been raising eyebrows for centuries! The castle's two drawbridges, still in good working order since it was completed in 1473, are shut every evening by the château's owner. The state rooms around the arcaded inner courtyard are airy, and decorated with finely carved stonework. Apart from French Revolution graffiti on the library fireplace, the building has survived the centuries remarkably undamaged. The château was originally the home of its architect, Jean Bourré, royal advisor and treasurer, who went on to design Langeais and Jarzé which similarly mark the transformation of Loire castles from military fortresses into palatial homes.

Accommodation and food around Plessis-Bourré

Château de Noirieux €€ *26 route du Moulin, Briollay; tel: 02 41 42 50 05, fax: 02 41 37 91 00.* Between Plessis-Bourré and Angers, this beautifully located, exceptional 15th- to 17th-century château-hotel is tranquil, well-equipped, and each bedroom has its own style. The restaurant – with a charming terrace – is outstanding, offering interesting seafood and fish dishes prepared with skill, imagination and flair, and a connoisseur's wine list.

Below
Château du Plessis-Bourré

CHÂTEAU DU PLESSIS-MACÉ❖❖

ℹ Château du Plessis-Macé €€ *13km NW of Angers on N162; tel: 02 41 32 67 93; open for 1-hr guided tours Jul–Aug daily 1030–1830, Jun and Sept Wed–Mon 1000–1200, 1400–1830, Mar, May, Oct, Nov daily 1330–1730, rest of year closed.*

Built as a dark, powerful fortress in the 11th and 12th centuries, Plessis-Macé was reconstructed as a luxurious palace 400 years later, after gradually falling into ruin. As part of the transformation, white tufa was added to decorate and lighten its appearance, and the building's fine Flamboyant Gothic stonework also dates from that period. Yet the château still has an impressively defensive character, with its battlements and broad moat. It's famous for the kings of France that stayed here, from Louis XI to François I. Plessis-Macé fell into ruin for a second time in the 19th century, and served a spell as a farmhouse before being bought and fully restored by the shipbuilding Walsh family from Nantes. Among several rooms visited on the tour of the house, one is the bedroom reserved for royalty. There's a private chapel with interesting Gothic panelling forming balconies. Around the courtyard are delightful balconies – one a hanging balcony built on a corner – where the household could safely watch jousting contests.

ST-FLORENT-LE-VIEIL❖

ℹ St-Florent Tourist Office *Pavillon de la Mairie; tel: 02 41 72 62 32, fax: 02 41 72 62 95, e-mail: off.tour.florentlevieil@ wanadoo.fr; open June–Aug 1000–1300, 1400–1900, May, Sept 1000–1200, 1400–1800, rest of year Mon, Thu and Fri 0900–1200, 1400–1700.*

☎ To arrange guided visits, *tel: 02 41 72 62 32, fax: 02 41 72 62 95.*

⊙ Market: *Fri pm.*

♦ Musical festival *Les Orientales – end June.*

ℹ Musée d'Histoire des Guerres de Vendée €€ *Pl. Jules et Marie Sourice; tel: 02 41 72 50 03; open Sat and Sun in season 1430–1830.*

A tranquil place nowadays, St-Florent was the scene of a bloody insurrection by Royalists in 1793: the fighting spread throughout the Vendée *département* to the south, and became known as the Vendéen War. The town has a **museum❖** about the uprising. On a high point overlooking the town, Republican citizens took refuge in the church – one of them the father of sculptor David d'Angers. Royalists locked them in and planned to massacre them, but Royalist leader Bonchamps insisted that the plan be abandoned. The sculptor showed his thanks by carving the marble bust of Bonchamps that forms his tomb inside the church. The esplanade by the church gives a broad view over town and river. On the little quayside by the Loire, a former salt-tax customs house has become a hotel.

Accommodation and food in St-Florent

Hostellerie de la Gabelle €–€€ *Quai de la Loire; tel: 02 41 72 50 19, fax: 02 41 72 54 38.* The salt tax was called *la gabelle*, hence the name of this pleasant little waterside hotel-restaurant in a former salt-tax collector's office. Family-run, charming and unpretentious, it offers comfortable accommodation and good cooking.

Château de Serrant❖❖❖

ℹ️ At the *Mairie*, St-Georges-sur-Loire; tel: 02 41 72 14 80, fax: 02 41 72 14 99.

🍴 Market: Thu.

ℹ️ Château de Serrant Just outside St-Georges-sur-Loire on N23, west of Angers; tel: 02 41 39 13 01, fax: 02 41 39 18 22; open, for guided tours only, June, Sept, Oct, 1–15 Nov 1020, 1120, 1420, 1520, 1620, 1720 (closed Tue), July–Aug 1020, 1050, 1120, 1420, 1450, 1520, 1550, 1620, 1650, 1720. 16 Nov–1 Jan Sat and Sun only 1020, 1120, 1420, 1520, 1620.

This elegant rural palace, cream-coloured under a black roof, keeps plenty of its former defences – solid walls, domed towers and a moat. A beautiful Renaissance covered stairway, known as the Escalier d'Honneur, with intricately carved balustrades under an elaborately painted ceiling, is the highlight of the interior. Such staircases would have led to the owner's private suites, guest bedrooms and the banqueting rooms used on special occasions. Built in 1546 but sympathetically extended over the next three centuries, it is still owned by the descendants of the Duc de La Trémoille who bought it in 1830. Before that, another owner had been the prosperous Nantes shipbuilder of Irish descent, Antoine Walsh. The splendid marble tomb of a previous owner, the Marquis de Vaubrun, can be found in the chapel. The rooms have kept their original exquisite furniture and decorations, including much priceless art, a fine collection of Flemish tapestries and a library of 12,000 books.

Suggested tour

Total distance: 146km, or 220km including the detours.

ℹ️ Angers Tourist Office 7–9 pl. Kennedy; tel: 02 41 23 50 00, fax: 02 41 23 51 19, e-mail: accueil@angers-tourisme.fr; open 15 June–15 Sept Mon–Sat 0900–1900, Sun and hols 1000–1300, 1400–1800, rest of year Mon 1100–1800, Tue–Sat 0900–1800, Sun 1000–1300. The area's main tourist office in Angers offers hotel reservations, currency exchange, booking for local events, and riverboat hire. Some villages in the region also have a small tourist office.

🌐 www.anjou.com/ (regional tourism site, French only); www.anjou.org/ (the economy of Anjou, in French and English);

Time: Allow 1 to 2 days.

Route: Start from **Angers** (*see page 138*). Leave the centre of town on r. Lise, by the Jardin des Plantes, continuing in the same direction (east) on av. Montaigne to join N147, in the direction of Saumur. After 3km, a right turn leads to **CHÂTEAU DE PIGNEROLLE ❶**, with its Communications Museum. A little further along the same road is the village of St-Barthélemy d'Anjou, where **Distillerie Cointreau** produces 28 million litres per annum of the region's famous orange liqueur. Visitors are taken around the distillery, and can wander in its museum. Continue on N147 to **CHÂTEAU DE MONTGEOFFROY ❷**.

Detour: It's a pleasant 17km along D61 to **BAUGÉ ❸**. Return along the same road to rejoin the route. From Montgeoffroy, return to N147 and cross over onto D55 – you pass through Gué-de-Mazé – heading to **St-Mathurin-sur-Loire**, where you cross the river. Follow D55 as it makes its way across the countryside to **CHÂTEAU DE BRISSAC ❹** on the far side of the village of Brissac (the commune is called Brissac-Quincé, as it combines two villages). The D130 continues west, reaching N160. Cross the main road and carry on to the village of Denée. Turn left there to follow the Loire downstream. At **Rochefort-sur-Loire**, you can take the bridge which crosses the Loire via the island of **BÉHUARD ❺**.

*www.loire-france.com/
(regional tourism site, French
only); www.francebalade.com
/ anjou/angers.htm (useful
regional site, French only);
www.ville-angers.fr and
www.angers-tourisme.com
(the official sites of the
region's capital).*

Autoroute *A11
(Paris-Nantes) passes
through the centre of the
region. It can also be
reached from east or west on
A85 or N147, and from the
south on A87 or N160.*

Anjou Festival, *from
about 20 June to 15
July, is one of France's
principal cultural and arts
festivals. The emphasis is on
theatre. Events take place
throughout Anjou.
www.festivaldanjou.com/*

It is possible to drive the short distance straight from here to St-Georges-sur-Loire and the Château de Serrant, but our route returns to the pretty south bank of the Loire. The river is much broken up here by islands and tributaries, as can be seen when the road climbs onto slightly higher ground following the **Corniche Angevine**, winding along the cliff face between Rochefort-sur-Loire and the appealing riverside village of **Chalonnes**, with cobblestone quay and a waterside church. The Loire is crossed here by a series of bridges that step from island to island – it's just 7km to St Georges-sur-Loire and **Château de Serrant**.

Detour: Before you take that route it's worth continuing further downstream for a few kilometres. Even after Chalonnes, the villages and road give excellent views, for example at Montjean-sur-Loire. Follow the south bank road as far as **ST-FLORENT-LE-VIEIL** ❻. Instead of heading back on the same road, cross the Loire and take N23 on the north side of the river direct to **CHÂTEAU DE SERRANT** ❼.

Drive to **CHÂTEAU DU PLESSIS-MACÉ** ❽. The fastest way to do this is to return on N23 to the Angers ring road (D106), join N162, and turn off left to the château after 6km. However, it is more enjoyable to drive north from St-Georges on the D961, turning right at **Bécon-les-Granits** and taking little D104 to Plessis-Macé. Follow N162 up to **Le Lion d'Angers**, a picturesque small town on the Oudon, a tributary of the nearby Mayenne. Its Église St-Martin is largely Romanesque, with 16th-century murals, and there's an 18th-century château. Take the road (D863) to Segré and **CHÂTEAU DE LA LORIE** ❾.

Return to Le Lion d'Angers, and leave the little town on the road which goes to Châteauneuf-sur-Sarthe, but after just 2km turn off right for **CHÂTEAU DU PLESSIS-BOURRÉ** ❿. The little D107 returns to Angers.

The Wines of Anjou

The area around Angers is noted for abundant and popular light wines, delicate and fruity whites and rosés, and some easy-drinking reds. The inexpensive, slightly sweet Rosé d'Anjou is one of Europe's favourites as a summer aperitif, or for outdoor parties and picnics. East of Angers, white wine vineyards grow close to the waterside on the Loire's right bank. South of Angers, vineyards massed along the pretty slopes above the Layon valley are famous for their sweet, golden wine.

Opposite
Château du Plessis-Macé

Angers

Ratings

Architecture	●●●●●
Tapestries	●●●●●
History	●●●●●
Restaurants	●●●○○
Winetasting	●●●○○
Museums	●●●○○
Children	●●○○○
Entertainment	●●○○○

This is the imposing, ancient capital of Anjou, land of the Plantagenets who, in the Middle Ages, became the royal line of England. Angers (pronounce it *'Ohnjay'*) makes sharp contrasts with the rest of château country. Instead of standing by the bright Loire, it turns towards the Maine, a tributary from the North. Instead of the familiar soft white stone called tufa, with its fairytale, sugar-icing look, the old heart of Angers, rising from its river bank, is dark slate. 'Black Angers', as it was known, still has a proud, resolute bearing, as one imagines the Plantagenets themselves may have had. And, instead of decorative Renaissance, its château is a daunting, dark medieval fortress. Its cathedral and church preserve fine Gothic architecture in the soaring Plantagenet style. Above all, the real treasures of the town are its tapestries, ancient and modern, especially the awesome Apocalypse Tapestry.

Getting there and getting around

ⓘ Angers Tourist Office *Angers Tourisme, 7–9 pl. Kennedy; tel: 02 41 23 50 00, fax: 02 41 23 51 19, e-mail: accueil@angers-tourisme.fr; open 15 June–15 Sept Mon–Sat 0900–1900, Sun and hols 1000–1300, 1400–1800, rest of year Mon 1100–1800, Tue–Sat 0900–1800, Sun 1000–1300.* **Summer annexe** *pl. de la Gare; open 15 June–15 Sept Mon–Sat 0900–1900, Sun and hols 1000–1300,*

By road
Angers lies a little north of the Loire. *Autoroute* A11 (Paris–Nantes) gives direct access to the town. It can also be reached from east or west on A85 or N147, and from the south on A87 or N160. All these main roads create a ring road around the whole town, while another square of boulevards encloses the central old quarter.

By air
Angers-Marcé airport is 20km northeast of the town centre on *autoroute* A11. The airport receives internal flights from Bourges, Clermont-Ferrand, Dijon, Lille, Lyon, Marseille, Montpellier, Mulhouse, Nice, Saint-Etienne, Strasbourg, Toulon and Toulouse. International flights arrive here from Amsterdam, Düsseldorf, Geneva, Milan, Turin and Munich. Airport information *tel: 02 41 33 50 00; reservations: 02 41 33 50 20; www.angers.aeroport.fr/*

Map of Angers showing: Musée J. Lurçat, Place du Tertre St-Laurent, Boulevard Arago, Quai Monge, MAINE, Pont de la Haute-Chaîne, Voie des Berges, Boulevard Ayrault, Rue de Rennes, Rue du Maine, Avenue Besnardière, St-Serge, Rue Boreau, Jardin des Plantes, la Trinité, Boulevard H. Arnaud, Quai R. Bazin, Quai Gambetta, Rue Thiers, Rue Maillé, Rue Boisnet, Place Molière, R. du Commerce, Boulevard Carnot, Centre des Congrès, Place Louis Imbach, Quai des Carmes, Pont de Verdun, Place de la Poissonnerie, Rue Parcheminerie, Rue du Mail, Nôtre-Dame, Rue Plantagenêt, Rue de la Roë, Rue Lenepveu, Boulevard Bessonneau, Quai Ligny, Rue Baudrière, Hôtel Pincé, Rue David d'Angers, Rue St-Maurille, Place du M^{al}. Leclerc, Prom. du Bout du Monde, Rue St-Aignan, Cathédrale, Place du Ralliement, Rue d'Alsace, Jardin du Mail, Château, du G. de Gaulle, Place Freppel, Rue Voltaire, Rue St-Julien, Rue Toussaint, Tour St-Aubin, Rue St-Martin, Rue St-Aubin, Rue Hanneloup, Galerie David d'Angers, Musée des Beaux-Arts, Rue des Lices, Boulevard de la M^{al}. Foch, Rue Hoche, Bd. du Roi René, Hôtel du Département, Place du Lycée

1400–1800. The tourist office offers hotel reservations, currency exchange, booking for local events, and riverboat hire.

Ⓦ www.ville-angers.fr and www.angers-tourisme.com (the town's official sites); www.francebalade.com/anjou /angers.htm (useful regional site. French only).

By rail
TGVs direct from Paris take 1hr 30mins. Other TGVs run direct to Lyon and Lille. There are frequent trains from Nantes, La Baule, Les Sables d'Olonne, Saumur and Tours.

Parking
There is plenty of car parking in the town, including in the squares near the boulevards, pl. Imbach, pl. François-Mitterrand, pl. Mendès-France and pl. Marechal Leclerc. In the town centre try pl. du Ralliement and pl. Freppel. On the other side of the river, there is ample parking in pl. de la Rochefoucauld-Liancourt.

Seeing the sights

A single low-priced ticket allows you to see all the major tapestries and most of the town's museums. Museums and other sights in Angers are open daily in season. Out of season they are closed Mon and some public holidays.

Markets: There's a market in town almost every day of the week. Main town centre markets are on Thu (square Jeanne d'Arc) and Sat (pl. Leclerc, pl. Imbach and pl. La Fayette). Others are, on Tue, in the Belle-Beille district, on Wed at La Fayette and Monplaisir, Thur at pl. Bichon, Fri at Grand Pigeon and Belle-Beille, on Sat in la Roseraie district, and on Sun at Monplaisir.

Anjou Festival, from about 20 June to 15 July, is one of France's principal cultural and arts festivals. The emphasis is on theatre. Events take place throughout Anjou, but mainly in Angers. Festival website: *www.festivaldanjou.com/*

Nightlife: Le Chabada 56 *blvd du Doyenné, tel: 02 41 96 13 40*, in the north of the town, is the main venue for live rock and pop. Late-night bars, some with music, are mainly on or near r. St-Laud in the old quarter.

Cathédrale St-Maurice
€ *Pl. Monseigneur Chappoulie; tel: 02 41 87 43 47; open daily morning and evening (hours variable) except some national hols.*

Guided tours

In summer, the tourist office organises 2-hr guided tours of the town and local sights, as well as a 'little tourist train' round the town centre, and taxi tours of the surrounding area.

Sights

Cathédrale St-Maurice✣✣

Standing in the centre of historic Angers, the cathedral is a good example of the 12th- and 13th-century Angevin Gothic style, although with unusual proportions and some later additions. The handsome west front is especially tall, and is entered by a 12th-century doorway with a fine tympanum above. The Calvary on the left is by the great sculptor David d'Angers. Rising above the façade are three towers, the middle one being a 16th-century Renaissance addition. Inside, the nave is one of the earliest and best examples of Plantagenet-style Gothic vaulting. There is an imposing organ and carved choirstalls of the 18th century, as well as fine stone carving and statuary, including Ste Cecilia in marble by David d'Angers. The 12th- and 13th-century stained-glass windows are magnificent, and there is a superb 15th-century rose window in the transept.

Château d'Angers✣✣✣

The sombre and imposing château that dominates Angers is quite different from the other Loire châteaux. This is decidedly more fortress than palace. Paler bands relieve its dark stone, but the overall impact is powerful and grim. It is one of the finest surviving examples of a French feudal castle.

Black Angers

The château's dark stone
once echoed the colour
of all else in the old town,
which became known as
Black Angers. It is built
mainly from locally
quarried slate. Only in
recent times have modern
building materials
lightened the town's
colour, especially by the
addition of suburbs in
white.

Left
Cathedral Façade, Angers

Overleaf
Angers Château

A massive structure, fortified by 17 round towers, the château stands on the site of an earlier wooden fortification. It was constructed in just 10 years, from 1230 to 1240, and was originally far more daunting than today. Its walls and towers stood much taller, and were surrounded by a broad, deep moat. During the Wars of Religion, one faction after another – Protestant and Catholic – used the château as a stronghold. In the 16th century, Henri III ordered that it be razed to the ground to prevent further use by hostile forces. Henri's order had only been partly carried out when he died, and the destruction of the castle was abandoned. The moat has been filled and planted out with beautiful flower gardens in the neat, geometric French style. The high ramparts walk, on the east side of the château, runs by another pretty garden.

Within the ramparts wall, the large **Ste-Genevieve Chapel**✦ was built in the 15th century by Louis II of Anjou and his wife Yolande of Aragon. Its door is especially notable for the exquisite foliage carvings. From the same period, the **Logis Royal**✦✦✦ houses the Royal Apartments, where superb 15th- and 16th-century Flemish tapestries are displayed, including the four which make up the remarkably rich Passion tapestry.

The highlight of the château – and of Angers – is the **Tapisserie de l'Apocalypse (Apocalypse Tapestry)**✦✦✦, displayed in the Grand Gallery which has been turned into an enclosed area with controlled atmospheric conditions designed to prolong the life of the fabric. It was commissioned by Louis I of Anjou. Based on drawings by Hennequin of Bruges, the manufacture was carried out in Paris by Nicolas Bataille and Robert Poinçon. It took them five years – from 1375 to 1380 – to complete the work.

Today, much of the tapestry is missing, and much is badly faded, but it is remarkable that anything survives of it at all considering that, during the French Revolution, the populace of Angers sacked the town's cathedral and renamed it as a Temple of Reason. Local people took the tapestry out and cut it into strips for use as rugs, curtains, bedspreads and furniture covers. Some 50 years later, an effort was made to recover the fragments and recreate the tapestry. Surprisingly, about two thirds was found and sewn back together. The length on display is about 100m, compared to the original length of 130m.

The Apocalypse Tapestry is in a series of dramatic panels, each depicting an element in the hallucinatory Revelations of St John, the final book in the New Testament. After vivid imaginings of a bloody Armageddon, it culminates in the victory of Christ and the Church over all the Earth.

Église St-Serge✦

At the other end of the town centre from the cathedral, Angers has a second exceptional example of the light, intricate Plantagenet Gothic vaulting in the former Benedictine abbey church of St-Serge. The 12th-13th-century chancel is particularly beautiful, while the 15th-century nave has stained glass of the 16th century.

The Plantagenets

The Plantagenets were a lordly dynasty of Angers who, under Geoffrey V (1131–1151), became monarchs of England. The name comes from the sprig of *plante à genet* – yellow-flowering broom – which Geoffrey liked to wear in his hair. His son Henri married the powerful heiress Eleanor of Aquitaine, and so added her vast domain in western France to the other Plantagenet territories. In 1154 he was crowned King Henry II of England, but continued to spend most of his time at the family's castle in Angers, incorporated into the structure of the later château. In 1205, the French captured Anjou and separated it from England. The ensuing war for possession of the Plantagenet territories in France was to last over 100 years, and was eventually won by the French crown. Under French rule, Anjou became a Duchy. The last of the Angers-born nobility was the scholarly and popular Good King René (1408–1480), Duke of Anjou, King of Naples and Count of Provence.

Galerie David d'Angers € *37bis r. Toussaint; tel: 02 41 87 21 03; open 15 June–15 Sept daily 0900–1830, rest of year 1000–1200, 1400–1800, closed Mon. Closed national hols.*

Galerie David d'Angers✧✧

One of Angers' most illustrious sons was the sculptor Jean-Pierre David (1788-1856), far better known simply as David of Angers. His greatest works were massive carved statues and portraits. Many on religious themes found their way into French churches, but he also executed busts of a wide variety of personalities such as writers, philosophers and historical characters. Plaster-cast copies of many of his works, and some originals, are displayed in this imaginatively restored, light-filled remnant of a former 11th-century abbey church.

Hôtel Pincé (Musée Turpin-de-Crissé)✧

Below
Galerie David d'Angers

Built in 1530, this Renaissance mansion near the main square was donated to the town in 1861. Today it is occupied by the eclectic Musée Turpin-de-Crissé. Originally privately owned, it consists of collections of the art and artefacts of various cultures, including Etruscan, Egyptian, Greek and Chinese. The highlight of the museum is a remarkable, extensive Japanese collection, with prints, masks, ceramics and all the accoutrements of a tea ceremony.

Musée des Beaux-Arts✧

The town's Fine Arts Museum occupies the Logis Barrault, a grand mansion built in 1487 by Olivier Barrault, who held such posts as Treasurer of Brittany and King's Secretary, as well as being mayor of Angers. The house was later occupied by Marie de Médicis and the governors of Anjou. The museum's substantial collection of paintings represents most of the French schools from the 13th to the 20th centuries, and is especially strong on the 17th to 19th centuries. There are also sculptures, and a floor devoted to local archaeology.

Hôtel Pincé (Musée Turpin-de-Crissé) €
32bis r. Lenepveu; tel: 02 41 88 94 37; open 15 June–15 Sept daily 0900–1830, rest of year 1000–1200, 1400–1800, closed Mon.

Musée des Beaux-Arts
€ 10 r. du Musée; tel: 02 41 88 64 65; open 15 June–15 Sept daily 0900–1830, rest of year 1000–1200, 1400–1800, closed Mon.

Musée Jean Lurçat et de la Tapisserie Contemporaine €€
4 blvd Arago; tel: 02 41 24 18 45; open 15 June–20 Sept Tue–Sun 0900–1830, rest of year daily 1000–1200, 1400–1800.

Musée Jean Lurçat et de la Tapisserie Contemporaine*[***]

While medieval tapestry is the treasure of Angers, especially the Apocalypse tapestry in the Château, on the other side of the river this museum celebrates modern tapestry. It is named for Jean Lurçat (1892-1966), reviver and master of tapestry design and weaving in modern times. The museum's centrepiece is Lurçat's famous latter-day version of the Apocalypse, in ten tapestries totalling 80m in length, called *Le Chant du Monde* (literally, 'song of the world'). It comes to a poignantly different conclusion from the original, reflecting the fears of the Cold War era in which it was made.

The museum occupies the former Hôpital St-Jean, or Hôtel-Dieu, the charity hospital founded by Henry II in 1175. Lurçat's tapestries, which have been displayed around the world, hang in the impressive *Salle des Malades*, the hospital ward, which dates back to the origins of the building and has a fine Plantagenet Gothic vaulted ceiling, supported by lovely slender pillars typical of the style. It continued to be used as a hospital until 1854. Note, too, the 17th-century Dispensary to one side, with its shelves of earthenware jars. Other parts of the former hospital display modern tapestries by other artists, and it is one of the world's leading sites for temporary exhibitions of modern tapestry. The former hospital also has an attractive Romanesque cloisters and garden, and a chapel.

Accommodation and food in Angers

Wine tasting

Just below the château you can learn about, sample and buy local wines at Maison du Vin de l'Anjou; *5 bis pl. Kennedy; tel: 02 41 88 81 13; fax: 02 41 86 71 84. Closed Jan–Feb.* They can also provide advice and information for wine-tasting in the vineyard region around the town.

Hotel Anjou and Restaurant La Salamandre €€–€€€ *1 blvd Foch; tel: 02 41 88 24 82, fax: 02 41 87 22 21, email info@hoteldanjou.fr; www.hoteldanjou.fr/* One of the best hotels in Angers, and one of the best restaurants, is an imposing building on the boulevard just south of the old centre of town. This long-established local favourite, now a Best Western, has plenty of character, with its stained glass, mosaics, and rooms in Art Deco style. The hotel is well-equipped and there is free parking, and a garden. The restaurant (in neo-Gothic style) offers well-prepared classic dishes.

Hotel de France €€–€€€ *8 pl. de la Gare; tel: 02 41 88 49 42; fax: 02 41 86 76 70.* One of the town's grander old hotels, located close to the TGV station, the France has a range of rooms from small and simple to larger and more luxurious. It has a couple of good, moderately priced restaurants – the simple, inexpensive Bistrot, and smarter Plantagenets.

Hotel du Mail €€ *8 r. des Ursules; tel: 02 41 25 05 25, fax: 02 41 86 91 20.* An appealing and friendly traditional small hotel in a quiet street in the old quarter.

Restaurant le Toussaint €€ *7 pl. Kennedy; tel: 02 41 87 46 20.* This classic gastronomic restaurant facing the château presents ambitious, elegant and skilful cooking accompanied by fine Anjou wines.

Suggested walk

Total distance: About 2km, or 4km including the detour.

Time: Although the town centre is very compact, the walk could take most of the day if you allow plenty of time to visit museums, admire façades, and step down side turns. Allow at least two hours more to include the detour.

Route: Start from the **CHÂTEAU** ❶. A peaceful old quarter separates the castle from the cathedral. Take r. St Aignan, passing some picturesque half-timbered houses on the right and the **Hôtel du Croissant** on the left. This grand 15th-century mansion is named for the knightly Order of the Crescent founded by Good King René, the 15th-century Duke of Anjou. Continue to the end where the street meets Montée St-Maurice, a long flight of steps climbing from the river to the **CATHEDRAL** ❷. There's an impressive view of the façade as you turn up the steps.

Behind the cathedral in pl. Ste-Croix, **Maison d'Adam** is a striking 15th-century half-timbered house noted for its apple tree supporting the corner turret, and for some remarkable wood-carving. Turn left into r. Chaperonnière to reach pl. du Ralliement, vivacious centre of town and bearer of much of its history. Overlooking the square is the imposing theatre, rebuilt in the 19th-century, while on the corner stands the Renaissance mansion **HÔTEL PINCÉ** ❸.

Detour: Continue from the square along r. Lenepveu and r. du Commerce via pl. Louis Imbach, and across blvd Carnot to reach **ÉGLISE ST-SERGE** ❹. Behind the church is the town's lovely **Jardin des Plantes** (Botanical Gardens), with a pool, an aviary and a small Romanesque church, as well as several rare tree species. Walk or take a bus along blvd Ayrault down to the river Maine. Across the water on the north bank is **MUSÉE JEAN LURÇAT** ❺. Returning to the south

Map labels:
Musée J. Lurçat **5**
Place du Tertre St-Laurent
Pont de la Haute-Chaîne
Voie des B
Boulevard Arago
Quai Monge
MAINE
Quai Gambetta
Boulevard Ayrault
Rue de Rennes
Rue du Maine
Avenue Besnardière
St-Serge **4**
la Trinité
Rue Thiers
Rue Boreau
Jardin des Plantes
Boulevard H. Arnaud
Rue Maillé
Rue Boisnet
Place Molière
R. du Commerce
Boulevard Carnot
Quai des Carmes
Pont de Verdun
Quai R. Bazin
Rue Parcheminerie
Rue du Mail
Place Louis Imbach
Centre des Congrès
Place de la Poissonnerie
Rue Plantagenêt
Rue de la Roë
Rue Lenepveu
Nôtre-Dame
Boulevard Bessoneau
Rue Baudrière
Hôtel Pincé **3**
Rue St-Maurille
Place du M^al. Leclerc
Quai Ligny
Prom. du Bout du Monde
Rue St-Aignan
Cathédrale **2**
Place du Ralliement
Rue David d'Angers
Jardin du Mail
1 Château
Place Freppel
Rue d'Alsace
A. du G. de Gaulle
Rue Toussaint **7**
Galerie David d'Angers
6
Tour St-Aubin
Rue Voltaire
Rue St-Julien
Rue St-Martin
Rue St-Aubin
Musée des Beaux-Arts
Rue des Lices
Bd. du Roi René
Hôtel du Département
Boulevard de la M^ll Foch
Rue Hanneloup
Rue Hoche
Place du Lycée

side, turn right from blvd Ayrault and, reaching r. du Mail, turn left to stroll through the old streets of the St-Laud area – r. St-Laud, r. des Poëlliers – back to pl. du Ralliement.

Leave pl. du Ralliement and walk up r. St-Martin to today's Prefecture, housed in the restored buildings of the former Benedictine abbey of St-Aubin, founded some 1500 years ago. There is a lovely glass-covered Romanesque arcade to the left of the courtyard. Cross r. des Lices to Tour St-Aubin, the abbey's surviving 12th-century belfry. Beside it, in the 500-year-old Logis Barrault, is the **MUSÉE DES BEAUX ARTS 6**. Skirt the museum to reach the entrance of **GALERIE DAVID D'ANGERS 7** in r. Toussaint. Promenade Bout-du-Monde leads back to the Château.

Le Loir: Vendôme–La Flèche

Ratings

Cave dwellings	●●●●●
History	●●●●○
Architecture	●●●●○
Scenery	●●●●○
Children	●●●○○
Son-et-Lumière	●●●○○
Activities	●●●○○
Winetasting	●●○○○

Just north of the Loire, and parallel to it, out of sight of the grandeur (and busy vacation traffic) of that immense, wide valley, lies a smaller and far less well-known river – and it, too, is called the Loir. While this Loir (with no 'e') is narrower and more homely, it also runs in a wide, fertile valley, and has white cliffs, distinguished vineyards, handsome villages, good restaurants and historic châteaux. Many rich abbeys and churches were built in the Middle Ages, as this was part of the pilgrims' route to Compostela. Flowing in leisurely meanders, the river cuts through the chalk, creating peninsulas and peaceful poplar-lined banks. Abundant fish and riverside farms have made this a prosperous place to live since time immemorial. There is riding, walking and river sports at several places along the Loir. The troglodyte dwellings hollowed out of the soft white waterside cliffs have been occupied since the Stone Age and are still used today.

CHÂTEAU-DU-LOIR*

ⓘ Château du Loir Tourist Office *Parc H Goude, 2 av. Jean-Jaurès; tel: 02 43 44 56 68, fax: 02 43 44 56 95, email: ot.loir.berce@wanadoo.fr; open June–Sept Mon–Sat 0930–1230, 1330–1830, Sun and national hols 1000–1200, rest of year Mon–Sat 1000–1230, 1500–1830.*

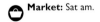 **Market:** Sat am.

Opposite
Château-du-Loir Hôtel de Ville

An important, bustling local centre, and a good base. However, the town itself offers little to see. And despite the name, it's not on the Loir and there's no château! Ruins of the castle keep, complete with dungeons, can be seen in the public park near the florid town hall.

Food and accommodation in and around Château-du-Loir

Grand Hôtel €€ *Pl. de l'Hôtel de Ville, tel: 02 43 44 00 17, fax: 02 43 44 37 58.* This decent, traditional family-run hotel and restaurant is in the centre, close to the former château site. Rates are very reasonable.

Le Védaquais €€ *Pl. de la Liberté, Vaas; tel: 02 43 46 01 41, fax: 02 43 46 37 60.* Located about 8km west of town, in a former village schoolhouse, this is a charming, unusual and comfortable place, though you may be accommodated in the annexe. The excellent restaurant offers local fish and a good selection of local wines.

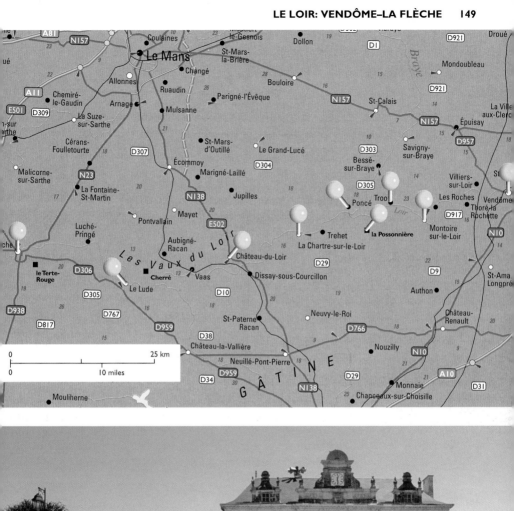

LA CHARTRE-SUR-LE-LOIR✣

ℹ️ La Chartre Tourist Office *In village centre; tel: 02 43 44 40 04, fax: 02 43 44 40 04.*

This appealing old town has an arm of the Loir running through it. Houses eat into the soft cliff face in the backstreets, which climb the hill of the southern edge of town. Some are right inside the cliff except for their front walls. Though with little to see itself, it is a popular base with good facilities, and is the centre for the sweet wines of the Jasnières *appellation*.

Accommodation and food in La Chartre

Hôtel de France €–€€ *pl. de la République; tel: 02 43 44 40 16.* A satisfyingly traditional family-run small hotel in the village square. Its popular restaurant is excellent, with an array of well-prepared local specialities at modest prices.

LA FLÈCHE✣

ℹ️ La Flèche Tourist Office *Blvd de Montréal; tel: 02 43 94 02 53, fax: 02 43 94 43 15, e-mail : otsi-lafleche@ libertysurf.fr; open June–Sept 0930–1230, 1400–1830 (Sun 1000–1200, 1400–1700), rest of year 1000–1200, 1400–1800, closed Sun.* Guided tours start from the tourist office at 1700 several days a week in summer.

🌑 Markets: Wed, Sat and Sun mornings.

🌑 Summer events – ask the tourist office for a list of concerts, theatre and shows.

Les Affranchis – the town's big festival of street entertainment and fun in early July.

Boule de Fort – the local game *boule de fort (see page 123)* is popular here; watch out for matches and tournaments.

Attractively sited on a bend in the Loir, this busy market town and local industrial centre has little to justify a long stay but rewards a passing visit. Its most famous building is the **Prytanée✣✣**, a leading military training academy at secondary school level, housed in the Baroque buildings of a former distinguished Jesuit college and chapel founded in 1604 by Henri IV, who spent part of his early years here. The philosopher and mathematician René Descartes ('I think, therefore I am') was among its many well-known former pupils. The school's library of 45,000 books includes priceless volumes, some as much as 500 years old. The ashes of the hearts of both Henri IV and Mary of Medicis are kept in a heart-shaped urn in the 17th-century Jesuit-style **Église St-Louis** that stands in the 16-ha formal gardens. The college played an important role in the colonisation of Quebec, and one of its pupils went on to become its first bishop. The town was the departure point for many who emigrated to the North American province. In the west of town, the Romanesque chapel **Notre-Dame-de-Vertus** has unusual Renaissance wood carvings. The old Château des Carmes (now the town hall) stands handsomely beside the Loir bridge and waterside public gardens.

Out of town 5km on the south side is **Le Tertre Rouge✣✣**, a large zoo located in a forest. The latest additions are great white wolves from the Arctic.

Accommodation and food in La Flèche

Le Moulin des Quatre Saisons €–€€ *2 r. du Géneral-Gallieni; tel: 02 43 45 12 12, fax: 02 43 10 31.* This old mill beside the Loir is now a

Chapelle de Notre-Dame-de-Vertus €
Beside cemetery off av. Rhin-et-Danube, usually open daily.

Le Tertre Rouge €€€
Route de Savigné (5km east of town on D104); tel: 02 43 48 19 19; open Apr–June daily 0930–1900, July–Sept daily 0930–2000, rest of year Mon–Sat 1000–1200, 1330–1730, Sun 1000–1730.

Prytanée €€ *r. Henri IV; tel: 02 43 48 67 04; open during school summer holidays: daily 1000–1200, 1400–1830, rest of year by appointment only. Entry ticket includes Église St-Louis.*

cheerful and easy-going restaurant offering a wide variety of imaginative dishes beautifully prepared and served. Excellent wine list, and good value.

Le Relais Cicero €€€ *18 blvd d'Alger; tel: 02 43 94 14 14, fax: 02 43 45 98 96.* This peaceful and comfortable hotel is close to the Prytanée. Furnished with antiques, it occupies a grand 17th-century mansion, originally part of a convent. There's a pretty garden, too.

Right
La Flèche, Prytanée

LE LUDE❖❖❖

ℹ Le Lude Tourist Office *Pl. F de Nicolay;* tel: 02 43 94 62 20, fax: 02 43 94 48 46.

☾ Events: *Printemps Culturel* (Cultural Springtime) – theatre, concerts, jazz, exhibitions, Mar–Apr; *Week-end des Jardiniers* (Gardeners' weekends) – plant shows and garden workshops at the château, early June; *Son-et-Lumière* – at the château every Fri and Sat, 12 June–5 Sept; *Les Journées Gourmandes* (Gourmet days) – music and gastronomy at the château, weekends 14 July–15 Aug.

🏛 Château du Lude €€ Tel: 02 43 94 60 09, fax 02 43 45 27 53, *www.chateauxcountry.com/ chateaux/lude; Open daily Apr–Sept only: grounds 0930–1200, 1400–1800, interior 1430–1800.*

A pleasant and attractive old town on the banks of the Loir, Le Lude's most splendid possession is the lovely **Château du Lude❖❖❖**, a strange, ornate construction, four-square with a massive tower at each corner, and surrounded by a broad dry moat with a footpath at the bottom. More approachable, less remote than many other such opulent dwellings, the château of Le Lude is one of the most enjoyable to visit in the Loir valley. Its *son-et-lumière* extravaganzas, telling the history of the château, are held in the grounds on the banks of the Loir almost every weekend throughout the season, with spectacular lights, fireworks, and 350 local people in period costume. Many other events are held in the house or grounds. Architecturally, the château is a curiosity, an almost amusing mix of conflicting styles, with a Gothic façade on the north wing, a pretty Renaissance south wing, and a plain white classical façade on the east side – a similar mix to that seen at the royal château of Blois. Yet the whole building and its gardens and terraces somehow create a majestic unity. Henri IV and Louis XIII were among houseguests before the Revolution. For the last 200 years the château has belonged to the same family and, although open to the public, it remains their private residence, very much with an air of being a grand family home. Inside, sumptuous rooms, fine pictures, Flemish tapestries, superbly restored Renaissance decoration, furnishings and period clothing are displayed.

Right
La Possonnière

Manoir de la Possonnière***

ⓘ Manoir de la Possonnière €€ *1 km south of Couture-sur-Loir; tel: 02 54 72 40 05; open for guided visits (45 mins) from about 1500–1730 on Sat, Sun and national hols in Apr, May, June, Sept, Oct, and 1–15 Nov. July and Aug tours from 1500–1830 Wed–Sun.*

A grand Renaissance country house in white stone, standing within walled grounds on the edge of green forest, La Possonnière was the birthplace and home of the 16th-century romantic poet Pierre de Ronsard. A prolific and immensely successful writer of sonnets, he was appointed Poet Laureate and travelled to Scotland with Princess Madeleine, James V's future wife. The mansion is sumptuously decorated. On the garden side of the house, Latin sayings are inscribed on the walls, while on the courtyard side is an elegant staircase tower.

Montoire-sur-le-Loir*

ⓘ Montoire Tourist Office *16 pl. Clemenceau; tel: 02 54 85 23 30, fax: 02 54 85 23 87; open Apr–Sept: Mon–Sat 1000–1200, 1500–1900; Sun and hols 1100–1300, rest of year: Tue–Sat 1000–1200, 1400–1800.*

ⓦ *www.montoire-sur-le-loir.net/ (useful independent local site).*

ⓐ World Folklore Festival – *mid-August; Loir Music Festival – July.*

ⓘ Chapelle de St-Gilles *€ 33 bis r. St-Oustrille; tel: 02 54 85 38 63; open according to demand.*

Château de Lavardin *€€ Route de Montoire, Lavardin; tel: 02 54 85 07 74; open daily 1100–1200, 1500–1800; guided tours on summer afternoons.*

St-Genest church *€ Grand Rue, Lavardin; open according to demand. If closed, enquire at town hall.*

Montoire's most infamous moment was on 24 October 1940, when Hitler met Pétain at the station here and urged him to support an invasion of the United Kingdom. Although Pétain enthusiastically ran France's collaborationist government, he refused to agree the invasion plan. The two men met at Montoire because the collaborationist but independent Government of France, based in Vichy, controlled everything south of the Loire, while France north of the Loire was under direct German rule. Today Montoire is a peaceful, appealing place, as it may have been then, too. There's a delightful view of the picturesque waterfront from the bridge. The Loir just here is a favourite with fishermen. Near the bridge on the south side stands the **Chapelle de St-Gilles***, with fine murals dating back to the 12th century. On a rocky spur behind rise the evocative ruins of Montoire's castle: for an impression of how the castle used to look, see the model in the town hall.

Take av. du Général de Gaulle out of town and follow the minor road for about 2 km upstream to the delightful hamlet of **Lavardin**, with its Gothic bridge and, poised on a rock above, the imposing ruins of the **Château de Lavardin****. Although only the keep and part of the ramparts survive, the castle was vast, and once covered a full four hectares. So daunting were its massive towers and triple walls that in 1188 the forces of Henry II and his son Richard the Lionheart were unable to take it, and turned away defeated. Later Henri IV succeeding in conquering the castle, and ordered it destroyed. In the village, Lavardin's Priory Church of **St-Genest*** is early Romanesque, and has remarkable murals, some of them 12th-century. Behind the church, the **Town Hall** contains two rooms dating back to the 11th century, partly reconstructed in the 15th century. From the viewpoint at La Rotte aux Biques a marked footpath leads alongside a succession of inhabited cave dwellings.

Mairie (Town Hall)
rooms € *Grand Rue,*
Lavardin; tel: 02 54 85 07
74; open Wed and Fri
1600–1900, Sat
0830–1200.

Accommodation and food around Montoire

Le Relais d'Antan €€ *6 pl. Capitaine-Vignau, Lavardin; tel: 02 54 86 61 33, fax: 02 54 85 06 46.* Rich and tasty fish and seafood dishes, followed by equally sumptuous desserts, are served at this friendly, highly rated restaurant in the pretty village of Lavardin.

PONCÉ-SUR-LE-LOIR*

ℹ️ **Poncé Tourist Office** *At the Mairie; tel: 02 43 44 45 32; open in season according to demand, but answering machine messages responded to all year.*

🏛️ **Château** €€ *D305; tel: 02 43 44 45 39; open Apr–Sept daily 1000–1200, 1400–1830, rest of year Sun only, same hours; 1-hr guided tours available.*

Paillard Mills Craft Centre €€ *D305; tel: 02 43 44 45 31; open Tue–Sat 0900–1200, 1400–1830.*

A 16th-century Renaissance **Château***** on a hillside dominates the village. Badly damaged by fire in the Revolution, much of the building was destroyed. But its great treasure survived – a superb staircase of stone, rising six flights beneath coffered ceilings exquisitely decorated with 130 mythological sculptures. The neatly geometric gardens, with lawns and greenery-covered walks, are beautiful too. The château's impressive dovecote survives, with its revolving ladders and 1800 nesting holes. There's a museum of local crafts and folk culture in one of the outbuildings. On the other side of town, in a converted 18th-century paper mill, you can watch glassblowers and other skilled craftsmen in action at the **Paillard Mills Craft Centre*** working in pottery, glass, metal, fabrics and wood. The Centre also puts on exhibitions, entertainments and markets from time to time. The village's 12th-century church contains interesting frescoes.

Overleaf
Le Lude Château

Right
Poncé-sur-le-Loir

Opposite
Carved staircase at Poncé

TROO❖

ⓘ **Troo Tourist Office** *At the Mairie; tel: 02 54 72 58 74 or 02 54 72 51 27, fax: 02 54 72 58 74; open daily Mar–Oct.*

Tours: ask the tourist office about the *train touristique* and guided walks.

This strange little village has several unusual features, especially the large number of cave houses rising up in tiers cut into the tufa cliffs. Their chimney stacks emerging from the ground strike a surreal note. Troo even has troglodyte streets and alleys – underground passageways and stairways – linking the subterranean homes. These underground galleries are known as *caforts*, originally from *caves forts*. Part of the village is beside the Loir, part on top of the escarpment, and part buried in the hillside. Troo is an ancient community, once fortified, with remnants of the old ramparts and a massive feudal mound called La Butte. The 11th- to 12th-century St-Martin Collegiate Church has an unusual square tower in Angevin style, and 15th-century woodcarving. Across the water, St-Jacques-des-Guérets church dates from the same period, and has exceptional murals that are almost 1000 years old; the best, in the apse, depict the *Crucifixion* and the *Resurrection of the Dead*. Maladrière Ste-Cathérine, opposite the *Mairie* on D917, is a 12th-century hospice. At the bottom of the village, the Grotte Pétrifiant is a stalactite cave where objects are 'petrified' by limescale while, at the top, is the *Grand Puits*, a large and deep covered well that is known for its echo.

Right
Troglodyte houses, Troo

Opposite
Flying buttresses,
Vendôme Abbey

VENDÔME*

Don't be deterred by the extensive surrounding industrial and residential areas. At its heart a delightfully attractive and interesting town, old Vendôme's location is striking, standing across different arms of the Loir which make a group of river islands below a castle-topped escarpment grandly called La Montagne. The Loir channels are crossed by many bridges, and the flowing water gives charm to the streets and parks. Although very ancient – there was a Gallic settlement here – the town grew around the **Abbaye de la Trinité***, founded in 1040 as a Benedictine community. For centuries the town was a place full of pilgrims, who would come to see the *Sainte Larme de Vendôme* (the 'Holy Tear of Vendôme'), a drop of liquid brought here from the Holy Land in the 11th century by Geoffrey Martel, Count of Anjou, who claimed that it was the tear shed by Christ on Lazarus' tomb. Most of the surviving abbey church, and especially its 16th-century west façade, is a masterpiece of delicate Flamboyant Gothic stonework. Set apart is the remarkably tall (80-m) 12th-century Romanesque bell tower. Inside the church, only the transept survives from the 11th century. Notice lovely 15th-century woodcarving on the stalls in the chancel.

In the 14th century, old Vendôme was ringed by fortifications, of which the handsome Porte St-Georges is a remnant. In the town's main square, Place St-Martin, you can see a 15th-century house called Grand St-Martin. Of the church which once stood on the square, only the Renaissance Tour St-Martin survives. The town hall, beside pleasant and shady Parc Ronsard in the town centre, was the college attended by Balzac – he hated it. There's also a 16th-century *lavoir* (wash house) on the edge of the park. It's a steep climb (some may prefer to drive) up to the sturdy 11th- and 14th-century **Château***, with its 16th-century dungeons. The Promenade de la Montagne, beside the castle, gives superb views over the town and the river Loir.

ⓘ Vendôme Tourist Information *Hôtel du Saillant, Parc Ronsard;* tel: *02 54 77 05 07,* fax: *02 54 73 20 81, e-mail: Ot.Vendome@wanadoo.fr;* open *1 May–10 June: Mon–Sat 1000–1230, 1400–1800, Sun and hols 1000–1300, 11 June–16 Sept: Mon–Sat 1000–1800, Sun and hols 1000–1300, 17 Sept–30 Apr: Mon–Sat.*

1000–1230, 1400–1800, closed Sun, except Easter weekend 1000–1300.

🔁 The town is on the N10 between Tours and Chartres. From Paris (about 2 hours' drive) take *autoroute* A10, then A11. Exit at Thivars (after Chartres), and take the N10 to Châteaudun, then Vendôme. Coming from the south, leave the A10 at Blois, and take the D957 to Vendôme. There are good railway links to towns in the region, and a TGV direct from Paris taking just 42 min.

🅿 There is parking in central pl. St-Martin, and in several signposted car parks around the town centre.

🔘 Guided tours: The tourist office organises 1–2hr themed guided walks throughout the summer. They also run guided tours on water. In addition, they organise afternoon tours, walks and events for 6–12-year-olds, such as 'Animals and people in the Middle Ages'.

🏛 **Abbaye de la Trinité €** *R. de l'Abbaye; tel: 02 54 77 26 13; open Wed–Mon 1000–1200, 1400–1800.*

Chateau € *Tel: 02 54 77 26 13, open daily 0900–1900 (June–Aug closes 2000). Walk up from pl. du Château, or drive via r. Ferme and faubourg St-Lubin.*

🎵 Festivals: International Guitar Festival – Apr, *www.vendomeguitarfest.com/*; Rockomotives – last weekend in Oct.

Accommodation and food in Vendôme

Auberge de la Madeleine €–€€ *6 pl. Madeleine; tel: 02 54 77 20 79, fax: 02 54 80 00 02.* Simple unpretentious comforts, and a straightforward and inexpensive restaurant, make this a good base or stopover.

Le Capricorne €€ *8 blvd de Tremault; tel: 02 54 80 27 00, fax: 02 54 77 30 63, e-mail: capricorne41@hotmail.com* A relaxed and welcoming hotel with pleasant rooms arranged around a garden, the hotel also has a choice of two reliable, good value eating places – one a simple bistro, the other a more ambitious restaurant.

Suggested tour

(W) *www.vallee-du-loir.com/* (site of the Association for the Development of the Loir Valley, with tourism pages focusing on travel offers and events. English and French); *www.chambordcountry.com* (website of the Loir-et-Cher *département*, featuring packages and special offers, and with pages for the main sights. English and French).

⇄ The Loir valley runs parallel to the Loire valley, approximately 40km north of it. Many roads, large and small, connect the two valleys. From Paris or the Channel, the main roads into the area are N10 and autoroute A11. TGVs travel direct to Vendôme from Paris, taking 42 mins.

Total distance: 152km.

Time: 2 days.

Links: From La Flèche you can travel 19km south via the D938 to link up with Baugé on the Western Châteaux tour (*see page 128*); or it is just 17km north on the N23 to La-Fontaine-St-Martin on the Sarthe tour (*see page 172*).

Route: Start from **VENDÔME ❶** on the Loir's picturesque north bank road, D5. At **Villiers-sur-Loir**, the church has 16th-century murals. There is also a good *cave co-operative* here selling white, red, rosé and sparkling wines of the Côteaux Vendômois, or you can buy direct from local producers in the village. From here **Rochambeau castle** can be seen on the far side of the river – if you want a closer look, take D67 and cross to the south bank, passing through **Thoré**. The route and the view are perhaps more interesting than the castle itself, and there are several cave dwellings here. Continuing on the north bank, the little river Boulon flows into the Loir in green water-meadows and reeds at **Le Guë-du-Loir**, where the Renaissance manor house La Bonaventure used to belong to the father of Henri IV, and later to the poet Alfred de Musset.

Instead of clinging to the riverside (via Asnières), take the direct road to **Les Roches l'Évêque**, where – just before entering the village – there are remarkable dwellings cut into cliff face, some with terraces and flowers around the entrances. It's a short distance into **MONTOIRE-SUR-LE-LOIR ❷**. Take the road to **TROO ❸**, its landmark belltower visible much of the way. Then continue as far as the left turn to **Vieux-Bourg** and follow the little riverside road to this small village. Cross the water into Artins and follow the roadsigns to **LA POSSONNIÈRE** manor **❹**. Pass through **La-Couture-sur-Loir** and cross the river back onto the north bank. Follow the river road through attractive villages of pale tufa houses, many quite grand. Just before **PONCÉ-SUR-LE-LOIR ❺**, notice its château high on the wooded slope to the right of the road. The route is very attractive along this stretch; passing by the vineyards of the Jasnières *appellation*, the road soon reaches **LA CHARTRE-SUR-LE-LOIR ❻**.

Leave town on D305 but, at resorty little **Marçon**, turn right past the attractive old church onto D61. Cross the river on a narrow bridge at **Le Port Gautier**, a former river port, and turn onto D64. It's a surprise, at the next village, to discover that Le Loir, like its grander namesake, has a **Vouvray**, and that this too is a wine-making village, simple and old-fashioned. From here comes very good Jasnières *appellation contrôlée* sweet wine. There's a tasting at the *Mairie* every summer weekend – look out for it. Follow the signs into **CHÂTEAU-DU-LOIR ❼**.

Left
Porte St-Georges, Vendôme

Below
Montoire-sur-le-Loire

On the menu

This is a good region in which to sample *rillettes*, *andouillettes*, *marmite sarthoise* and confectionery called *Roseau du Loir*. Among its wines, the reds, rosés and whites of the Coteaux du Loir, and the sweet wines of Jasnières are well worth trying and buying.

Travel on the south bank road (via Nogent-sur-Loir) to **Vaas**. This is horsebreeding country, with many stables and stud farms. The waterside at Vaas, with its working corn mill and local museum (*tel: 02 43 46 70 22*) and its old *lavoir* (wash house), is picturesque. There's a good hotel-restaurant here (see *Château du Loir*) and a river beach and watersports, as well as riding, while just north in the Bercé Forest there are marked walking trails. Just beyond, the **Cherré** archaeological site stands at the junction of the D305 and D188. It's the site of a Gallo-Roman settlement occupied until the 4th century. You can see the remains of its theatre and some other structures. Continue into **LE LUDE ❽**. Travel on either side of the river for **LA FLÈCHE ❾**. If taking the main D306, south of the river, you first reach **Le Tertre Rouge** beside the road on the left.

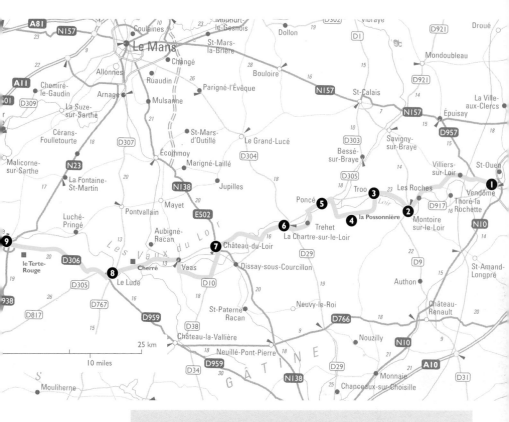

On the troglodyte trail

The Loir meanders through a valley cut into the tufa over 2 million years ago and, in many places, its white cliffs rise up to 60m from the valley floor. Quarrying of the soft white stone has left behind networks of caves and galleries, used as refuges in times of war, as places of pagan and Christian worship, as homes, barns, wine cellars, mushroom farms and even museums.

The stretch of river valley between Montoire and Vendôme is especially well-supplied. In Lavardin you'll find a rare example of a troglodyte restaurant, the appropriately named Le Caveau (*tel: 02 54 85 31 11*). At Les Roches l'Éveque there is a chapel with 14th-century frescoes, while Thoré la Rochette boasts some 15 wine cellars that can be visited by arrangement with the *Mairie* (*tel: 02 54 72 80 82*). Just outside Villiers-sur-Loir, on the hillside at St-André, a 700-m path leads to a troglodyte hamlet. Exhibitions and guided tours take place at weekends July–Sept (*tel: 02 54 72 90 83*). Also at St-André is a mushroom farm offering tours of its galleries and selling its produce, as well as a troglodyte picnic area with a wood fire (*tel: 02 54 72 78 10*).

Finally, if all this has given you a taste for troglodyte life, ask at local tourist offices about *gîtes troglodytes*.

Le Mans

Ratings

Architecture	●●●●●
Sport	●●●●●
Roman remains	●●●○○
History	●●●○○
Gastronomy	●●●○○
Museums	●●●○○
Shopping	●●●○○
Entertainment	●●○○○

For many, the name Le Mans is inextricably linked with the epic 24-hour motor race and dismissed from a cultural point of view. That's a mistake, as this riverside town has a fine renovated medieval heart that, in turn, is enclosed within a large Roman city wall, legacy of the Gallo-Roman town, *Vindinium*. The town centre is divided in two: the mainly modern sector, with shops, banks and administrative buildings, and *Le Vieux Mans* spread out on the hilltop. Thanks to its scores of half-timbered houses, cobblestone streets and quiet courtyards, it has become a very fashionable place to live. Subtle illumination and a plethora of restaurants enhance its appeal at night. A major tunnel, from the 1870s, cuts under the old town and is named for aviator Wilbur Wright (1867–1912) who undertook aviation trials here. Other Le Mans residents included Kings Henri II (1139–89) and Jean le Bon (1319–64), and the poet Paul Scarron (1610–60).

Getting there and getting around

ℹ Le Mans Tourist Office r. de l'Étoile; tel: 02 43 28 17 22, fax: 02 43 28 12 14; open Mon–Sat 0900–1800, Sat 0900–1200, 1400–1800, Sun 1000–1200. www.ville-lemans.fr

By road
Le Mans is located at a central point in France: two major autoroutes (the A11 from Nantes to Paris and the A81 from Rennes) meet here. Access to Paris, 205km away, takes just 2 hrs.

By rail
The TGV links Le Mans with Paris, Montparnasse in 54 min.

By air
The nearest international airport is Paris-Orly.

Parking
Le Mans' street parking is generally metered. The best option is to

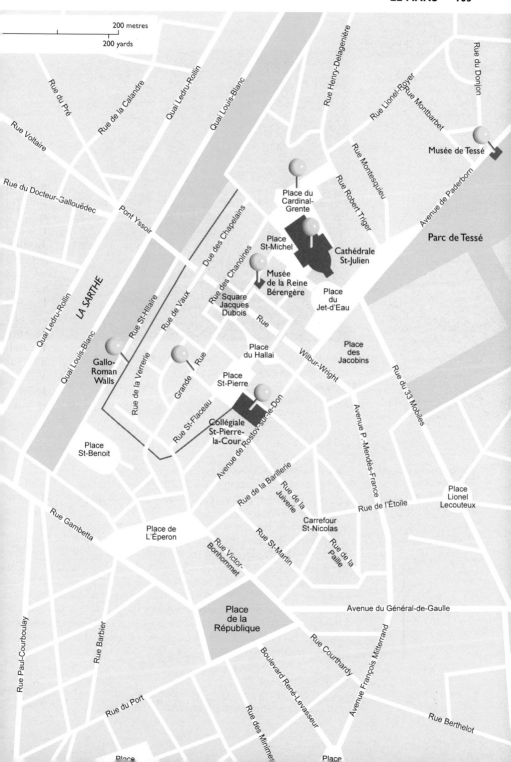

200 metres

200 yards

Rue du Pré

Rue Voltaire

Rue de la Calandre

Rue du Docteur-Gallouédec

Quai Ledru-Rollin

Quai Louis-Blanc

Rue Henry-Delagenière

Rue du Donjon

Rue Lionel-Royer

Rue Montbarbet

Musée de Tessé

Rue Montesquieu

Rue Robert Triger

Avenue de Paderborn

Parc de Tessé

Pont Yssoir

Due des Chapelains

Place du Cardinal-Grente

Place St-Michel

Cathédrale St-Julien

LA SARTHE

Rue St-Hilaire

Rue des Chanoines

Musée de la Reine Bérengère

Place du Jet-d'Eau

Quai Ledru-Rollin

Quai Louis-Blanc

Rue de Vaux

Square Jacques Dubois

Rue

Place des Jacobins

Rue du 33 Mobiles

Rue de la Verrerie

Rue

Grande

Place du Hallai

Wilbur-Wright

Gallo-Roman Walls

Place St-Pierre

Rue St-Flaceau

Collégiale St-Pierre-la-Cour

Avenue de Rostov-sur-le-Don

Avenue P.-Mendès-France

Place St-Benoit

Rue de la Barillerie

Rue de la Juiverie

Rue de l'Étoile

Place Lionel Lecouteux

Rue Gambetta

Place de L'Éperon

Rue Victor-Bonhommet

Rue St-Martin

Carrefour St-Nicolas

Rue de la Paille

Rue Paul-Courboulay

Rue Barbier

Place de la République

Avenue du Général-de-Gaulle

Rue Courthardy

Avenue François Mitterrand

Rue du Port

Boulevard René-Levasseur

Rue des Minimes

Rue Berthelot

Comité Départemental du Tourisme
40 r. Joinville, Le Mans; tel: 02 43 40 22 50, fax: 02 43 40 22 51,www.tourisme. sarthe.com; open Mon–Thur 0900–1230, 1400–1745, Fri 0900–1330, 1400–1730.

Right
Le Mans cathedral

leave your car in the underground parking in pl. des Jacobins, or head for the area slightly south of the centre around Église Notre-Dame-du-Pré (where street parking is still free). Then cross the pont Yssoir and you are next to the *Vieille Ville*.

Sights

Cathédrale Saint-Julian *Open 0800–1200, 1400–1900, July–Aug 0800–1900.*

Cathédrale Saint-Julien✦✦✦

Consecrated in the name of the first bishop of Le Mans, this is one of France's finest Romanesque cathedrals. Its imposing western portal, nave and finely-carved stone capitals date from the end of the 11th century, while the choir and apse chapels are all 13th-century. It's worth walking round the cathedral's exterior to admire the 82 flying buttresses which sustain the roof – works of art in themselves. The 12th-century stained-glass windows depicting biblical scenes (including the celebrated 1140 interpretation of the *Descent from the Cross*) are matched by other magnificent works executed in the 13th and 15th centuries. The tomb of Charles IV (d. 1472) is the work of celebrated Sicilian sculptor, Francesco Laurana. Leaning against a corner of the Western Portal, like a shrouded figure, stands an ancient menhir attesting to the significance of this site in pagan times.

Gallo-Roman walls✦✦

Some 1700 years ago, the Gallo-Romans constructed these sturdy walls, towers and tunnels around their 9-ha town, *Vindinium*.

Musée de la Reine Bérengère € 7–11 r. de la Reine Bérengère; tel: 02 43 47 38 80; open Mon–Fri 1000–1230, 1400–1830, Sun 1000–1230, 1400–1830 (free of charge Sun pm).

Musée de Tessé €€ 2 av. de Paderborn; tel: 02 43 47 38 51; open Tue–Sun 0900–1200, 1400–1800, closed Mon except July & Aug.

Right
Roman walls

Subsequent generations have built on these ancient fortifications, embellishing them with carved designs, coloured stonework or geometric brick decorations. The Tours Madeleine and du Vivier are particularly fine.

Grande Rue✦✦✦

This is a focal point in the *Vieux Mans* for it still retains a number of interesting 15th- and 16th-century façades with some quirky details and plenty of grandiose portals. The listing Maison d'Adam et Éve (the superb two-figure relief that gave the house its nickname is now believed to represent Bacchus and Ariane) was built for the astrologer, Jean de l'Épine. It represents French Renaissance architecture at its finest. The Maison des Deux Amis, once property of the 15th-century poet Nicolas Denizot, has an intriguing sculpted image of two figures outside, giving it its common name. The Maison du Pilier Rouge, on the corner of the r. du Pilier Rouge and Grande Rue, is named for the 16th-century twisted barleysugar stone column with red paintwork that supports part of the house's façade. Nearly opposite is the 16th-century pillar giving the Maison du Pilier Vert its sobriquet.

Musée de la Reine Bérengère✦

This historical and ethnographic museum, built in the mid-15th century, holds some beautiful paintings of old Le Mans, including work of local painter Jules-Alfred Hervé-Mathé (1868–1953), a collection of locally produced pewterware and a fine range of pottery and faïence from the Sarthe and Maine regions.

Musée de Tessé✦✦

Once the home of the influential Tessé family, this museum now houses a fascinating and eclectic collection of old paintings including works by Philippe de Champaigne, Georges de la Tour, Nicolas Tournier and the Sienese painter, Pietro Lorenzetti.

Place du Cardinal-Grente✦

Located in front of the cathedral, this square is characterised by the elegant 16th-century Hôtel du Grabatoire, now the city's bishopric. In much the same style but with a delightful round corner tower, is the Maison de la Tourelle, decorated with stone lucarne windows.

Above
Vieux Mans

Festivals and events

Time out from sightseeing

The **Parc de Tessé** is a pleasant place to relax, as is the 5-ha **Jardin d'horticulture**, a classified garden, nearby on r. de Flora. It was conceived in part as a formal French garden, and in part as an English one. The French rose garden is not to be missed, while the English-style park-garden, with its lake, islands and waterbirds, is always popular with the young.

• Spring Festival – beginning April, Onion Festival first Fri in Sept;
• Les Quatre Jours du Mans – festival during first fortnight of Sept;
• Les 24 heures du Mans – for cars, staged from Sat to Sun during the middle to end of June each year; for motor bikes it is staged in April, and for lorries/utility vehicles in October. *www.ville-lemans.fr* or *www.lemans.org*

Les 24 Heures du Mans

In June 1906, the first Automobile Club de la Sarthe endurance race was staged on regional roads. The drivers raced 130km between Le Mans, Saint-Calais and La Ferthé Bernard. Through the years it gained in prestige to become a 24-hour endurance test, for all classes of motorcars, and is now held each June on a 13.6km-long circuit just south of Le Mans. The record distance clocked up has now exceeded 5000km during the 24 hours.

Accommodation and food in and around Le Mans

Auberge de la Foresterie €€ *route de Laval; tel: 02 43 51 25 12, fax: 02 43 28 54 58; open all year.* Five minutes out of town, a tranquil, modernised hotel with full services and excellent restaurant.

Hotel Chantecler €€ *50 r. de la Pelouse; tel: 02 43 14 40 00, fax: 02 43 77 16 28; open all year.* A very well-kept hotel in a quiet part of town not far from railway station and river. No restaurant.

Auberge des Matfeux €€€ *D147 at Arnage (9km); tel: 02 43 21 10 71, fax: 02 43 21 25 23.* In a traditional auberge, a classical French menu is served with elegance.

Le Grenier de Sel €–€€ *26 pl. de l'Eperon; tel: 02 43 23 26 30; fax: 02 43 77 00 80; open daily except Sun pm.* A bright restaurant in an attractive period building, serving a good traditional menu with local specialities.

La Ciboulette €€ *14 r. de la Vieille-Porte; tel: 02 43 24 65 67; closed Sat & Sun.* A gourmet address which offers consistently good food.

Suggested walk

Total distance: About 1.5km.

Time: Allow about 4 hours to enjoy this walk.

Route: The **PLACE DU CARDINAL-GRENTE** ❶ in front of the cathedral's western portal, is a good spot to admire the **CATHEDRAL** ❷ itself before walking eastwards past the menhir and along the cathedral's flank, to pl. St-Michel. Behind you, note the southern portal: it's a beautiful 12th-century entrance in carved stone. At No 1, the rather run-down Renaissance house was once owned by Scarron.

Backtrack a few metres and turn left into r. Bérengère. In the elegant building on the left is the **MUSÉE DE LA REINE BÉRENGÈRE** ❸. Continue this narrow street into the Square Jacques Dubois where, on the corner ahead, stands the **Maison du Pilier Rouge**. Turn left, past the café, in r. du Pilier Rouge which leads through the **place du Hallai**, past the **Hôtel de Ville**, built on the former Plantagenet royal palace, and into the Place St-Pierre. On the south side are the 14th-century remains of the **Collégiale St-Pierre la Cour** which overlook the vestiges of Le Mans' **Roman baths**. Leave the Place by **r. de la Écrivisse** and head for the **GRANDE RUE** ❹. Turn left and walk downhill until you reach the turning on the right into **r. St-Pavin de la Cité**, a quiet

Above
House of Adam and Eve, detail of carvings

Above
River view at Le Mans

La Obéissante

The French automobile industry has Le Mans resident Amédée Bollée (1844–1917) to thank for the debut of the car. His first vehicle, making its appearance in 1873, was oddly named *La Obéissante* (the obedient one). He was the first person to place the motor in the front of the driver, rather than behind. His likewise-named son (1867–1926) carried on the research, but concentrated on speed rather than utility.

street which curves back and runs into **r. du Bosquet**. Straight ahead at the bottom of this street are the imposing portals of the **Hôtel de Vaux**, former residence of painter, J-A Hervé-Mathé. The tranquillity and gardens of r. de Vaux make it a prime residential address. Turn left and walk along to the flight of steps that leads through the **GALLO-ROMAN WALLS** ❺ and out to the grassy lawns along **r. St-Hilaire** and the river. Walk northwards along the walls to opposite the Pont Yssoir, catching a glimpse of the Romanesque **Église Notre-Dame-du-Pré**, once part of the female Benedictine Abbaye St-Julien-du-Pré, before turning towards the long flight of steps that lead up to the **r. des Chanoines**. Turn left here and walk along to the end of the road which rejoins the Place du Cardinal-Grente. Although it is not in *Vieux Mans*, the **MUSÉE DE TESSÉ** ❻, just 500m along the **ave de Paderborn** from the cathedral, should also be visited.

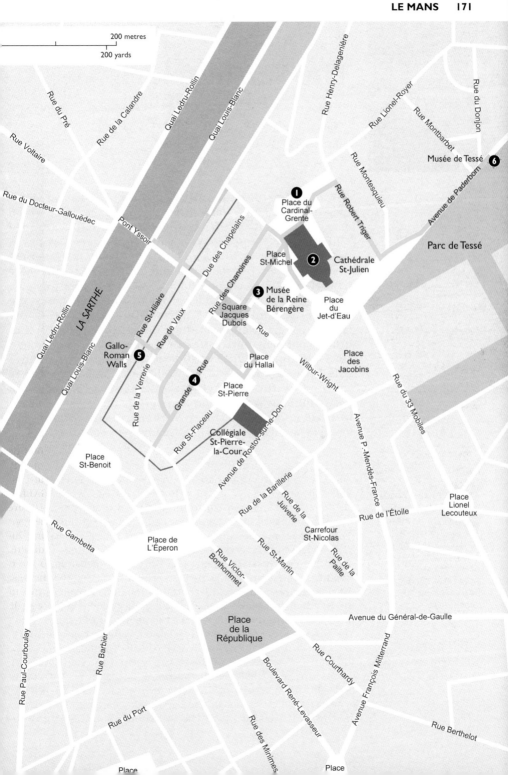

200 metres
200 yards

Rue du Pré

Rue Voltaire

Rue de la Calandre

Quai Ledru-Rollin

Quai Louis-Blanc

Rue Henry-Delagenière

Rue Lionel-Royer

Rue Montbarbet

Rue du Donjon

Musée de Tessé **6**

Rue du Docteur-Gallouédec

Pont Yssoir

LA SARTHE

Quai Ledru-Rollin

Quai Louis-Blanc

Due des Chapelains

Rue des Chanoines

Rue St-Hilaire

Rue Montesquieu

Rue Robert Triger

Parc de Tessé

Avenue de Paderborn

1
Place du
Cardinal-
Grente

Place
St-Michel

2 Cathédrale
St-Julien

3 Musée
de la Reine
Bérengère

Place
du
Jet-d'Eau

Square
Jacques
Dubois

Rue

Gallo-
Roman
Walls **5**

4

Rue de Vaux

Rue de la Verrerie

Grande Rue

Place
du Hallai

Place
St-Pierre

Wilbur-Wright

Place
des
Jacobins

Rue du 33 Mobiles

Rue St-Flaceau

Collégiale
St-Pierre-
la-Cour

Avenue de Rostov-sur-le-Don

Place
St-Benoit

Place
St-Pierre

Rue de la Barillerie

Rue de la
Juiverie

Carrefour
St-Nicolas

Rue de l'Étoile

Avenue P. Mendès-France

Place
Lionel
Lecouteux

Rue Gambetta

Place de
L'Éperon

Rue Victor-
Bonhommet

Rue St-Martin

Rue de la
Paille

Rue Paul-Courboulay

Rue Barbier

Place
de la
République

Avenue du Général-de-Gaulle

Rue Courthardy

Avenue François Mitterrand

Rue du Port

Boulevard René-Levasseur

Rue des Minimes

Rue Berthelot

Place

Place

The Sarthe

Ratings

Churches	●●●●
Châteaux	●●●●
Forests	●●●●
Gardens	●●●
Children	●●●
Scenery	●●●
History	●●
Gastronomy	●●

Surrounding the city of Le Mans is the *département* of the Sarthe, taking its name from the navigable river which diagonally cuts it in two. Like the Loire, the Sarthe provided a lifeline and transport system for the villages and towns that grew along its banks and, like the Loire, it has retired from continuous transport and now accommodates the more leisurely traffic of boating holidaymakers. Within this area are some large forested tracts, such as the Perche, once the sparring ground of the English and French during the Hundred Years' War. From those distant times, we still find historic dolmens, ancient feudal manors and little churches. Small towns and villages still boast traditional, Renaissance half-timbered houses and old washhouses. Sometimes barely touched by the advancing centuries, the role of these communities was to support and nurture the noble residence in their midst. Give this area the time and attention it deserves and its rewards will be many.

ABBAYE DE L'ÉPAU❖❖

Abbaye de l'Épau
€€ Le Mans (near exit for motorway); tel: 02 43 84 22 29; open Mar–Sept 0930–1200 and 1400–1800, Oct–Feb 0930–1200 and 1400–1730.

Le Man's soulless modern suburbs are in direct contrast to the serenity of this Cistercian Abbey – one of France's most attractive – founded in 1229 by Queen Bérengère (Richard the Lionheart's widow) who also ended her days here. The Abbaye de l'Épau was torched during the Hundred Years' War but was partially rebuilt between 1400–44. The coloured glass windows in the choir date from this rebuilding, while the grey and black glass window antedates this, having been designed in the 13th century while there was a ban on the use of coloured glass. The Abbey is laid out around grassy cloisters, with the collegial church to its north side. The beautifully-vaulted Salle Capitulaire, probably the most impressive part of this Abbey, shelters the stone effigy of Queen Bérengère, while the bare interior of the deconsecrated church highlights the simplicity of Cistercian architecture. Three chapels are of moderate interest, though one has an odd altarpiece showing the *Martyrdom of Saint Sebastian*. The Sacristy has been restored to its

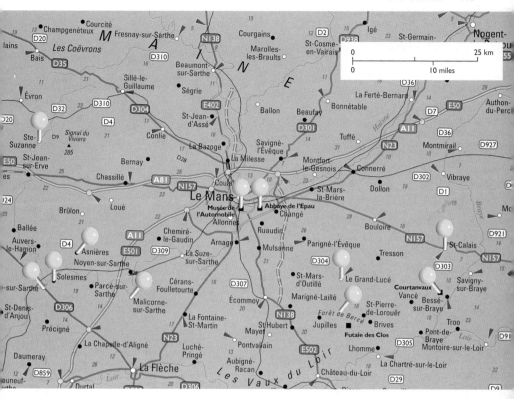

original state and boasts a couple of beautifully carved capitals and 14th-century wall paintings; so, too, the renovated the dormitory (now also used for seminars) that is believed to have been constructed before the rest of the Abbey buildings.

Accommodation and food near the Abbaye de l'Épau

Novotel €€€ *Blvd. R-Schumann; tel: 02 43 85 26 80, fax: 02 43 75 31 76; open year round.* A large and very comfortable hotel just minutes from the Abbey and the centre of Le Mans. Its restaurant has a good reputation with locals.

ASNIÈRES-SUR-VÈGRE❖❖❖

There are parts of rural France where you dream of going back in time. In Asnières-sur-Vègre, you are plunged into another era, one in which the painter John Constable would feel at home. A pretty little river weaving lazily between its banks, ducks paddling nonchalantly on its

ⓘ Association de Patrimoine Asnières-sur-Vègre; tel: 02 43 92 40 47. Open July & Aug Tue–Sun 1630, Apr–June & Sept, Sun only, 1630 for guided visits.

waters, thick foliage drooping into the stream, ancient houses along crooked little roads, and a stone bridge which has witnessed the passage of wheels and pedestrians for over 800 years. This is a gem of a village and one that, for its own preservation and for visitors' pleasure, should ban cars from its centre. Each way you turn there is an old building to admire: the solid small church dedicated to St-Hilaire boasts a fine cycle of wall paintings depicting scenes from the *Life of Christ*, executed nearly 1000 years ago (look at those terrified chaps in chain mail cringing at the demons from hell, and the wonderful rendition of *Christ's Baptism*); the Cours d'Asnières, a 13th-century manor house with a pepperpot tower, is a massive limestone building, with attractive ochre-coloured mortar and a very severe grey slate roof; have a look at the old *pigeonnier* (dovecote) in the field behind it. The Vieux Pont one of the focalpoints of the village, is next to the mill and leads over the Vègre to the medieval building known as the Basse Cour. There is also a notable washhouse around the Fontaine de Saint-Aldic.

Accommodation and food in Asnières-sur-Vègre

Right
Asnières café

Opposite
Cloisters, Abbaye de l'Épau

Manoir des Claies €€ *La Malvoyère; tel: 02 43 92 40 50, fax: 02 43 92 65 72. Open Apr–mid-Nov.* This is a large, privately-owned *chambres d'hôtes* in a restored building dating from the 15th century. Comfortable and secluded. Meals on request.

COURTANVAUX ❖

🏠 Château de Courtanvaux €
Bessé-sur-Braye; tel: 02 43 35 34 43; open Easter–1 Nov daily except Tue. Guided visits 1000, 1100, 1500, 1600, 1700 and 1800.

The attractive entrance gate, designed with twin rounded towers and decorative windows, and the beautifully maintained parkland, suggest the château's former grandeur, but the large, high-ceilinged rooms of this château are disappointingly bare. There are guided tours when the building is not hosting more lucrative private functions. However, the gardens are open irrespective of these. A château was originally erected here in Gothic times but most of what we see today is 15th- and 16th-century and was last owned by the Montesquiou family (the Comtesse was Napoleon's governess) who sold it to the state in 1976. The

cobblestone courtyard affords a good point from which to look at the stone castle's different styles. Beyond it you can enjoy its pretty, formal French garden and lush parkland. With over 70ha of woodland, a lake and a small river – all accessible by good footpaths – this is probably the most attractive part of the château.

Food near Courtanvaux

La Petite Auberge €–€€ *Bessé-sur-Braye, 2km south of town, on D303; tel: 02 43 44 45 08, fax: 02 43 44 18 57; closed mid-Jan, Mon pm and Tue, out of high season.* A popular, rustic restaurant with pretty decoration. Creative cuisine using fresh, local produce.

FÔRET DE BERCÉ✧✧

The 5 379-ha Fôret de Bercé is a vast area, the remains of an extensive Gallic forest, thickly wooded with beech, chestnut and oak trees – it is a rare treat for the nature lover and amateur ornithologist. Over the centuries Bercé has been protected by royal warrant and, although Colbert tried to extend it westwards in 1669, he chose inhospitable land which was fit for little more than pine trees. Selective logging is permitted in parts of the forest and, amid the brackens hidden by the dappled light, there are often huge piles of stacked logs. There are numerous places to picnic, walk and drive through this area: if you don't follow the suggested route (*see page 182*), try going on the D13, through **Jupilles** and then via the die-straight avenue from Rond-Wautot to the Rond-du-Clocher and out via **St-Pierre-du-Lorouër**.

Don't miss the Chêne Boppe, a huge and ancient oak tree, the Futaie des Clos, where trees still date from the 1650s and the Fontaine de la Coudre, source of the River Dinan.

LE GRAND-LUCÉ✦✦✦

Château de Grand-Lucé €€ *9 pl. de la République; tel: 02 43 40 85 56, fax: 02 43 40 94 97, www.sarthe.com/visiter/cult/grandluce.htm; open May–Sept 1000–1900, mid–end–Apr weekends & hols only 1000–1900, closed Mon.*

Grand-Lucé is a fine 18th-century château in neoclassean style with 30ha of equally magnificent gardens. It was built for Jacques III Pineau de Viennay as a summer residence between 1760–64 (unfortunately he died just as it was completed), and is light and airy in ambience, designed to incorporate the new ideas of the French Enlightenment. The gardens include greenhouses, wooded park, vegetable gardens and, of course, a formal French garden.

MALICORNE-SUR-SARTHE✦✦

Malicorne Tourist Office *3 pl. du Guesclin; tel: 02 43 94 74 45, fax: 02 43 94 59 61, www.villemalicorne.fr; open Apr–Sept daily 0900–1230, 1430–1900, rest of year Wed–Sat 0900–1200, 1400–1700.*

Château de Malicorne €€ *Tel: 02 43 94 74 75; open daily July–Aug except Mon & Tue 1030–1200, 1500–1800.*

Faïenceries d'Art de Malicorne *18 r. Bernard-Palissy; tel: 02 43 94 81 18; open Mon–Sat 0900–1200, 1400–1830, Easter–Sept Sun 1400–1830.*

Faïenceries du Bourg-Joly *16 r. Carnot; tel: 02 43 94 80 10; open Mon–Sat 0900–1200, 1400–1830, Easter–Sept Sun 1400–1830.*

Right
Malicorne faïence

A quintessentially French town with its languid river, pleasure boats and elegant 18th-century brick and stone architecture, Malicorne is, however, better known for its unusual faïence. Potters have been working here since 1747, and much of the work that they produce is still decorated by hand. Its trademark style is created by cutting away shapes in each piece, and by enlivening its white base with details in colour. Bowing to the changes in taste, the major producers in Malicorne now also create faïence that follows contemporary trends. The **Musée de la Faïencerie d'Art de Malicorne✦✦** traces the development of the craft, while the two major **factory outlets✦✦** welcome visitors. The old mills used for grinding material for the ceramic industry, the town's renovated 17th-century château✦ and its delightful 11th-century **Église Saint-Sylvestre✦✦** are all in the western part, as you come in from Sablé or Parcé.

**Musée de la Faïencerie
d'Art de Malicorne €**
*Open Tue–Sat 0900–1100,
1400–1615, Sun & hols
1400–1645.*

Market: Fri am.

Food in Malicorne-sur-Sarthe

Restaurant La Petite Auberge € *Pl. du Guesclin; tel: 02 43 94 80 52;*

Musée de l'Automobile de la Sarthe✧✧✧

**ⓘ Musée de
l'Automobile de la
Sarthe €€** *Tel: 02 43 72
72 24; open daily Oct–May
1000–1800, June–Sept
1000–1900..*

Below
Musée de l'Automobile

This museum will seduce even those not interested in racing or cars. It is laid out beautifully in a modern hangar-like building near the famous circuit and is divided into two sections. The first starts with the origins of the vehicle, and includes steam-run examples dating from 1769, vehicles pioneered by Nicolas Joseph Cugnot and James Watt. Then there are the first 'bikes' dating from 1861, each with a big front wheel and small back one. From the turn of the 20th century

and its early years there are some beautiful cars: a Peugeot dating from 1906–10, a 1930s Mercedes, a Rosengart cabriolet, even a Bugatti and, in the midst of these antiquities there is an 'exploded' 1990s Renault that shows how all the component parts of a modern car fit together. The second part of the museum is dedicated to cars – and motor bikes – which have taken part in the 24-hour endurance race. Between these two sections a walled area with dozens of video screens play back footage of historic moments in racing.

SABLÉ-SUR-SARTHE❖❖

Sablé Tourist Office Pl. Raphaël-Elizé; tel: 02 43 95 00 60, fax: 02 43 92 60 77; open Mon–Sat 0930–1230, 1400–1800.

P The best places to leave a car are either in front of the Château or in the pl. de la République.

Église de Notre-Dame € Open daily 0800–1200, 1500–1900.

Markets: Mon am and Fri am.

Cruising the Sarthe: For short trips contact Crosière Sabolienne tel: 02 43 95 93 13, fax: 02 43 95 99 14; for residential houseboats contact Anjou Navigation, Sablé-sur-Sarthe tel: 02 43 95 14 42; fax: 02 43 92 26 06.

Situated at the confluence of three rivers, Sablé evolved as a port for transporting sand (sable in French) on the Sarthe and as a bridging point across this large river. Today, transport is in the form of pleasure boats that ply the river and its basins, while its economy has shifted from sand and anthracite to agriculture and tourism. Its charm lies in its little island, formed by the rivers and the unexpected backwaters that encircle its oldest part. The town is dominated by the 18th-century Château des Colberts, named for Colbert de Torcy, Marquis de Sablé and nephew of the better-known Jean-Baptiste Colbert (minister to Louis XIV), who commissioned its construction in 1711. Colbert erected this handsome building on the site of a much earlier fortified castle. Unfortunately, it is closed to the public as it now houses the Bibliothèque de France's centre for book restoration. The town's rather unattractive neo-Gothic church, the **Église de Notre-Dame**❖❖, was built at the end of the 19th century on the site of its previous church. The building doesn't entice visitors, which is a pity for it houses some magnificent stained-glass windows (including the huge Crucifixion commissioned by the Dukes of Nemours in 1494) which, declared a Historic Monument in 1894, were reinstalled in the modern church and have been subsequently painstakingly restored. Sablé still boasts homes constructed between the 15th and 18th centuries, some to be found along the Grande Rue, while the pl. Raphaël-Élize (where the tourist office is, and where the weekly market is held) is an elegant example of 19th-century architecture.

Accommodation and food in Sablé-sur-Sarthe

Hôtel Le Saint-Martin €–€€ 3 r. Haute St-Martin; tel: 02 43 95 00 03. A traditional-style hotel, on the south side of the centre, with a better-known gastronomic restaurant, closed Mon.

Villa Roma € 1 r. de l'Île; tel: 02 43 92 43 93; open daily except Mon. This is a popular pizzeria but its biggest draw is its position right by the Sarthe, where it has a pleasant terrace overlooking the river.

SAINT-CALAIS✷✷

St-Calais Tourist Office
Pl. de l'Hôtel de Ville; tel: 02
43 35 82 95, fax: 02 43 35
15 13; open Tue–Sat
1000–1230, 1500–1830.

 Market: Sun am.

Karileph, the saint who indirectly gave his name to this town, was a monk from the Auvergne who founded a simple abbey here in the sixth century. The large 15th-century **Église Notre-Dame**✷ is dedicated to this pious fellow. With its ornate Italianate façade one would expect a decorative interior: this is not the case. Massive Gothic columns support a high ceiling, leaving the huge nave bare. Karileph's 7th-century shroud, a very rare piece of religious reliquary, is kept in the *Mairie*. Ask to see it or look out for a postcard of this unusual cloth. Among the town's most attractive aspects are its shady *quais* running along banks of the River Anille. Built to protect the town from flooding, they are beautifully maintained and a favourite rendezvous with locals. The old *lavoir* or washhouse is a particularly fine example of its type and worth a visit. The renovated La Halle, with its fancy decorative brickwork, is once more the site of the Sunday market and is also used as a public meeting hall.

Food in Saint-Calais

Below
Dolmen, Ste-Suzanne

Restaurant Le Saint-Antoine €-€€ *8 pl. St-Antoine; tel: 02 43 35 01 56, fax: 02 43 35 00 01; open daily except Sun pm and Mon.* Good and imaginative cuisine in this pleasant restaurant just behind the church.

SAINTE-SUZANNE**

ⓘ Ste-Suzanne Tourist Office *13 r. de la Cité; tel: 02 43 01 43 60, fax: 02 43 01 21 12; open Apr–Oct Mon–Sat 1000–1230, 1400–1900, winter Mon–Sat 1330–1730.*

ⓜ Musée de l'Auditoire € *7 Grande Rue; tel/fax: 02 43 01 42 65; open summer daily 1400–1830 (Sun to 1800).*

Château de Sainte-Suzanne € *Open daily July–Aug 1000–1900, May, June & Sept 0900–1800, Oct–Apr daily except Mon 0930–1230, 1330–1730.*

Dolmen des Erves € *Open at all times.*

Topped by towers and turrets, Sainte-Suzanne is still encircled by its fortified walls, forming a perfect, shield-shaped, little medieval town of crooked stone buildings and narrow streets perching above the River Erve. This is definitely a place to park and stroll, to soak up its historic atmosphere. William the Conqueror camped outside the town, and it was a strategic point in the Hundred Years' War. Medieval life is on show in the small **Musée de l'Auditoire*** where, through documents, exhibits and life-sized maquettes, the daily life of Sainte-Suzanne's predecessors takes form. Tangible evidence of the town's past includes the remains of the 11th-century rectangular dungeon and the handsome but smallish 17th-century **castle***. However, Sainte-Suzanne's history dates back even further, as the neolithic **Dolmen des Erves*** attest. These stones were erected some 6500 years ago and their site, just 2km north of town, may be visited. There is no information concerning these stones actually on site so it's best to pick up a leaflet from the Tourist Office before heading out there.

Accommodation and food in Sainte-Suzanne

Hôtel Restaurant Beauséjour €–€€ *4 r. de la Libération; tel: 02 43 01 40 31; fax: 02 43 01 46 21; open daily in summer, closed Sun in winter.* A small hotel with a popular restaurant. The menu features traditional cuisine with some interesting additions.

SOLESMES**

ⓜ Église de l'Abbaye de Solesmes € *Open 0915–1815; services in Gregorian chant at 1000, 1300, 1350, 1700 & 2030.*

With its honey-coloured stone buildings and profusion of flowers, Solesmes could just as easily be in England's Cotswolds. The village is beautifully maintained and breathes a gaiety that the austere 19th-century Abbaye Saint-Pierre de Solesmes – reminiscent of Mont-Saint-Michel – lacks. The Abbey (still occupied by the Benedictines) dates from the 11th century and is closed to the public, but its 11th- to 16th-century **church*** is open, and attending a service sung in Gregorian chant is a memorable occasion. A shop near the entrance to the abbey sells recordings made by the brothers, as well as books about this ancient and beautiful form of worship. Of particular note in the church are its Renaissance sculptured 'Saints of Solesmes' and the extraordinary rendition of *Christ's Entombment*, a three-dimensional work composed of many different figures and sculpted architectural elements, dating from 1496.

Accommodation and food in Solesmes

Grand Hôtel de Solesmes €€–€€€ *16 pl. Dom Gueranger; tel: 02 43 95 45 10, fax: 02 43 95 22 26, web: www.chateauxhotels.com/solesmes.* Open year-round, this attractive period mansion has been renovated to form a mid-sized hotel with a notable gastronomic restaurant.

Suggested tour

ⓘ Comité Départemental du Tourisme *40 r. Joinville, Le Mans; tel: 02 43 40 22 50, fax: 02 43 40 22 51, e-mail: tourisme.SARTHE@cg72.fr, http://tourisme.sarthe.com; open Mon–Thur 0900–1230, 1400–1745, Fri 0900–1330, 1400–1730.*

Total distance: 240km.

Time: 2 days.

Links: The N138 south of Écommoy links with Château-du-Loir on the Loir: Vendôme–La Flèche tour (*see page 148*).

Route: Leave **Le Mans** (*see page 164*) on the N157 (and continue for 3km past the University), then branch off right for some 33km on the D28 via Bernay and Torcé-Viviers-en-Charnie. Here you turn left and drive right through the village, leaving on the D9 to **SAINTE-SUZANNE ❶**. The best view of this small town is from behind the château or as you leave, southwards, just off the D7. The road goes due south, at first through the forest of Grande Charnie, crosses the motorway and leads into Epineux-le-Séguin. Here we cut across to the Vègre Valley by turning left onto the D560 and arrive at Polle-sur-Vègre. The stretch of the D190 southwards is very pretty, and meanders down to medieval **ASNIÈRES-SUR-VÈGRES ❷**. The D22 leads towards the larger town of **SOLESMES ❸**.

Following the banks of the River Sarthe, and passing by **Juigné-sur-Sarthe** (there's a great view back up to the village as you cross the iron bridge) the D138 leaves the countryside behind for the busy town of **SABLÉ-SUR-SARTHE ❹**.

Getting out of the car: The gardens of the château at Juigné are delightful, with panoramic views.Cross the main D306 highway and head for the car park at the edge of the old town. The Sarthe's course is sinuous, but the straight D309 heads to the stone town of Parcé-sur-Sarthe. Pick up the D8 which hugs the river for a while and heads southeast to the attractive town of **MALICORNE ❺**. The same D8 continues towards the deciduous Forest of Courcelles.

It is another cross-country run from here via the quaint village of **La Fontaine Saint-Martin**. Stop and look at the few old buildings that cluster around the privately-owned château. Of interest is the house belonging to Louis Simon, a self-taught peasant, who leaned to read and write, played six instruments and found employ as sacristan, aubergist and tax collector. Here you change to the D32 to Écommoy, and turn south on the N138. Just 8km later, at St-Hubert, the D13

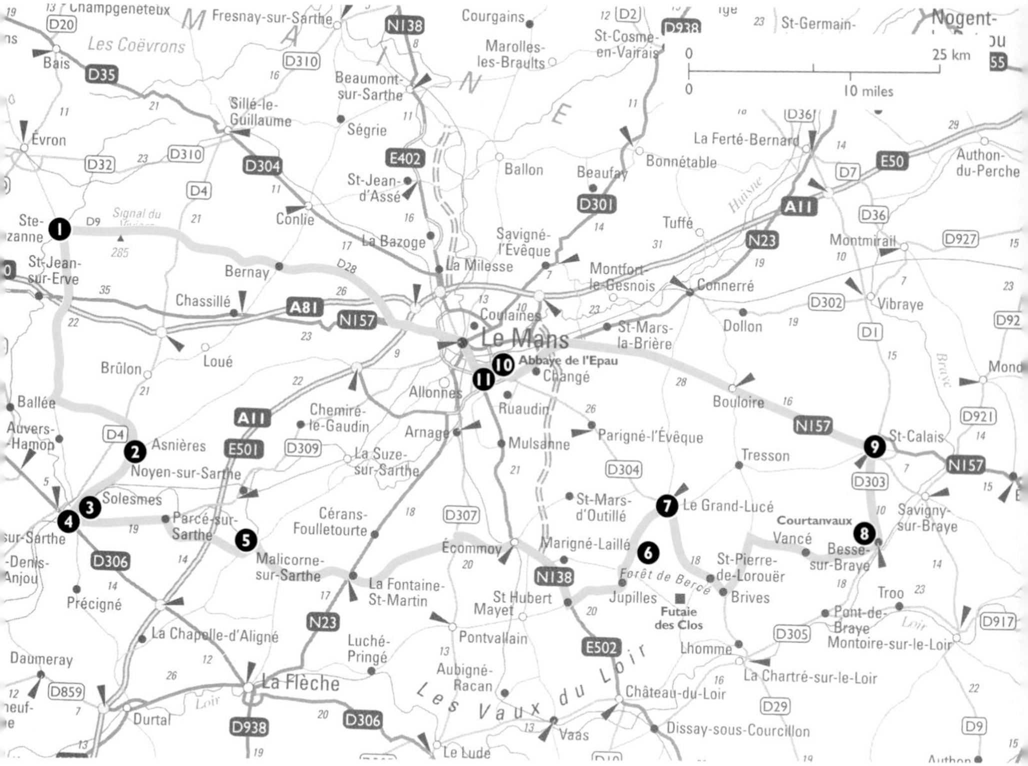

Map labels: Champgeneteux, D20, Fresnay-sur-Sarthe, N138, Courgains, 12 (D2), St-Cosme-en-Vairais, D938, 23, St-Germain-, Nogent-, ou, 55, Les Coëvrons, Marolles-les-Braults, 0, 25 km, Bais, D35, D310, Beaumont-sur-Sarthe, 16, 8, N, E, 0, 10 miles, Sillé-le-Guillaume, 16, Ségrie, 11, La Ferté-Bernard, D36, 29, Authon-du-Perche, Évron, D32, 23, D310, D304, 21, Ballon, Beaufay, Bonnétable, D7, E50, St-Jean-d'Assé, D4, 11, D301, Conlie, 16, Savigné-l'Évêque, 14, Tuffé, All, D36, Ste-zanne, D9, Signal du..., 285, 21, La Bazoge, 17, La Milesse, 31, N23, Montmirail, D927, 15, St-Jean-sur-Erve, 35, Bernay, D28, Montfort-le-Gesnois, Connerré, 19, 10, 7, 23, Chassillé, A81, N157, Coulaines, 13, 10, 23, St-Mars-la-Brière, Dollon, 19, D302, Vibraye, D1, D92, 22, 23, Brûlon, Loué, Le Mans, Abbaye de l'Epau, Changé, 28, Mond, Ballée, Chemiré-le-Gaudin, Allonnes, Ruaudin, 26, Bouloire, 16, D921, Auvers-Hamon, D4, All, E501, D309, Arnage, Mulsanne, Parigné-l'Évêque, N157, St-Calais, 14, Asnières, La Suze-sur-Sarthe, Tresson, N157, Noyen-sur-Sarthe, St-Mars-d'Outillé, D304, D303, 15, Solesmes, Cérans-Foulletourte, 18, D307, Le Grand-Lucé, Courtanvaux, Vancé, Savigny-sur-Braye, Parcé-sur-Sarthe, 19, St-Pierre-de-Lorouër, Bessé-sur-Braye, 8, Malicorne-sur-Sarthe, 14, Écommoy, 20, Marigné-Laillé, Forêt de Bercé, Brives, 18, Troo, 23, Précigné, La Fontaine-St-Martin, 17, N138, St Hubert, Jupilles, Futaie des Clos, Pont-de-Braye, D305, Montoire-sur-le-Loir, D917, La Chapelle-d'Aligné, N23, Luché-Pringé, Pontvallain, E502, Lhomme, Daumeray, D859, 12, 26, Aubigné-Racan, Château-du-Loir, La Chartre-sur-le-Loir, 22, neuf-e, 7, Durtal, D938, 20, D306, Les Vaux du Loir, 13, Vaas, Dissay-sous-Courcillon, D29, D9, Le Lude, Authon, D4, D306, D859, D7, D302, D303, D304, D305, N157, N138, N23

crosses this road and you turn left to enter the **FÔRET DE BERCÉ** ❻. This large area is crisscrossed with roads and tracks but you remain on the D13, a pretty road through the thick forest that passes through Pruillée-l'Eguillé and goes on to **LE GRAND-LUCÉ** ❼. Fork right as you enter the town and the château is on your right. Leave by the D304 towards La Chartre-sur-le-Loir and head along the increasingly attractive road to Brives. You take the left turn onto the D64 which joins the D63 in Courdenmache and heads north through pockets of wooded area to St-George-de-la-Couée. Turn in the direction of Vancé on the D176 and the D34 which leads towards the woodmilling town of Bessé-sur-Braye. It's just a further 1km north to the château at **COURTANVAUX** ❽.

Picking up the D303 again, it's a 15-minute drive to **SAINT-CALAIS** ❾ on the River Anille. The main Le Mans road skirts St-Calais and heads northwest, arriving at the city just by the **ABBAYE DE L'ÉPAU** ❿. Although the abbey is in the midst of the suburbs, it is well signposted. Before returning to the centre of Le Mans, take the fast N23 ring road, following the signs to the **Circuit Automobile** and then signs to the **MUSÉE DE L'AUTOMOBILE DE LA SARTHE** ⓫. The road back into the heart of Le Mans is well indicated.

Chartres

Ratings

Architecture ●●●●●

History ●●●●●

Medieval art ●●●●●

Views ●●●●○

Restaurants ●●●○○

Museums ●●●○○

Children ●●○○○

Shopping ●●○○○

The name Chartres at once brings to mind not a town but a building: the beautiful early Gothic stonework and famous stained glass of one of Europe's best-known churches. For over 700 years crowds of pilgrims have been admiring it, marvelling at it, and praying in it. For the modern visitor, there is the added rarity of seeing a medieval cathedral that has hardly been changed since the day it was completed. Yet Chartres is not just a cathedral. It is also a busy working town, one of the oldest in northern France, with a rich religious history going back to Druidic times, and a medieval quarter at its centre, picturesque with lanes and waterside cottages and stone bridges across the river Eure. As well as the cathedral, there are many other impressive historic churches. Once reached by the pious only after long journeys on foot, Chartres is now an easy and popular day trip from Paris, and an ideal stopover between the Channel and the Loire.

Getting there and getting around

❶ Chartres Tourist Office Pl. de la Cathédrale; tel: 02 37 18 26 26, fax: 02 37 21 51 91, e-mail : chartres.tourism @wanadoo.fr; open daily Apr–Sept Mon–Sat, 0900–1900 and Sun 0930–1730, Oct–Mar Mon–Sat 1000–1800 Sun 1000–1300, 1430–1630.

By road
Chartres is an easy 100-km drive from Paris on *autoroute* A11. From the Channel ports, the best way to reach the town is via Rouen, on expressway N154. A busy ring-road bypasses Chartres completely, while another inner ring-road, made up of separate boulevards, avoids the old centre. Take any turn to the *Centre Ville*.

By air
Paris-Orly international airport is under an hour's drive away.

By rail
Trains leave from Paris approximately every 2 hours during the day; the journey takes around 1hr. There are rail links to Le Mans, Nancy, Tours, and other major towns in the region.

0 — 200 metres
0 — 200 yards

Boulevard Charles Péguy
Promenade des Charbonniers
Rue Muret
Rue du Massacre
Boulevard Jaurès
Avenue Bethouart

St-André ✗

Musée des Beaux-Arts

Rue du Cardinal-Pie

Centre International du Vitrail

Rue du Cheval-Blanc

Cathédrale Notre-Dame

EURE

Rue de la Tannerie

Boulevard du M^{al} Foch

Rue Porte Guillaume

Rue du Fg. Guillaume

et

Place Jean Moulin

d'Harleville

R. du Soleil d'Or

Rue des Changes

Rue des Écuyers

Rue de la Foulerie

Maison Picassiette ➡

Place Morard

Rue Noël Balley

Place du Cygne

Place Marceau

Rue Marceau

Rue des Greniers

Rue St-Pierre

St-Aignan

R. du Bois-Merrain

R. de la Poêle-Percée

Place des Halles

Rue St-Michel

St-Pierre

Boulevard Chasles

Boulevard Chasles

Place Pasteur

Rue Pétion

Boulevard de la Courtille

Rue Chanzy

W *www.ville-chartres.fr/ (official site of the town of Chartres. Incomplete. English and French); www.chartres.com/ (independent site promoting Chartres, English and French); www.diocesechartres.com/ (official site of the Chartres diocese and cathedral. French only).*

Markets: Sat am in r. des Changes. Flower market Tue, Thur, Sat in r. du Cygne.

Festivals: There are important concerts and other musical events throughout the year, including Musical Saturdays and Lyric Days. *Festival de Jazz* – March; *Harpsichord Festival* – May; *Le Festival International d'Orgue* (International Organ Festival) – July–Aug.

The Theatre de Chartres *blvd Chasles; tel: 02 37 18 27 27* puts on frequent performances ranging from children's shows to modern dance.

Parking
There is car parking off the inner ring-road boulevards.

Guided tours
Tours of the Old Town available through the tourist office, either with a guide or with a 1-hr audio-cassette. It is also enjoyable to get an overview of the town from a horse-drawn carriage or on the little train.

Sights

Cathédrale Notre-Dame✦✦✦
One of the great buildings of the world, this UNESCO World Heritage Site does not disappoint when you arrive. Vast and beautiful, it is heralded from afar by two curiously dissimilar spires, one simple and elegant, the other higher, fussier, more elaborately Gothic, soaring high above the rooftops of the town. Constructed at speed – it was completed in 25 years – and incorporating the west front and the crypt of its late Romanesque predecessor, which had been destroyed by fire in 1194, the new building employed revolutionary new Gothic ideas to create a masterpiece of grace and craftsmanship. By good fortune, it escaped serious damage during the Wars of Religion, the Revolution and the two World Wars.

Right
Cathedral interior

Cathédrale Notre-Dame € *cathedral tel: 02 37 21 75 02, fax : 02 37 36 51 43, tour office tel: 02 37 28 15 58, e-mail: visitecathedrale@diocesecha rtres.com; open Mon–Sat 0730–1915, Sun and hols 0830–1915 (hours sometimes vary). www.unesco.org/whc/sites/81 .htm (UNESCO webpage on Chartres Cathedral).*

On the west front, the Romanesque triple doorway of the Royal Portal includes a multitude of small figures and statuary. The impressive tympanum above the central doorway shows *Christ in Majesty*. The south tower is the Romanesque survivor, while the taller north tower in Flamboyant Gothic style was added in the early 16th century. The sharp contrast between the two is intriguing and pleasing. Around to the right of the building, the beautiful South Porch is also richly carved.

The most striking features on entering the building are its massive dimensions (it has the widest nave of any church in France), and the phenomenal quantity and quality of richly coloured stained glass. The three rose windows, especially, are remarkable. The effect is, of course, at its most vivid on a sunny day. In all, there are more than 150 windows, their total surface area adding up to an astonishing 2 600sq m. The colour and workmanship of the glasswork, depicting Biblical stories, is exceptional. The finest of the windows are the west rose window, the *Tree of Jesse* window, also on the west side, and the *Blue Virgin* window in the apse close to the south door.

During the Middle Ages, the building was often filled with people sleeping inside it, many of them sick and hoping for a miracle cure. The labyrinth laid into the nave floor (these used to be a common feature of churches) was followed by pilgrims on their knees, and symbolises the Way of the Cross; it usually took about an hour to complete. In the absidal chapel is displayed the Veil of the Virgin, which pilgrims worshipped as a sacred relic.

Visiting the cathedral

Explanatory signs (in English) are displayed around the cathedral. Tours in English, starting from the gift shop, are offered twice daily at 1200 and 1445 by the noted authority on the cathedral, Malcolm Miller. If there are fewer than 12 participants, a tour may be cancelled.

Tours of the crypts Apr–Oct 1100 (except Sun and hols), 1415, 1530, 1630, 1715 (in high season), Nov–Mar 1100 (except Sun and hols), 1615.

Centre International du Vitrail € *5 r. du Cardinal Pie; tel: 02 37 21 65 72, fax: 02 37 36 15 34, www.centre-vitrail.org/PA/pa.htm; open daily 0930–1230, 1330–1800.*

Centre International du Vitrail*

Close to the cathedral is the remarkable International Stained Glass Centre. It is housed in the beautifully restored 13th-century vaulted crypt of the Greniers de Loëns, originally the grain warehouse of the cathedral chapter. Dedicated to research and education, the centre has a vital role in the preservation and development of stained glasswork. Demonstrations by skilled artists, hands-on workshops and classes, a museum and a documentation centre reveal the secrets of designing and making stained glass both in the Middle Ages and today.

Above
Cathedral clock

🛈 **Maison Picassiette**
€ *Off r. St-Barthelemy;
tel 02 37 34 10 78; open
from about Easter to end-
Sept 1000–1200,
1400–1800, closed Tue
(and sometimes Mon).*

Maison Picassiette*

Raymond Isidore (1900–64) was one of those eccentrics whose obsession eventually comes to be admired. Every day, after work, this local tramway conductor would set to work using fragments of broken glass, glazed pottery, pieces of smashed plates and other scraps to make sculptures, mosaics and murals all over his house and garden, even covering furniture. Guided tours of his home show the mosaic of Jerusalem, a replica of the cathedral, and numerous other works.

🛈 **Musée des Beaux-
Arts** € *29 Cloître
Notre-Dame; tel: 02 37 36
41 39; open Wed–Mon,
1000–1200, 1400–1700
(or 1800). Closed Tue, Sun
am, and national hols.*

Musée des Beaux-Arts*

The Fine Arts Museum, located inside the former Bishops' Palace adjacent to the cathedral, displays small but important collections of paintings and other artwork from the 15th–20th centuries. Highlights include a fine group of tapestries, some interesting portraits, and 12 large enamels depicting the Apostles, made in 1547 by Léonard Limousin. More modern work includes a collection of paintings by Vlaminck, and frequent interesting temporary exhibitions.

Previous page
Rose window,
Cathédrale Notre-Dame

Accommodation and food in Chartres

Mid-priced chain hotels can be found near the railway station and on the boulevards around the town centre.

Grand Hôtel Monarque €€€ *22 pl des Epars; tel: 02 37 21 00 72; fax: 02 37 36 34 18.* This landmark establishment stands on the edge of the old town centre. A fine 18th-century façade covers an older, well-preserved mansion with spacious, attractively decorated rooms. The restaurant is one of the best in town, with a noted wine cellar.

Hôtel de la Poste €-€€ *3 r. du Géneral-Koenig; tel: 02 37 21 04 27, fax: 02 37 36 42 17.* Situated just outside the old centre, and not far from the cathedral, this is a good, reliable, mid-priced hotel, family-run and comfortable. There is a moderately priced restaurant.

St-Hilaire €€ *11 r. Pont St-Hilaire; tel: 02 37 30 97 57, fax: 02 37 30 97 57.* A small, charming and friendly place beside pont St-Hilaire over the Eure, the restaurant strongly features the best of all that is local to Chartres and its region.

Suggested walk

Total distance: About 2km, or 4km with the detour.

Time: 2 hours.

Route: Start from the west side of the **CATHEDRAL ❶** and walk over to parallel r. du Cardinal Pie for the **CENTRE INTERNATIONAL DU VITRAIL ❷**. Continue along this street for the **MUSÉE DES BEAUX-ARTS ❸**, behind the cathedral. Follow **Tertre St-Nicolas** down towards the river. The Romanesque church of **Saint-André**, on the left, was once the place of worship for a densely populated working-class district alongside the riverbank. Now deconsecrated, it is used for concerts and exhibitions. Reaching the River Eure, cross on the footbridge to **r. de la Tannerie**, following this upstream past restored old houses and picturesque washhouses, and views of the cathedral. Walk as far as **pont du St-Hilaire**.

Detour: At pont du St-Hilaire, turn away from the river on **r. de la Porte Morard**, and cross the next arm of the Eure to reach pl. Morard. Leave the square on the street on the left to r. **Saint-Barthelemy**. **MAISON PICASSIETTE ❹** is signposted.

On pont St-Hilaire, with its attractive view downstream, cross back over to the left bank to reach the church of the former 6th-century Benedictine **Abbey of St-Pierre** (originally St-Père-en-Vallée), which

has beautiful 13th-century early-Gothic stained-glass windows. The building itself was constructed mainly in the 12th and 13th centuries, but includes remnants of much older structures. The porch-belfry is pre-Romanesque, and may date as far back as the 10th century.

Wander on r. St-Pierre and r. des Ecuyers through the old quarter, perhaps turning off right along r. Perrault and r. aux Juifs for part of the way. Several beautiful old houses line the steep narrow streets and lanes; some date back to the 14th, or even the 13th, century. Go up r. du Porte Cendreuse to **r. des Changes**, where there are many lovely old houses. Double back along r. des Grenets to see **St-Aignan** church, which has good stained glass and is attached to the town's original ninth century ramparts. From r. du Porte Cendreuse, **r. de la Pie** leads into central pl. Marceau and pl. du Cygne. **R. du Soleil d'Or** leads back down into r. des Changes, where you turn left to return to the cathedral.

Right
Vieux Chartres

0   200 metres

0   200 yards

Boulevard Charles Péguy

Promenade des Charbonniers

Rue Muret

Rue du Massacre

Boulevard Jaurès

Avenue Bethouart

St-André ✗

Musée des Beaux-Arts

Rue du Cardinal-Pie

❸

Centre International du Vitrail ❷

Rue du Cheval-Blanc

EURE

Rue de la Tannerie

Boulevard du M^{al} Foch

❶

Cathédrale Notre-Dame

Place Jean Moulin

arleville

Rue Porte Guillaume

Rue du Fg. Guillaume

R. du Soleil d'Or

Rue des Changes

Rue des Écuyers

Rue de la Foulerie

Maison Picassiette

❹➜

Place Morard

Rue Noël Balley

Place du Cygne

Place Marceau

Rue St-Pierre

Rue des Grenets

Rue Marceau

R. du Bois-Merrain

R. de la Poêle-Percée

St-Aignan

Place des Halles

Rue St-Michel

St-Pierre

Boulevard Chasles

Boulevard Chasles

Place Pasteur

Rue Pétion

Boulevard de la Courtille

Chanzy

Eure-et-Loir

Ratings

Windmills	●●●●●
History	●●●●
Medieval architecture	●●●●
Museums	●●●
Dungeons	●●●
Activities	●●●
Châteaux	●●●
Scenery	●●

The relatively flat land surrounding the major city of Chartres falls into the *département* of Eure-et-Loir which, in turn, takes its name from the two major rivers which flow through it. In the eastern part, it is a land of wide open spaces ideal for the cultivation of cereals and, in the western part, a landscape of undulating hills and a patchwork of forests that forms the region of the Perche. By the Middle Ages the local gentry were growing in power and authority, with the result that they expanded and fortified their substantial residences, and constructed impregnable dungeons to protect themselves in times of siege. Its proximity to Paris meant also that royalty were often present in its châteaux. But if castles and towers are one feature of the landscape, the other rather more quaint feature are the scores of windmills that break the often-flat horizon of the Beauce's cereal lands.

BONNEVAL*

Bonneval Tourist Office *Logis des Trois Marchands, pl. de la Mairie;* tel: 02 37 47 55 89, fax: 02 37 96 28 62, open Wed–Sat & Mon June–Aug 1000–1200, 1500–1800, Sun and hols 1000–1200, Sept daily except Tue 1000–1200, 1500–1900, winter daily except Wed & Thur am.

Market: Mon all day.

Just 14km north of its better-known neighbour, Châteaudun, Bonneval is a small fortified town beside the Loir. It grew up in the 14th century around the Benedictine Abbaye de Saint-Florentin, the remains of which are now occupied by a psychiatric hospital behind a grandiose entrance gate. It's an engaging little town of old stone buildings, towers and gates, and many man-made channels which run into the Loir. The Gothic Église Notre-Dame in the centre of Bonneval dates from the 13th century and has an attractive rose window.

Accommodation and food in Bonneval

Hostellerie du Bois Guibert €€ *Hameau de Guibert;* tel: 02 37 47 22 33, fax: 02 37 47 50 69, e-mail: boisguibert@châteauxhotels.com, www. châteauxhotels.com/boisguibert A relatively inexpensive hotel (for its

Joncherets
Joncherets
St-Rémy-sur-Avre
Houdan
Montfort-l'Amaury N191
Trappes
Tillières-sur-Avre
N12
Chevreus
Laons
Dreux
D936
St-Léger-en-Yvelines
N10
Verneuil-sur-Avre
Vernouillet
D929
D983
Brézolles
D4
Coulombs
Forêt de Rambouillet
Rambouillet
D941
N939
Tréon
Nogent-le-Roi
La Férte-Vidame
D4
Maillebois
D928
Tremblay-les-Villages
D26
Épernon
D906
Pierres
St-Arnoult-en-Yvelines
D11
Châteauneuf-en-Thymerais
Maintenon
Longny-au-Perche
D941
Senonches
Thimert-Gatelles
N154
D906
Gallardon
Belhomert-Guéhouville
Digny
Joug
Ablis
D918
Eure
Courville-sur-Eure
D939
Lèves
N10
La Loupe
D918
D928
Mainvilliers
Luisant
Auneau
N191
Rémalard
Bretoncelles
N23
Luce
Chartres
Béville-le-Comte
Sainville
Condé-sur-Huisne
Bailleau-le-Pin
Thivars
Sours
Voise
Ouarville
D15
D921
Dammarie
D7
Nogent-le-Rotrou
Illiers-Combray
N10
D935
Moutiers
A10
Thiron Gardais
Chassant
Le Gault-St-Denis
Voves
N154
E05
N20
D955
Alluyes
Viabon
Ymonville
BEAUCE
Unverre
Brou
Bonneval
Sancheville
Janville
Outarville
Toury
Authon-du-Perche
D13
D921
D955
Orgères-en-Beauce
D927
La Bazoche-Gouet
Logron
Loigny-la-Bataille
Aschères-le-Marché
Montmirail
D927
Arrou
Terminiers
Neuville-a
Courtalain
D927
Harville
D935
Artenay
D921
Châteaudun
D927
Patay
D5
Chevilly
Droué
Niverville
Mondoubleau
Cloyes-sur-le-Loir
La Ferté-Villeneuil
D955
ORLÉANAIS
N20
D97
D921
D924
D925
Épieds-en-Beauce
D3
Saran
Fleury-les-Aubrais
N157
La Ville-aux-Clercs
Morée
Ouzouer-le-Marché
Coulmiers
St-Jean-de-Braye
Équisay
N157
Binas
St-Jean-de-la-Ruelle
Orléans
D957
Savigny-sur-Braye
Meung-sur-Loire
St-Ay
Olivet
Bessé-sur-Braye
St-Ouen
Oucques
D917
Marchenoir
Sandillon
Thoré-la-Rochette
Vendôme
Josnes
Cléry-St-André
N20
D917
Selommes
A10
Beaugency
N10
N152
Lailly-en-Val
D103
Jouy-le-Potier
D921
D957
D924
Mer
St-Laurent-Nouan
La Ferté-St-Aubin
D9
St-Amand-Longpré
D951
Suèvres
Menars
La Ferté-St-Cyr
A71
E05/E60
La Chaussée-St-Victor
E0
Renault
Blois
D766
Chambord
D925
D922

25 km
10 miles

comfort and style), located in a 17th- to 18th-century manor house. Its highly-rated gastronomic restaurant has an innovative and excellent menu.

CHÂTEAUDUN✤✤

ⓘ Châteaudun Tourist Office *I r. de Luynes; tel: 02 37 45 22 46, fax: 02 37 66 00 16; open mid-June–mid-Sept Mon–Sat 0900–1200, 1400–1830, Sun 1000–1200, rest of year, Mon–Sat 0900–1200; 1400–1800, closed public hols.*

ⓘ Château de Châteaudun *€€ Tel: 02 37 94 02 90; open Apr–Sept 0930–1815, and until 1900 in June and July, rest of the year 1000–1230, 1400–1700, closed major public holidays.*

Musée des Beaux-Arts et d'Histoire Naturelle *€ 3 r. Toufaire; tel: 02 37 45 55 36; open Oct–Mar 0930–1200, 1330–1700; Apr–June & Sept 0930–1200, 1330–1800, July–Aug 0930–1830, closed Tue out of high season and 1 Jan, 1 May & 25 Dec.*

Grottes du Foulon *€€ r. des Fouleries; tel: 02 37 45 19 60, fax: 02 37 45 80 02; open June–Sept 1000–1200, 1400–1800, Apr–May 1400–1800, winter Sat, Sun and public hols, 1400–1800, closed Mon.*

Ⓜ Market: Thur all day.

The small town of Châteaudun, situated on a rocky outcrop overlooking the valley of the Loir, grew from the foundations of a sixth-century fortification which was largely rebuilt into a **château**✤✤ during the 12th century. Despite its proximity to Chartres, it remains a provincial town with relatively few tourists. The heart of the *Vieille Ville* is the castle, once the property of Joan of Arc's companion, Jean de Dunois, a building erected in medieval and Gothic style with Renaissance additions. Its most important features include the 30m-high, circular dungeon, used as a bolt hole during times of war or siege, which was originally accessible only from the second floor. Its pepperpot tower is a much later addition. Next to it, the Sainte-Chapelle shelters some fine 16th-century sculpture while the exquisite French and Flemish tapestries in the château are breathtaking. The gardens, too, are interesting for they are the recreation of a medieval garden, complete with medicinal herbs.

Beyond the castle walls lies the largely pedestrian-only *Vieux Quartier,* the oldest part of Châteaudun which was spared the catastrophic fire of 1723. An area of cobblestone streets, ancient buildings and quiet courtyards, it merits leisurely exploration. Within this area the huge Hôtel Dieu, founded in 1062 but remodelled in the 18th and 19th centuries, and the Church of the Madeleine, once part of the Abbey of the same name, are impressive sights. Near the pl. du 18 Octobre, the geographic centre of Châteaudun, lies the **Musée des Beaux-Arts et d'Histoire Naturelle**✤✤ with an eclectic display of over 2 500 stuffed birds, plus archaeological items from Egypt and local sources.

Also beyond the ancient city walls and accessible from the Loir valley below, are a series of grottoes, the limestone **Grottes du Foulon**✤✤, which, after a guided tour, are enlivened with a *son-et-lumière* performance.

Accommodation and food in Châteaudun

Hôtel Saint-Michel *€€ 28 pl. du 18 octobre; tel: 02 37 45 15 70, fax: 02 37 45 83 39.* An inexpensive small hotel in the centre of town, within easy walking distance of all the principal sights.

Les Trois Pastoureaux *€–€€ 31 r. André Gillet (corner r. du Coq); tel: 02 37 45 74 40, fax: 02 37 66 00 32.* A warm welcome in this restaurant located just a few minutes' walk from the centre. A gastronomic and creative cuisine, all prepared in-house, using local ingredients.

Le Saint-Louis €€ *41 r. de la Republique; tel: 02 37 45 00 01.* A combination of comfortable hotel, brasserie, restaurant, pizzeria and piano bar, with the bonus of a delightful terrace for summer dining. The brasserie in particular is a favourite with locals.

Right
Châteaudun Château

GALLARDON*

The slim remains of what was once a circular 12th-century dungeon bring history buffs to Gallardon. This was part of Gallardon's former castle which was razed in 1421 by the Dauphin, Charles VII. In the main square there is also a well-preserved carved timber-frame house, known simply as the Maison de Bois. It dates from the 16th century and boasts 88 carved wooden columns and old, diamond-shaped, glass windowpanes. The church, dedicated to Saints Peter and Paul, was first consecrated in the 11th century and enlarged to its present form in the 16th century. It has a carved wooden vault and old stained-glass windows.

Food in Gallardon

Restaurant Le Commerce € *12 pl. de l'Église; tel: 02 37 31 00 07.* Next to the church, with inexpensive traditional menus. Inside and outside seating.

ILLIERS-COMBRAY*

For Marcel Proust *cognoscenti*, a trip to Illiers-Combray is *de rigueur*. For the rest of us, it is perhaps less of a highlight. It was here in the medieval town of Illiers (on the pilgrimage route to Santiago de Compostela) that the celebrated author spent some of his youth and drew inspiration for his great work, *À la Recherche du Temps Perdu*, 'In Search of Lost Times'. The **Musée Marcel Proust**, located in the home (Maison de Tante Léonie) where the author stayed with his aunt, displays documents, photos and family memorabilia. The **Jardin du Pré Catelan***, created by Proust's Uncle Jules in 1850, offers a pleasant detour on the banks of the River Loir. Immortalising the town of Illiers under the imaginary name of Combray, a decision was taken on the centenary of Proust's birth in 1971 to rename the town Illiers-Combray.

Food in Illiers-Combray

Le Florent € *Pl. du Marché; tel: 02 37 24 10 43; closed Sun pm, Mon & Wed pm.* Offering well-prepared and presented food, this restaurant rightly has a good reputation with its local clientele. Good wine cellar.

Marcel Proust

Considered by many to be France's greatest author, Marcel Proust (1871–1922) was born in Paris but spent some of his school holidays with his paternal aunt, Elizabeth (Léonie) and her husband, Jules Amiot. However, suffering from hayfever and severe asthma, the young writer had to forsake his visits as he grew up. After Léonie's death in the rainy autumn of 1886, he saw their house for the last time. His visit brought back his impressions of Illiers, its homes and inhabitants, and of childhood walks along the Thironne in neighbouring Méréglise. These images marked Proust and were to provide the inspiration for *Du Côté de Chez Swann*.

Right
Musée Proust, Illiers-Combray

MAINTENON❖❖

ⓘ Maintenon Tourist Office *Pl. Aristide Briand; tel: 02 37 23 05 04; open Apr–Sept, Mon, Wed, Thur, Fri 1430–1800, Sat 1000–1200, 1430–1800.*

ⓘ Château de Maintenon *€€ Tel: 02 37 23 00 09; open Apr–Oct daily 1400–1800, Sun & hols 1000–1200, 1400–1800, Nov–Mar Sat, Sun and hols 1400–1700, closed Tue & Christmas week.*

A pretty town straddling the Eure and bursting with flowers, Maintenon might not have made its mark on the tourist circuit were it not for its most famous resident, Françoise d'Aubigné, the Marquise de Maintenon. Widow of poet Scarron but later to become the secret wife of Louis XIV, she bought the property in 1674, revamping the feudal castle into an elegant **château**❖❖ and employed noted landscape architect, Le Nôtre, to lay out the park and gardens. Vauban's unfinished aqueduct (commissioned by Louis XIV to bring water to Versailles) provides an unexpected backdrop. Beside the entrance to the château is the Église Saint-Nicolas, built in 1521 by Jean Cottereau (1458–1530), François I's treasurer. Nearby, in Maintenon-Pierres, there is a beautiful medieval garden, the **Jardin Medieval de Bois-Richeaux**❖, pleasantly laid out and full of interest to gardeners and laypeople alike.

Accommodation and food in Maintenon

Jardin Medieval de Bois-Richeaux € Tel: 06 11 88 20 20; open daily 1000–1200, 1400–1800.

🟠 **Market:** Thu am.

⛰ For a bird's eye view of Maintenon in the early morning, a local company offers hot air ballooning trips. Montgolfières Air-Magic €€€ 5 r. de l'Aqueduc, Houx; tel: 02 37 32 38 06, fax: 02 37 27 10 20.

Le Saint Denis € 5 pl. Aristide Briand; tel: 02 37 23 00 76, fax: 02 37 27 10 20, e-mail: hallier.jerome@wanadoo.fr In the heart of town, this is a pleasant small hotel. Its great draw is the cool, riverside restaurant behind it.

Le Bistro d'Adeline € 3 r. Collin d'Harville; tel: 02 37 23 06 67, closed Sunday and Monday. This charming little restaurant just along from the château serves good, old-fashioned home cooking at low prices. Its size and value means it's always busy, so book in advance.

NOGENT-LE-RETROU❖❖

ℹ **Nogent-le-Retrou Tourist Office** 44 r. Villette Gâté; tel: 02 37 29 68 86, e-mail: nogent28tour@infoonie.fr; open Mon–Fri 0800–1200, 1330–1730, Sat 0900–1200, 1400–1700, Sun at Château 1000–1200, 1400–1800.

🏰 **Château Saint-Jean** € Tel: 02 37 52 18 02 open May–Oct 1000–1200, 1400–1800, Nov–April 1000–1200, 1400–1700, closed 1 Jan, 1 May, 1 Nov & 25 Dec.

Mausoleum of the Duke of Sully R. de Sully; open daily 0900–1630.

🟠 **Market:** Sat all day.

Capital of the forested region of the Perche, and rising above the River Huisne, Nogent-le-Retrou is a delightful market town, with some historic old homes and ancient churches. It is best-known for its **Château Saint-Jean**❖❖, containing the **Musée du Perche**❖, and for its attached 1 000-year-old dungeon. The visible origins of the town date back to the Middle Ages (though it may well date from Roman times) when the knoll above the river was walled and a fortification erected. In the tenth century, the first of the powerful Retrou family took up residence, giving his name to the burgeoning town. The two Demoiselles d'Armagnac, daughters of the beheaded Duc of Nemours, inherited the castle in 1503 and are responsible for much of its current aspect. In 1624, the Duc de Sully assumed ownership of the castle and built a small pavilion on the northern side. The museum documents the history of Nogent-le-Retrou and displays items relating to country life in the Perche. Within the town, the white marble **Mausoleum**❖ of Sully and his wife, Rachel, can be visited in the Rotunda next to the recently renovated Église Notre-Dame. The latter was once the chapel of a hospice for pilgrims en route to Santiago de Compostela.

Accommodation and food around Nogent-le-Retrou

Moulin de Villeray €€€ route de Rémalard, near Condeau (8km from Nogent); tel: 02 33 73 30 22, fax: 02 33 73 38 28, www.chatotel.com and

Le Château de Villeray €€€ same details. A choice between staying in the hotel complex built around an old windmill or in the 17th-century château. Either way, the service and rooms are impeccable. The cuisine at the Moulin is arguably the best in the region.

Le Lion d'Or €€ *28 pl. Saint Pol; tel: 02 37 52 01 60, fax: 02 37 52 23 82, www.logisdefrance.fr* An old-fashioned, small and surprisingly quiet hotel in the main square in the centre of Nogent.

La Papotière € *3 r. Bourg le Comte; tel: 02 37 52 18 41, closed Monday.* In a Renaissance building, this offers an interesting and innovative cuisine, including their own duck foie gras.

Suggested tour

① Comité Départemental du Tourisme *10 r. du Docteur Maunoury, Chartres; tel: 02 37 84 01 00, fax: 02 37 36 36 39, e-mail: cdt28@wanadoo.fr, www.chartrescountry.com or www.eureetloirtourism.com; open Mon–Fri 0900–1300, 1400–1800 but not open to public visits.*

🏛 Guided tour of Moutiers' historic mill *Tel: 02 37 99 93 25; by appointment only.*

Le Grand Moulin, Ouarville € *Tel: 02 37 22 13 87; guided visits Sun pm.*

Parc des Félins d'Auneau €€ *Château d'Auneau; tel: 02 37 31 20 20, fax: 02 37 31 26 28, e-mail: auneau@cerza.com; open May–Sept 0930–1900, Oct–Apr 1000–1600.*

Total distance: 240km, and 15km for the detour.

Time: Allow 2 days.

Links: A fast national road connects Châteaudun with Orléans (*see page 242*) while another good national road links Nogent-le-Retrou with the city of Le Mans (*see page 164*).

Route: Leave **Chartres** (*see page 184*) on its northern side (following directions initially to Drieux) and branch off in the suburbs onto the D906 which goes to **MAINTENON ①** and Rambouillet. Crossing the River Eure, you leave Maintenon on the D18 and pass under the high arches of Vauban's aqueduct. Following the River Voise, the road leads to **GALLARDON ②**. Leave by the D116 in the direction of Auneau. This town is probably best known for its collection of wild cats, **Les Félins d'Auneau**, some 25 species of which are now housed within the grounds of the 14th-century château. Leave Auneau on the D71 and drive 9.5km southwards before turning left onto the D939 to **Ouarville**. Rising to a height of 10.85m, with sails extending over 14m, the Grand Moulin is a local landmark and is visible from the road as you near the village of Ouarville. Take the D117 via Louville-la-Chenard to enter **Moutiers-en-Beauce**. The 18th-century wooden mill is just beside the D117 leaving the village on the south side. Continue on this road to **Ymonville** where there is another interesting mill. Keep following the D107 southwards through large tracks of open fields to Orgères-en-Beauce. Here, you'll pick up the faster D927 in the direction of **CHÂTEAUDUN ③**, or you may follow the detour first.

Detour: For aficionados of windmills, there is a superb, restored example of a stone windmill at **Niverville**. Take the D144 via Harville and cross the D955 heading for Morgues and Niverville. In its present form, the Moulin à Vent de Frouville-Pensier is largely 19th-century, though its origins date back to the 13th. It is open from 1430–1830 in summer. From Niverville, pick up the D31 back towards Châteaudun.

Auberge de l'Abbaye € *15 r. du Commerce, Thiron-Gardais; tel: 02 37 49 54 18, fax: 02 37 49 49 17; closed Sun pm and Mon.* A modest, traditional auberge restaurant on the main road, offering local specialities and grills in the garden area, during summer.

Exit on the N10 in the direction of Chartres, passing Flacey, and drive for another 5km when you take the slip road into the centre of **BONNEVAL** ❺. Back on the N10, turn left onto the D281 just after the end of town. It leads to **Alluyes**, a pretty village straddling the River Loir. Note its round dungeon, similar to that of Châteaudun, now integrated into a building that forms part of the local psychiatric hospital. The D281 continues from Alluyes for another 10km, when it joins the D941 and enters **ILLIERS-COMBRAY** ❻. Onwards through the sometimes-wooded Perche by the picturesque D922, via Chassant and Thiron-Gardais. This town grew up around its Église Abbatiale de la Sainte Trinité built during the 12th to 13th centuries. Only its church remains, just by the main road. From here it is just 14km to **NOGENT-LE-RETROU** (6). The N23 is the quickest way to return to Chartres.

Windmills

Windmills have been part of the landscape in the Beauce plains since the Middle Ages. They were used to grind the local oats or wheat. Those that remain date from the 17–19th centuries and are built of wood or stone, with either wood or canvas panels. Constructed on a central pivot, they have the unique distinction of a long, wooden 'tail' which is used to rotate the whole building in order to catch the wind at the best angle. The Beauce style of mill was copied throughout Europe and adapted for not only milling flour, but cutting and pulping wood for paper.

Right
Moutiers Windmill

Nonancourt
St-Lubin-des-Joncherets
St-Rémy-sur-Avre
Houdan
Montfort-l'Amaury
N191
N12
Trap
N26
N12
Verneuil-sur-Avre
Tillières-sur-Avre
N10
17
Che
Dreux
D936
St-Léger-en-Yvelines
Rambouillet
N191
Laons
Vernouillet
D983
St-Arnoult-en-Yvelines
D4
Brézolles
D929
Coulombs
Forêt de Rambouillet
N12
La Férte-Vidame
N939
Tréon
Nogent-le-Roi
Épernon
D906
D4
Maillebois
D928
Tremblay-les-Villages
D26
Châteauneuf-en-Thymerais
Pierres
Maintenon
Senonches
D941
Thimert-Gâtelles
N154
Gallardon
Digny
D906
Jouy
Belhomert-Guéhouville
A11
N10
Ablis
D918
Courville-sur-Eure
D939
Léves
Auneau
Béville-le-Comte
La Loupe
Mainvilliers
Luce
E50
N
D918
D928
Rémalard
Luisant
Chartres
D24
Bretoncelles
Bailleau-le-Pin
Sours
Voise
Sainville
Condé-sur-Huisne
N23
Thivars
D7
Ouarville
D15
Dammarie
Moutiers
A10
Nogent-le-Rotrou
D921
D935
N154
A10
E05
Illiers-Combray
N10
Voves
Thiron Gardais
D922
Le Gault-St-Denis
Ymonville
BEAUC
Chassant
D941
D281
Viabon
Outan
D955
Ceton
Alluyes
Sancheville
Janville
Authon-du-Perche
Unverre
Brou
Bonneval
Orgères-en-Beauce
D13
D921
Logron
Loigny-la-Bataille
La Bazoche-Gouet
D955
Terminiers
 Aschère-le-Marc
D36
Montmirail
Arrou
D927
D935
Artenay
Neu
Vibraye
D927
Courtalain
Harville
Patay
D5
Chevilly
D921
Châteaudun
D144
N20
D1
Droué
Niverville
ORLEANA
D955
N20
Mondoubleau
Cloyes-sur-le-Loir
La Ferté-Villeneuil
Épieds-en-Beauce
D3
Séran
Fleury-les-Aubrais
St-Calais
D924
D925
St-
de-
N10
Coulmiers
St-Jean-de-la-Ruelle
Orléans
N157
La Ville-aux-Clercs
Morée
N157
Ouzouer-le-Marché
Binas
D303
Meung-sur-Loire
St-Ay
Olivet
Savigny-sur-Braye
D957
St-Ouen
D917
Marchenoir
A10
Cléry-St-André
N20
Bessé-sur-Braye
Oucques
Josnes
Beaugency
La Fe
St-A
Thoré-la-Rochette
Vendôme
D917
N152
D103
Jouy-le-Potier
Troo
Selommes
Montoire-sur-le-Loir
N10
Mer
St-Laurent-Nouan
D951
D957
D924
La Ferté-St-Cyr
A71
D9
St-Amand-Longpré
Suèvres
Menars
E05
0   25 km
0   10 miles
D766
Renault
E05/E60
Blois
La Chaussée-St-Victor
Chambord
D925
D972

Longny-au-Perche

donnai
D941
D11
D922
E50

Blois

Ratings

Architecture	●●●●●
Châteaux	●●●●●
History	●●●●●
Entertainment	●●●●
Restaurants	●●●
Museums	●●●
Shopping	●●●
Children	●●●

From across the river, the elegant buildings of Blois, in pale and dark grey, stepping up in long terraces to the town's lofty château, look supremely dignified. The vast Royal Château, first constructed over a thousand years ago on an easily defended ledge of rock rising from the Loire, has been substantially rebuilt and enlarged in different reigns and under different regimes. Yet it remains the heart of Blois. From their rocky platform, the château façades look down upon the steep streets, lanes and stairways of the old town. In these narrow streets stand many Renaissance mansions, often built by the officials, courtiers, financiers, friends and hangers-on of the French kings. Yet, though proud of its historic, aristocratic and royal connections, Blois is thoroughly vivacious, busy and productive, a modern commercial centre for the surrounding rural area. It is noted for excellent local produce, high-quality pâtisserie and confectionery, and good restaurants.

Getting there and getting around

ℹ Blois Tourist Office
Pavillon Anne de Bretagne, 3 av. Jean Laigret; tel: 02 54 90 41 41, fax: 02 54 90 41 49, email: info@loiredeschateaux.com; open 16 Oct–14 Apr Mon 1000–1230, 1400–1800, Tue–Sat 0900–1230, 1400–1800, Sun & hols (except 25 Dec and 1 Jan) 0930–1230, rest of year 0900–1900, Sun & hols 1000–1900. The tourist office offers a wide variety

By road
The town is two hours' drive from Paris. Many roads converge on Blois, coming from every direction. *Autoroute* A10 and N152 on the north bank of the Loire, and the quieter D751/D951 on the south bank, connect Blois to Tours and Orléans. On reaching the town from any direction, head for the *Centre Ville*, and then for the château.

By rail
There are frequent local trains from Tours and Orléans.

Parking
There is a large multi-storey car park, partly underground, less than five mins' walk from the château.

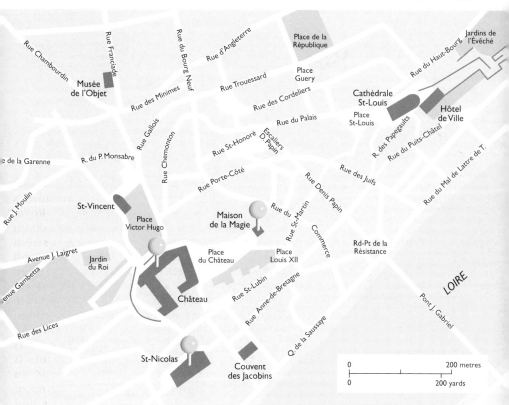

of services, including hotel reservations, currency exchange, booking for local events and tours.

W *www.loiredeschateaux. com* (Blois tourism site); *www.ville-blois.fr/* (the town's official site).

Markets: Tue, Thur, Sat, Sun weekly, and second Sun of each month. Local produce market every Thur pm in July–Aug.

Guided tours

Free tours of the Old Town on request, depending on numbers; ask at the château. Tours by horse-drawn carriage start in front of the château.

Combined ticket

A low-priced all-in-one ticket (*Billet Jumelé*) gives access to the château, a *son-et-lumière* and the Maison de la Magie, or any two. Available at the château.

Right
Château gardens

Sights

Festivals and events: Conteries Mars – Mar (annual themed town carnival and festival); Son-et-Lumière at the château ('Ainsi Blois vous est conté') – 29 Apr–16 Sept (except 13 July), 2200 nightly; free summer classical concerts at the château (Salle des Etats Généraux) – July–Aug, 3 times per week, 1800; Music Festival – jazz and classical street performances in Old Town.

Château Royal de Blois €€ (includes museums) Pl. du Château; tel: 02 54 90 33 33, fax: 02 54 90 33 31, email : docchateau@ville-blois.fr; open daily all year (except 25 Dec and 1 Jan) Jan–Mar, Oct–Dec 0900–1230, 1400–1700, Apr–June, Sept 0900–1800, July–Aug 0900–1930.

Château Royal de Blois***

On the outside wall of the château, the Flamboyant Gothic brick and stone main entrance faces onto pl. du Château. Once a walled farmyard, this is now a large, attractive and sunny plaza with a tree-shaded esplanade. Peaceful gardens to one side give a good view across the town and river. Set in the wall above the château's main gate is a 19th-century equestrian statue of Louis XII. To the right is the gable end of the 13th-century Salle d'Etats, and to either side the window corbels are decorated with robust stone carvings.

The fortified entrance gives access to the château's bright, spacious inner courtyard, recently restored. Four entirely dissimilar styles of architecture, representing four eras of French history, almost completely enclose the paved courtyard: from the feudal period, two 13th-century Gothic structures stand diagonally opposite one another; the late-Gothic (Louis XII) wing and chapel on the left; the exquisite Renaissance (François I) wing on the right, with its stupendous open staircase; and the 17th-century classical wing directly ahead.

The repeated crowned porcupine motif was the emblem of Louis XII, while the crowned salamander was the chosen symbol of François I. It is striking that just 14 years passed between the construction of the Louis XII and François I wings. In that time a revolutionary change in taste had been brought about by exposure to Italian design during the Italian war campaigns. Notice Italianate decoration on Gothic structures. The builder of the classical section was Gaston d'Orléans, brother of the king, Louis XIII. The architect was Mansart. He had already demolished about half of the existing château to construct the new wing, and was already knocking down the lovely Renaissance wing when his work stopped abruptly in 1638 when Louis XIII had a son (meaning Gaston was no longer next in line to the throne). Note the strange break between the two wings, and the off-centre position of the spiral staircase. Go inside the classical wing to see Mansart's intriguing and beautiful cupola. Gaston's demolitions also created the gap between the church and the new wing, giving access to the terrace, with magnificent town and river views. The church contains modern stained glass by Max Ingrand.

Inside François' Renaissance section, the Royal Apartments on the first floor are decorated with bright floor tiles, colourful patterned walls, painted beams and gilded fireplaces. In the Galerie de la Reine, the floor has recently been laid with surprising new glazed floor tiles in blue, yellow, black and white. Apparently, these are based on historical evidence. In the smaller Study, the narrow gilded wood panelling is original, and supposedly conceals secret hiding places. On the second floor are Henri III's apartments and the Guise Hall, devoted to a museum of paintings on the theme of the 1588 assassination of

Chronology of the château

10th century: built by Thibault I.

12th century: Count of Blois marries William the Conqueror's daughter; their son Stephen becomes Count of Blois and King of England.

1440: Charles d'Orléans demolishes part of feudal fortress and rebuilds in brick and stone.

1462: future Louis XII born in the château; after 1498 it is the principal royal residence.

Early 16th century: François I frequently in residence, adds Renaissance wing.

1588: Henri III has Duc de Guise assassinated at the château; three days later Catherine de Medicis (the king's mother) dies in the château.

1635: Gaston d'Orléans commissions Mansart to demolish château and rebuild in classical style. Completes just one wing before stopping in 1638.

Above
Château interior
Overleaf
Château courtyard and staircase

the Duc de Guise. He was killed on 23 December 1588, in the king's bedchamber. His brother, the Cardinal of Lorraine, was also murdered. The influential Guise and his followers were fanatically anti-Protestant, wished to form an alliance with Spain, and seemed intent on deposing the king.

Returning to the first floor, the **Musée des Beaux-Arts** (Fine Arts Museum) contains a large number of 16th- and 17th-century portraits, several good later works, and many Brussels tapestries. Pass through the guardroom to reach the large restored *Salle des Etats-Généraux* (the meeting place of the medieval French Parliament). This is the oldest part of the château, as well as one of the oldest and largest surviving feudal assembly halls in France. Despite a spell in the 19th century as an army gymnasium, it is in excellent condition, with an impressive ceiling of twin barrel vaults supported by central pillars. Here, free classical concerts are held on summer evenings. On the ground floor, a **Musée Archéologique** (Archaeological Museum) is located in former château kitchens.

Église St-Nicolas €
R. St-Lauren; open daily.

Église St-Nicolas*

Formerly a Benedictine abbey church, St-Nicolas was built in an interesting experimental transitional style in the early 12th-century when the Gothic style was a novelty. Inside, there is some good stone carving, interesting stained glass and a 15th-century altarpiece. An unusual dome covers the crossing. The large abbey and its ecclesiastical quarter once played an important part in the life of medieval Blois. The abbey's 18th-century dependencies, in classical style, stretch down to the Loire.

Maison de la Magie
€€€ 1 pl. du Château;
tel: 02 54 55 26 26, fax: 02 54 55 26 28; open Apr–Sept daily 1000–1300, 1400–1800, rest of year Wed, Thur and weekends 1000–1230, 1400–1730.

Maison de la Magie*

A huge and implausible dragon pokes its six heads through the windows of this large 19th-century brick-and-stone mansion opposite the château, dedicated to Robert Houdin. The 'father of modern magic', Houdin – no relation to the famed Houdini – was a brilliant illusionist and entertainer. The museum gives some background to this art form, and many amusing examples. The underground *Théâtre des Magiciens* stages excellent conjuring shows (at 1145, 1530 and 1700 daily).

Below
Statue of Houdin

Accommodation and food in Blois

Streets in the town centre have dozens of inexpensive brasserie-style eating places, with tables set outside in summer. Chain hotels in all price ranges can be found close to the town centre.

Au Rendezvous des Pêcheurs €€ 27 r. du Foix; tel: 02 54 74 67 48, fax: 02 54 74 47 67. Relaxed and enjoyable, one of the best restaurants in town, this Michelin-rosetted address is near the river, a few paces downstream from Église St-Nicolas. The speciality is imaginative fish and seafood dishes perfectly prepared, but game, sauces, vegetables and desserts are all excellent too. There is a good value set menu and local wine list.

L'Orangerie du Château €€€ 1 av. J Laigret; tel: 02 54 78 05 36, fax: 02 54 78 22 78. This is the place for a special treat in Blois, top of the range, a classic, elegant, traditional restaurant. Being located inside the château's Orangerie, just off pl. Victor Hugo at the foot of the Façade des Loges, adds to the pleasure. Cooking with flair, using the best ingredients, accompanied by an excellent wine list and crisp, friendly, efficient service.

Le Bistrot du Cuisinier €-€€ *20 quai Villebois-Mareuil; tel: 02 54 78 06 70, fax: 02 54 74 81 75.* Right beside the water on the south bank, close to the bridge, this convivial and informal bistro with its big dining room has a wonderful view of the town. It makes a point of specialising in wine rather than any particular style of cuisine. For all that, the food is very good, with local dishes emphasised despite periodic specials from around the world. Excellent value for money. Keeps relatively late hours, too – you can order until 2330.

Suggested walk

Total distance: About 3km.

Time: Half a day.

Links: Blois is the point at which three tours meet and can be linked: The Grand Châteaux: Tours–Blois (*see page 54*); Blois–Orleans (*see page 230*); and Cher and the Sologne (*see page 214*).

Route: Start from pl. Victor Hugo (or square Augustin-Thierry), at the foot of the château. On the square's north side is the 17th-century Jesuit church of St-Vincent. On the west side of the square, the **Jardin du Roi** is a last small remnant of the once extensive park and gardens of the château (which reached about as far as today's SNCF railway station). Nearly opposite is the charming Renaissance **Pavillon Anne de Bretagne** (now the tourist office) and **Orangerie**, which were once in the king's gardens and directly accessed by footbridge from the château's Royal Apartments. Along one side, pl. Victor Hugo is overlooked by the impressive **Façade des Loges**, the exterior of the château's Renaissance wing, a long, Italianate, elegant terrace, four storeys high, of which two storeys are open galleries or *loges* (from Italian *loggia*).

Walk up the steps that lead from pl. Victor Hugo to r. de la Voûte-du-Château and up past the Loges façade to reach pl. du Château, the fine traffic-free space in front of the **CHÂTEAU ROYAL DE BLOIS ❶**. Before entering the château, admire the quiet rose gardens on the far side of the square; they have a good view down to the river, crossed by the town's beautiful old bridge. After visiting the château, **MAISON DE LA MAGIE ❷** is at the far end of the square.

At the south-western corner of pl. du Château (that is, at the far left-hand end of the château as seen from the square), a flight of steps leads steeply down to r. St-Lubin. Turn right into this street, and right again, to see the **Façade Gaston d'Orléans**, the imposing exterior of the château's classical wing. Steps down from r. St-Lubin lead to **ÉGLISE ST-NICOLAS ❸**. Near the back of the church, in r. Anne-de-

Above
Place du Château

Bretagne, the town's Natural History and Religious Art museums are housed in former abbey buildings. Walk along **r. St-Lubin**, which has houses dating to the 15th–16th centuries, to busy pl. Louis XII, the main square, destroyed in 1940 and rebuilt. Take r. St Martin and cross r. du Commerce – convivial, crowded, pedestrianised old shopping streets – into r. des Trois Clefs. Cross over r. Denis Papin, the main street of the town; ironically, it is named in honour of the great 17th-century physicist, a native of Blois who, being Protestant, was driven out of the town and hated the place for the way it had treated him and his family.

There are interesting old façades, several half-timbered, along all these streets. Turn right down **r. des Juifs**, so-called for the Jewish community of about 200 living here in the Middle Ages. Thirty-five members of the Jewish community were burned alive on 26 May 1171 after 'the Jews' were blamed for the death of a child. The whole community was again arrested in 1181 and freed after payment of a crippling ransom. There is no Jewish community here today. There are

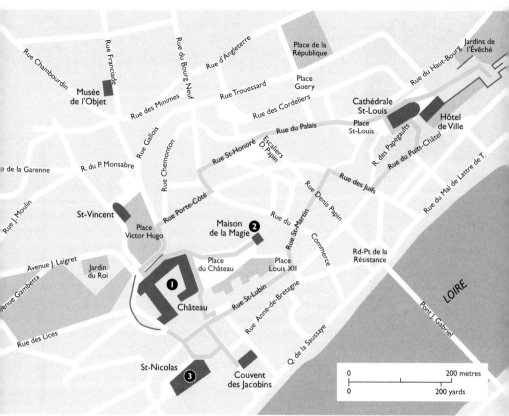

fine Renaissance houses in the street; especially at No 3, **Hôtel Condé**, which was built in 1540, and has a gallery and spiral staircase in the courtyard. Turn left for **r. du Puits Chatel**, where again there are several fine mansions, some with courtyards based on that of the château (note Nos 3, 5 and 7). Off to the left, via the atmospheric little Petits Degrés St-Louis, is the **Cathédrale St-Louis**, an ancient church rebuilt (in Gothic style) in the 17th century. It stands on a steep ledge overlooking the river. Behind the church and lower down the slope is the town hall, with beautiful rose gardens, and a little beyond are the **Jardins de l'Évêché** (The Bishops' Gardens), which afford wonderful river views.

Walk along r. du Palais and r. Denis Papin, backstreets with occasional wide views across the town and river. Nos 56–48 r. Denis Papin have 16th-century arched shopfronts; the façade of No 50 displays the salamander of François I. At the end of the street, turn left and right to follow the wide r. Porte Côté back to pl. Victor Hugo.

Cher and the Sologne

Ratings

Châteaux	●●●●
Children	●●●●
Activities	●●●●
Nature	●●●●
Picturesque villages	●●●
History	●●●
Wildlife	●●●
Gastronomy	●●●

The Sologne was one of the country's great gaming grounds in pre-Revolution days. Royal hunting lodges, elaborate châteaux amid huge parklands, and smaller royal towns pepper a landscape of forests, marshes, small lakes and undulating hills that thin out as they extend towards the Cher and the Loire valleys to the west and north. Amid this bucolic background, the battles between Catholic and Protestant were waged during the Wars of Religion, while the intrigues of kings and courtiers were played out in their favourite châteaux and noble mansions. Nature lovers find the peace and beauty of the Sologne a tonic after city life, while many of the châteaux have nurtured alternative attractions – small zoos, the rearing of exotic birds and animals, and small museums presenting local lifestyles – in their spacious parks. A region of poor, sandy soil, the Sologne is known today for its excellent strawberries and asparagus, and its variety of game and wines, all of which constitute a regional cuisine to delight the gourmet.

BEAUREGARD❖❖

Château de Beauregard €€
Cellettes; tel/fax: 02 54 70 36 74; open Apr–Sept 0930–1200, 1400–1830, July–Aug 0930–1830, Oct–Mar 0930–1200, 1400–1700 except Tue. Closed Jan and the first 3 weeks in Dec.

Originally a hunting lodge for François I, this château passed into the hands of Jean du Thier, Henri II's Secretary of State, and it was he who, in the middle of the 16th century, commissioned the Cabinet des Grelots, a small room decorated in oak, carved and gilded, as his own study. The intricate work, depicting man's varied occupations, was executed by master craftsman and cabinetmaker to Henri II, Italian Scibec de Carpi, who had also undertaken work at Fontainebleau. In 1617, Beauregard belonged to Paul Ardier, a former treasurer to Henri IV. During his time he hosted Cardinal Richelieu (*see page 101*) who had been travelling with King Louis XIII and his court when the King stopped at Blois to meet his mother, Marie de Medicis. Fearing a conspiracy, Richelieu slipped away with his faithful musketeers and took shelter in Beauregard. It was Ardier who commissioned the celebrated Galerie des Illustres. It's the equivalent of a 'who's who' of France's royals and notables, as well as famous foreign personalities,

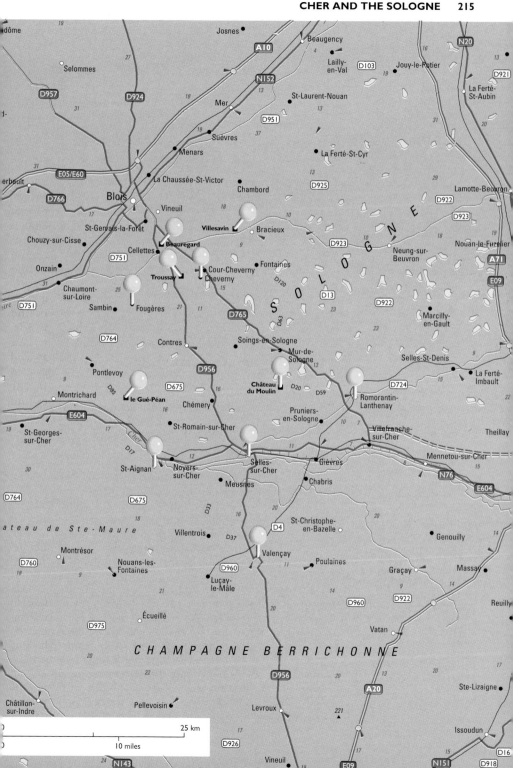

dôme

Josnes

Beaugency

A10

N152

Selommes

D957

D924

D103

Jouy-le-Potier

N20

D921

La Ferté-St-Aubin

Lailly-en-Val

St-Laurent-Nouan

Mer

D951

E05/E60

Suèvres

Menars

La Chaussée-St-Victor

La Ferté-St-Cyr

D925

Lamotte-Beuvron

D922

erbault

D766

Blois

Vineuil

Chambord

D923

O   G   N   E

D923

St-Gervais-la-Forêt

Villesavin

Bracieux

Neung-sur-Beuvron

Nouan-le-Fuzelier

Chouzy-sur-Cisse

Cellettes

Beauregard

D751

Cour-Cheverny

Fontaines

D120

A71

Onzain

Troussay

Cheverny

D13

E09

Chaumont-sur-Loire

Sambin

Fougères

D765

D922

Marcilly-en-Gault

D751

S   O   L   O   G   N   E

D764

Contres

Soings-en-Sologne

Mur-de-Sologne

Selles-St-Denis

Pontlevoy

D956

D675

Château du Moulin

D20

D59

Romorantin-Lanthenay

D724

La Ferté-Imbault

Montrichard

le Gué-Péan

Chémery

E604

St-Georges-sur-Cher

St-Romain-sur-Cher

Pruniers-en-Sologne

Villefranche-sur-Cher

Theillay

D17

St-Aignan

Noyers-sur-Cher

Selles-Sur-Cher

Gièvres

Mennetou-sur-Cher

N76

D764

D675

Meusnes

Chabris

E604

âteau de Ste-Maure

Villentrois

D33

D37

D4

St-Christophe-en-Bazelle

Genouilly

Montrésor

Nouans-les-Fontaines

Valençay

Poulaines

Graçay

Massay

D760

Luçay-le-Mâle

D960

D922

Reuilly

Écueillé

D960

Vatan

D975

C H A M P A G N E   B E R R I C H O N N E

Châtillon-sur-Indre

Pellevoisin

Levroux

A20

D956

Ste-Lizaigne

Issoudun

D926

Vineuil

E09

N151

D918

N143

D16

25 km

10 miles

Above
Beauregard Château

for it includes 327 portraits. Hundreds of eyes focus on you as you wander around the gallery. Look down, too: the blue Delft tile floor in this Gallery is a fine piece of 17th-century faïencework. The south gallery holds some impressive Belgian tapestries as well as various items of remarkable period furniture. The château is currently in private hands and the owners live in the left wing.

In complete contrast to the historical aspect of this château, the owners commissioned a modern garden in the 70-ha park that was created by a notable contemporary French landscape gardener, Gilles Clément.

Food near Beauregard

Bernard Noël Restaurant de la Roselle €€ *15 r. de la Rozelle, Cellettes; tel: 02 54 70 31 27, fax: 02 54 70 35 48, closed Sun pm and Mon, also Thu pm out of season.* This is a gourmet restaurant of some repute in a lovely 18th-century mansion.

CHÂTEAU DE TROUSSAY✥✥

Château de Troussay €-€€
Cheverny; tel: 02 54 44 29 07; open Apr–June & Sept 1030–1230, 1400–1830, July–Aug 1000–1900, Oct weekends 1030–1230, 1400–1730.

Hidden in a lovely tract of woodland is the privately owned Château of Troussay. It probably dates back to 1450 – though the first deeds are from 1545 – and, extraordinarily, this building has only been sold twice (in 1732 and 1900) during the last 600 years. It was constructed for Robert Bugy who was controller of the all-important salt reserves in Blois under François I. It was subsequently owned by the 19th-century historian, Louis de la Saussaye, who was responsible for much of its embellishment. His portrait hangs in the salon Louis de la Saussaye. What we see today is a gentleman's residence, a mansion with human proportions and symmetrically designed service buildings either side of the *Cour d'honneur*. The best views of this ensemble are from the park, behind the château – it wasn't designed to be seen from today's entrance – where the decorative stonework is far more appreciable. The château's ceilings and furniture keep up its 18th-century ambience. A small Musée de Sologne is lodged in the old stables and distillery and displays a collection of traditional farming and agricultural implements.

Accommodation and food near Troussay

Château du Breuil €€€ *Route de Fougères, Cheverny; tel: 02 54 44 20 20, fax: 02 54 44 30 40, www.chateauxhotels.com/breuil; closed mid-Nov–mid-Mar. Restaurant closed Sun & Mon out of season.* In its own wooded parkland, this 18th-century château has been remodelled into a smallish luxury hotel. Good restaurant.

CHEVERNY***

Cheverny Tourist Office *Av. de Cheverny, Cour-Cheverny; tel: 02 54 79 95 63, fax: 02 54 76 96 24; open Apr–mid-Nov daily 1000–1900, closed winter.*

Château de Cheverny €€€; *tel: 02 54 79 96 29, fax: 02 54 79 25 38, www.chateau-cheverny.fr; open Apr–Sept 0915–1845, Oct–Mar 0915–1200, 1415–1700 (until 1730 in Mar and Oct).*

Market: *Cour-Cheverny, Tue pm.*

This is one of the most classic of the Loire châteaux and is well-organised for tourists, children included. Huge parking areas usher in visitors and encourage them to get out and walk. The immaculately-maintained château dates from the 17th century – it was built between 1604–34 by the Count Hurault de Cheverny – and its slate roof and cool stone façade have not been altered since. The château will seem familiar to lovers of Hergé's *Tintin* – his fictitious Château Moulinsart was inspired by this castle. The château is beautifully furnished in period style with dozens of rare items, and the decoration of some of its principal rooms is exquisite. Among the most interesting is the Salle d'Armes with a fine collection of ancient arms and Gobelin tapestries, and the King's bedroom with its magnificent painted ceiling and stone fireplace held aloft by atlantes figures, its tapestries and its rich silk baldaquin bed. The 17th-century tapestries in the Tapestry Chamber are woven copies of works by the famous Flemish painter, Teniers. Visitors to the 100-ha park have a choice of discovering the woodlands and fauna by either a small electric car, by boat on the château's canal or by foot. Cheverny is also noted for its hunting, and it boasts a 90-strong pack of hounds. Their afternoon feeding time is a popular occasion with younger visitors.

Accommodation and food in Cheverny

Le Beguinage €€ *D 765, Cour-Cheverny; tel: 02 54 79 29 92, fax: 02 54 79 94 59, www.multimedia.com/beguinage/* A lovely and tranquil *chambres d'hôtes* with an established garden, just outside the centre. An excellent base for regional visits.

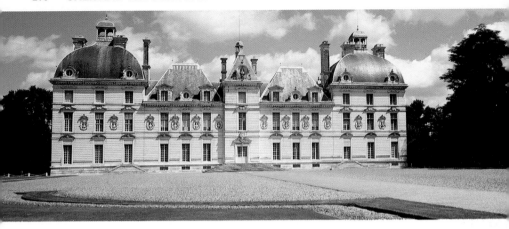

Above
Cheverny

Hôtel des Trois Marchands €€ *Pl. de l'Église, Cour-Cheverny; tel: 02 54 79 96 44, fax: 02 54 79 25 60, www.hotelde3marchands.com* A mid-sized hotel in the centre of town, with garden and highly-rated restaurant. The ambience is that of Louis XIII elegance, and all dishes are made entirely in the kitchens. There is also a less expensive grill restaurant, La Grignotière.

Restaurant Le Pichet €-€€ *Pl. de l'Église, Cheverny; tel: 02 54 79 97 23, fax: 02 54 79 24 09; open daily in season, closed Sun and Mon out of season.* Cleverly located at the château's exit gates opposite the little church (worth a quick look, too), a small traditional restaurant with outdoor and indoor seating.

FOUGÈRES-SUR-BRIÈVRE*

🛈 Château de Fougères € *tel: 02 54 20 27 18; open Apr–Sept daily 0930–1200, 1400–1800, Oct–Mar Wed–Mon 1000–1200, 1400–1630, closed 1 Jan, 1 May, 1 & 11 Nov, & 25 Dec.*

Amid pine forests and fields of asparagus sits the small town of Fougères. It unfurls around its **château*** built by Pierre de Refuge, Louis XI's treasurer at the turn of the 15th century. No pure architectural lines here. His sturdy concept of architecture was tempered by the more attractive additions commissioned subsequently by his son-in-law, Jean de Villebresme, with the result that it's a bit of a hotchpotch. Flat arches, towers capped with pointed roofs and a Renaissance gallery inspired by the château

Right
Fougères Château

at Blois, the building was entirely constructed, unusually for its importance, by local artisans.

Accommodation and food near Fougères-sur-Brièvre

Relais des Landes €€-€€€ *Ouchamps; tel: 02 54 44 40 40, fax: 02 54 44 03 89; open Mar–Nov.* Just 5km from Fougères, this is a luxurious hotel, housed in a converted mansion and its cottages. Excellent gourmet restaurant.

Gué-Péan✢

Château du Gué-Péan €€ *Monthou-sur-Cher; tel: 02 54 71 37 10; open July–mid-Sept 1030–1230, 1400–1830.*

This privately-owned château, dating from the 16th and 17th centuries, is only open in summer, but its beautiful situation in the Forêt Choussy, and its collection of furniture, make it worth the effort. It is said that it was here that Louis XII's widow, Anne de Bretagne, secretly married her lover, the Duke of Suffolk. The fine château with asymmetrical towers (three are round with pepperpot roofs, the fourth has a bell-shaped roof) has an important *Cour d'honneur*, entirely enclosed by the château and its ancillary buildings. The chapel, library and dungeon are of particular note.

Right
Gué-Péan

LE MOULIN❖❖

Château du Moulin
€€ *Lassay-sur-Croisne;*
tel: 02 54 83 83 51; open
Apr–Sept daily 0900–1130,
1400–1830, Oct–mid-Nov &
Mar weekends 0900–1130,
1400–1730, closed Wed
and mid-Nov–Mar.

This beautiful, fortified château is hidden in the forests just near the village of Lassay-sur-Croisne. It was built in 1492 by royal architect J de Persigny for Philippe du Moulin, captain to Charles VIII. Complete with its original dungeon, round towers, an impressive keep and its water-filled moat, this privately-owned (and still inhabited) castle presents a picture-postcard image of a Renaissance château.

ROMORANTIN-LANTHENAY❖❖❖

**Romorantin-
Lanthenay Tourist
Office** *pl. de la Paix; tel: 02
54 76 43 89, fax: 02 54 76
96 24; open Mon
1000–1215, 1400–1830,
Tue–Fri 0845–1215,
1330–1830, Sat
0845–1215, 1330–1800.*

P Parking Pl. Jean
Moulin, in the south
or pl. de la Paix, in the
centre.

Tarte Tatin

The two 19th-century Tatin sisters made culinary history at the Solognot village of Lamotte-Beuvron. They invented (though one wonders if it was by accident) the much-loved French dessert, *tarte Tatin*, in which the standard apple pie is reversed and the caramelised apples appear sitting on their pastry base.

When the 1498 plague threatened Amboise, young François I fled with his mother to take up residence in his château in Romorantin. Not much of the château now exists in this beautiful town – the sub-prefecture occupies the remains – but there are plenty of ancient homes, built of brick and wood, and a number of watermills. Romorantin grew up as an important drapery centre, and the materials for its trade were prepared in the numerous mills along the River Sauldre, one of which was still active in 1970. The **Musée de Sologne**❖❖ is situated in a couple of these renovated (and built onto) buildings, the Moulin du Chapitre and the Moulin de la Ville. Once used to mill flour and oil, and for pressing raw materials for fabric, these mills now house an interesting collection dedicated to the life, history and economy of the Sologne including that of its capital, Romorantin-Lanthenay.

Romorantin's other trump card is its collection of old buildings that line the various arms of the River Sauldre, some still half-timbered and almost all in good condition. The **Musée d'Archéologie**❖ is a must just for its 600-year-old building, the Carroir Doré. Its brick and timber walls are embellished by finely-carved, wooden columns. Saint Michael about to stab the dragon is particularly well-preserved. The collection (small, as is the building) incorporates finds from the region including prehistoric tools, Gallo-Roman pottery, and medieval locks. Nearby, on an islet encircled by more arms of the river, is the well-kept **Parc Ferdinand Buisson**❖, a quiet and favourite place for Romorantin locals to relax. It backs onto the very elegant 19th-century mansion that now houses the *Mairie*. Lastly, Romorantin-Lanthenay is somewhat better known today as the centre of Matra car production, a company with close links to Renault (Matra pioneered the *Espace*, for instance, which Renault markets). The **Espace Automobiles Matra**❖❖, an exhibition of 50 of Matra's vehicles including racing, experimental and saloon cars, is open to the public in the old Beaulieu factory once responsible for producing Super 8 movie cameras.

Accommodation and food in Romorantin-Lanthenay

🏛 **Musée de Sologne €**
tel: 02 54 95 33 66;
open Apr–Oct daily 1000–
1800, hols 1400–1800,
Nov–Mar 1000–1200,
1400–1800, Sun & hols
1400–1800, closed Tue.

Musée d'Archéologie €
21 r. de la Pierre; tel: 02 54
76 22 06; open June–Sept
except Thur, Sun & public
hols 1430–1830.

**Espace Automobiles
Matra €€** 17 r. des
Capucins; tel: 02 54 94 55
55, fax: 02 54 94 55 56;
open Mon & Wed–Sat
0900–1200, 1400–1800,
Sun 1000–1200,
1400–1700, closed 1 Jan,
1 May and 25 Dec.

🛒 **Markets:** Wed all
day, Fri am.

Grand Hôtel du Lion d'Or €€€ 69 r. *Georges Clemenceau; tel: 02 54 94 15 15; fax: 02 54 88 24 87; web: www.hotel-liondor.fr* A member of the prestigious *Relais & Châteaux* group, this largely Renaissance mansion has been beautifully converted to a small luxury hotel. Its award-winning gourmet restaurant also has a remarkable selection of fine wines.

Restaurant Le Colombier €€ *18 pl. du Vieux-Marché; tel: 02 54 76 12 76.* A surprising find – a little way from the centre but a very good restaurant with imaginative gourmet cuisine. Also a small inexpensive hotel.

Auberge de Lanthenay €€ *Pl. de l'Église, r. Notre-Dame-du-Lieu (2 km from centre); tel: 02 54 76 09 19, fax: 02 54 76 72 91; closed Christmas and New Year period, first half July, Sun pm & Mon.* Perennially popular restaurant with gastronomic and local cuisine, and a family-run inn with ten rooms. Good, friendly service. Book early for weekend meals.

The Sologne

The Sologne is a vast area of often-misty ponds, dense heath and extensive forests. Conifers, birches and oaks hide a prolific wildlife: indeed, under the Second Empire some 340 châteaux were built for hunting. In those days game was everywhere; today the area counts just 20 different species of mammal but 200 species of bird. And, in its 3000-odd ponds, there are carp, tench, pike and perch. It is a haven for nature lovers.

SAINT-AIGNAN❖❖

ℹ️ **St-Aignan Tourist
Office** 26 pl. Wilson;
tel: 02 54 75 22 85, fax: 02
54 75 50 26; open Mon–Sat
1000–1230, 1430–1830,
summer Sun 1000–1200,
1500–1800.

🅿️ Park in front of the
Hôtel de Ville.

This town is best known for its white lions in the **Zoo Parc de Beauval**❖❖❖, 4km to the south. It is a fine place to visit, especially with children, but the medieval town also has plenty of charm. It is a place to park and walk through its tiny alleys, exploring streets with ancient homes such as the 15th-century, half-timbered house or the Gothic Maison de le Prévôté formerly the Palais de Justice. The château is not open for visits but the **Église Collégiale de Saint-Aignan**❖❖❖ merits a serious visit. This Romanesque church – one of the Loire region's finest – has superb capitals and a fabulous series of original 11th- to 15th-century frescoes in the choir, in a chapel dedicated to Saint John, and above all in the crypt, which was the site of its previous church, the Église Saint-Jean. No need for a guide here as, for a small fee, a pre-

In summer, there are 90-min cruises on the *Val-du-Cher* from the embarkation point on the Cher. *Tel: 02 54 71 40 38.*

Église Collégiale de Saint-Aignan € *R. Constant; open 0800–1200, 1400–1900.*

Zoo Parc de Beauval €€ *tel: 02 54 75 50 00, fax: 02 54 75 50 01, www.zoobeauval. com; open daily 0900–dusk.*

Market Sat all day.

recorded *son-et-lumière* show lights up and explains each space in turn. The energetic can climb up the bell tower and view medieval Saint-Aignan from a novel angle. Crowning the skyline is the château – remains of which date back to the 9th and 11th centuries: Foulques Nerra (*see page 103*) took the town in 1030 and remodelled part of the fortified castle. It then became the home of the Ducs de Beauvillier. The castle is not open to the public, but the views over the River Cher from the far end of the *Cour d'Honneur* are impressive.

The much-publicised zoo is certainly worth a visit, especially for the young. It was conceived to help conserve endangered species and has evolved into a centre dedicated to research and conservation, offering help and financial assistance in countries requiring conservation measures. Various different climatic environments have been recreated on the 15-ha estate, including tropical greenhouses and savannah grasslands. The large collections of cats and primates are a big attraction, but it is interesting to find that they also have over 2000 birds, many of which are tropical and spectacularly plumed. One of the most delightful and newer aspects of the zoo is the introduction (to the public) of its nursery where abandoned young are bottle-fed and reintegrated as they mature with their respective species.

Accommodation and food in and around Saint-Aignan

Grande Hôtel Saint Aignan €–€€ *Quai Jean-Jacques Delorme; tel: 02 54 75 18 04, fax: 02 54 75 12 59; closed part-Feb, part-Nov; out of season Sun, Mon and Tue am.* A pretty, small hotel right on the banks of the Cher offering comfortable rooms and a good restaurant.

Hôtel Le Clos du Cher €€ *Rte de St-Aignan, Noyers-sur-Cher; tel: 02 54 75 00 03, fax: 02 54 75 03 79, www.chateauxhotels.com/closcher; closed Wed pm and Thu out of season.* Located in parkland, this restored, 18th-century home has been converted into a comfortable, small hotel. There is also a restaurant offering regional menus.

Restaurant Chez Constant € *Pl. de la Paix; tel 02 54 75 10 75, closed Mon and Tue except high season.* This pleasant restaurant is named for Constant Ragot, the mayor of St-Aignan. It offers diners a good traditional menu, and friendly service.

Below
St-Aignan, view from Château

SELLES-SUR-CHER✥

ⓘ Selles Tourist Office *Pl. Charles de Gaulle; tel/fax: 02 54 95 25 44; open Tue–Sat 0900–1200, 1400–1800.*

ⓘ Musée du Val-de-Cher € *Pl. Charles de Gaulle; tel/fax: 02 54 95 25 44; open June–Aug Tue–Sun 1000–1200, 1430–1800.*

🛒 Market Thur all day.

It is a pity that you can't visit the Renaissance Château at Selles, for its impressive profile reflecting in the waters of the Cher hints at a once-grandiose past. Content yourselves with the Église Saint-Eusice. This Merovingian church dates back some 1500 years (have a look at the ancient sixth-century sarcophagus containing the remains of Saint Eusice in the crypt, and the paintings in the apse depicting his life) though much of its form shows its 13th- to 16th-century remodelling. In the main square, pl. Charles de Gaulle, the small **Musée du Val-de-Cher✥** has a collection of items showing ancient farming methods and traditional old costumes.

Right
Selles church façade

Accommodation and food in Selles-Sur-Cher

Le Lion d'Or €–€€ *14 pl. de la Paix; tel: 02 54 97 40 83, fax: 02 54 97 78 36.* This staging point has been feeding travellers since 1664 and, although its interior is modern, it is still a favourite rendezvous. Apart from the restaurant, it also has five bedrooms.

Selles-sur-Cher cheeses

Selles-sur-Cher is known for its soft round goat's cheese, which has its own *appellation contrôlée*. Round or cylindrical, rolled in herbs or left to mature on its own, it is one of the fine cheeses from the Sologne area. For more cheesy know-how and the chance to sample local produce, visit the *Fromagerie P Jacquin & Fils €, off the D 956 (between Selles and Valençay), tel: 02 54 95 30 60, fax: 02 54 97 47 46; open by appointment only Feb–Oct daily except Sun & public hols 0830–1130.*

Overleaf
Selles-sur-Cher

VALENÇAY*

Valençay Tourist Office 2 av. de la Résistance; tel/fax: 02 54 00 04 42; open May–Sept daily 0930–1900, winter 0930–1230, 1400–1800.

www.cc.valençay.fr

Château de Valençay €€–€€€; tel: 02 54 00 15 69, fax: 02 54 00 02 37; open Apr–mid-Nov daily 0930–1800 (until 1930 July–Aug), Nov–Feb Sat/Sun & hols 1400–1700, Mar Mon–Fri 1400–1700, Sat/Sun & hols 1000–1700, closed 1 Nov.

Market: Tue am.

This Renaissance château, just inside the Berry, took its inspiration from Chambord. It was built around 1540 but bought in 1803 by the Prince of Talleyrand (Napoleon's Foreign Minister) who revamped it to entertain foreign dignitaries. Its excellent proportions lend themselves to fine decoration, and all the rooms are well-furnished with period pieces and reflect the personalities of those who once inhabited them. These numbered the Duchess of Dino, Talleyrand himself (look out for the elaborate clothing worn by the handicapped Prince) and Ferdinand, later King of Spain. The large underground kitchen was the domain of the illustrious Chef Carême. Beside it, the cellars still boast a magnificent, albeit dusty, collection of wines. The Park is also a big draw and very child-friendly. Apart from deer, there are llamas and other exotic creatures. The peacocks, ducks and geese have the free run of the formal French garden. During the summer months, costumed actors bring the castle back to life: fencing matches take place, the kitchen bustles with activity as Chef Carême 'prepares a meal' and the courtiers move through the state rooms.

Accommodation and food in Valençay

Hôtel Le Relais du Moulin €–€€ 94 r. National; tel: 02 54 00 38 00, fax: 02 54 00 38 79; closed mid Nov–1 Apr. A modern, mid-sized hotel, with pool, just 800m outside town. Two restaurants with local and gourmet menus.

Valençay cheese

Gourmets should look out for Valençay's goat's cheese. This creamy, crumbly delight is formed in the shape of a pyramid with a flat top – it is best enjoyed with a local red sauvignon wine such as the AOC Valençay or Reuilly.

VILLESAVIN*

Château de Villesavin €€ Tour-en-Sologne; tel: 02 54 46 42 88, fax: 02 54 46 09 49; open mid-Feb–May 1000–1200, 1400–1900, June–Sept 1000–1900, Oct–Nov 1000–1200, 1400–1800, Dec Sat–Sun & school hols 1000–1200, 1400–1800.

This Renaissance-style château only rises two storeys yet creates an imposing impression with its elegant wings. Although it is used for receptions, it is also open to the public on guided tours. Some 350 diadems form part of its unusual collection of objects and costumes grouped around the theme of marriage. On display, too, are a series of horse-drawn carriages and, a highlight for kids, their herds of breeding donkeys.

Right
entrance to Villesavin

Accommodation and food near Villesavin

Au Bistrot d'Arian € *231 route d'Arian, Tour-en-Sologne; tel/fax: 02 54 46 42 85.* A small restaurant with a shady garden, conveniently situated for Villesavin. Traditional and regional dishes, and friendly service.

Suggested tour

❶ Comité Départemental du Tourisme de Loir-et-Cher *5 r. de la Voûte du Château, Blois; tel: 02 54 57 00 41, fax: 02 54 57 00 47, www.tourismloir-et-cher.com; open Apr–Sept Mon–Fri 0900–1900, Oct–Mar 0900–1200, 1400–1800.*

Ⓦ *www.sologne-fr.com; www.chambordcountry.com*

❶ La Magnanerie €€ *4 chemin de la Croix-Bardin, Bourré; tel: 02 54 32 63 91; open daily except Tue Apr–Oct, guided visits at 1100, 1400, 1500, 1600 & 1700.* Raising silk worms.

Total distance: About 165km.

Time: Allow 2–3 days. The distances are not particularly great but there are so many interesting sights that it's impossible to do them justice in less than 2 days.

Links: From Montrichard, the D176 heads westwards to Chenonceaux on the Grand Châteaux: Tours–Blois route (*see page 54*). Were you to travel 20km south from Valençay to Levroux, you'd link up with the Berry route (*see page 270*), while at Bracieux the D120 leads straight to Chambord, on the Blois–Orléans route (*see page 230*).

Route: Leaving **Blois** (*see page 204*) by the southbound D956, it is just 8km to the small village of Cellettes. Turn first left, following the signs for **BEAUREGARD ❶**. It's just a short road through the corn fields to the château. Leave by the same route into Cellettes and drive through the town, branching off to the left on the D77 signposted to Bracieux and **CHEVERNY ❷**. The nearby town (1km) of **Cour-Cheverny**, on the D765, is a better bet for a hotel and for dining. Leaving the château at Cheverny, make for the D52 and turn left at the junction. It is just 1km to the turning marked **TROUSSAY ❸**.

La Ville Souterraine €€
*40 route des Roches, Bourré,
tel: 02 54 32 35 15, fax: 02
54 32 56 09; open daily
Palm Sunday to mid-Nov
1000–1800.* Champagne-
style wine cellars,
mushroom cellars, and
troglodyte village.

**Musée Archéologique
€€** *Mairie de Thésée-la-
Romaine; tel: 02 54 71 40
20; open daily July–Aug
except Tue 1430–1830,
Easter–June & Sept–mid
Oct, weekends & public hols
only 1500–1800.*

**⚫ Restaurant-Hôtel
de l'Ecole €–€€**
*12 rte de Montrichard,
Pontlevoy; tel: 02 54 32 50
30, fax: 02 54 32 33 58.* A
handsome-looking small
hotel with an elegant
restaurant, *La Closerie*,
garden dining in fine
weather. Personalised
service and warm welcome.

**Hostellerie du Moulin
de la Renne €€** *11 rte de
Vierzon, Thésée-la-Romaine;
tel: 02 54 71 41 56, fax: 02
54 71 75 09; closed from
mid-Jan–mid-Mar, Sun pm
and Mon.* A small hotel just
behind the old watermill, on
the D176 road towards
Noyers-sur-Cher.
Traditional restaurant
decorated in rustic style.
Pleasant gardens.

**⚫ Bernard Robin – Le
Relais €€€** *1 av. de
Chambord, Bracieux; tel: 02
54 46 41 22, fax: 02 54 46
03 69, e-mail:
robin@relaischâteaux.fr*
Renowned chef Bernard
Robin welcomes diners to
this award-winning
restaurant in an old
coaching house.

You pick up the D52 again leaving Troussay and head southwest towards **Sambin**, arriving in the pretty town of **FOUGÈRES-SUR-BRIÈVRE ❹**. Its large, fortified château is on the left, just across the River Brièvre. Continue along the D52 to **Sambin** and turn left onto the D764 in the direction of **Pontlevoy**. The vast and impressive Abbaye de Pontlevoy has recently been renovated to become the Centre European American, a cross-cultural educational institute. It is a pleasant place to stop and stroll. There is an interesting open-air exhibition of sepia photographs placed strategically around town, showing how Pontlevoy looked a century ago. Take the D85, marked to **Monthou-sur-Cher**, and turn in the direction of the signposted **GUÉ-PÉAN ❺**.

The small road back to the River Cher, via Monthou, comes to **Thésée-la-Romaine**. This pleasant town was once an important Gallo-Roman site. Renowned for its pottery, it has a remarkable small museum with archaeological finds from this era and the remains of its second-century town walls; it is also known for its troglodyte homes. From Thésée, take the bridge across the river, marked to **Pouillé**. The D17 follows the Cher and takes you towards **SAINT-AIGNAN ❻**, crowned by its château. It is a pleasant run eastwards along the D17. There is an historic dovecote on the right side of the road, at **La Colombier**, just short of Couffy. The D33A and the D33, to the south of **Meusnes**, follow the small River Modon. At Villentrois you take a left onto the D37 which passes through the thick **Forest of Gâtiné** before joining the D956 at **VALENÇAY ❼**. The straight D956 heads for the Cher, and the town of **SELLES-SUR-CHER ❽**. Take the exit road from the north of Selles to the highway, N76, and turn eastwards. This will bring you to the capital of the Sologne, **ROMORANTIN-LANTHENAY ❾**. Leave Romorantin by the D59, which is marked to Gy-en-Sologne, and then turn onto the D20 in the direction of **Lassay-sur-Croisne** where the moated **CHÂTEAU DU MOULIN ❿** is located just 1km away.

The D20 goes to **Mur-de-Sologne**, a little town in the heart of this flat area. Onwards on the D63 via **Courmemin**, where you turn onto the D120 to **Fontaines-en-Sologne** and continue the road to **Bracieux**. This town is known for little else than its highly rated restaurant, one of the region's best. At the junction just before the town, take the D102A to Arian, for just over the river Beuvron is the château of **VILLESAVIN ⓫**. The simplest way back to Blois is to pick up the D102 and head back for Cour-Cheverny, turning right at the main junction onto the D765.

dôme

19

Selommes

D957

D924

31

Josnes

27

27

18

Mer

D951

13

Suèvres

19

37

Menars

E05/E60

La Chaussée-St-Victor

Chambord

Blois

D766

Vineuil

18

St-Gervais-la-Forêt

17

Chouzy-sur-Cisse

Cellettes

1 Beauregard

Villesavin **11**

Bracieux

Onzain

D751

14

Troussay **3**

2 Cour-Cheverny

Cheverny

9

Fontaines

Chaumont-
sur-Loire

31

25

Sambin

4 Fougères

21

11

D765

15

Contres

Soings-en-Sologne

Mur-de-
Sologne

Pontlevoy

D956

23

Montrichard

D675

16

Château
du Moulin **10**

D20

D59

E604

D85

le Gué-Pêan **5**

Chémery

16

St-Romain-sur-Cher

Pruniers-
en-Sologne

St-Georges-
sur-Cher

17

13

Romorantin-
Lanthenay **9**

19

D17

12

N76

Villefranche-
sur-Cher

St-Aignan **6**

Noyers-
sur-Cher

8

Selles-
sur-Cher

Gièvres

D764

D675

Meusnes

Chabris

N76

E604

D956

Château de Ste-Maure

18

Villentrois

16

20

St-Christophe-
en-Bazelle

D760

Montrésor

D37

7 Valençay

Genouilly

D4

18

Nouans-les-
Fontaines

9

11

Poulaines

Massay

D960

Luçay-
le-Mâle

Graçay

D975

21

Écueillé

20

D960

D922

Reuilly

CHAMPAGNE BERRICHONNE

Vatan

Châtillon-
sur-Indre

20

Pellevoisin

22

D956

20

13

20

17

Ste-Lizaigne

A20

Levroux

25 km

10 miles

D926

221

Issoudun

D16

Clèry-St-André

20

N20

Beaugency

4

Lailly-
en-Val

D103

Jouy-le-Potier

D921

19

St-Laurent-Nouan

La Ferté-
St-Aubin

20

13

La Ferté-St-Cyr

13

29

Lamotte-Beuvron

D925

D922

D923

10

18

19

D923

Neung-sur-
Beuvron

Nouan-le-Fuzelier

A71

10

E09

D120

D63

D13

D922

23

Marcilly-
en-Gault

13

Selles-St-Denis

D724

15

La Ferté-
Imbault

22

10

7

Theillay

7

Mennetou-sur-Cher

8

15

30

14

9

14

9

14

17

17

Blois–Orléans

Ratings

History	●●●●●
Châteaux	●●●●●
Entertainment	●●●●
Activities	●●●
Winetasting	●●●
Museums	●●●
Scenery	●●
Children	●●

At Orléans, the Loire has turned west to face the sea, and opens out to create a region of cultivation and plenty in the broad river plain. It is also a region of heath and forest, once preserved as hunting lands for the nobility. As it continues downstream, the river valley carves into the soft rock of the Beauce plateau on the north bank, and forms fertile meadows from sandy alluvial deposits on the south bank. The Loire itself is often seen only from afar. Much of the history of France has been made on this stretch of the valley. At Blois, Joan of Arc had her standard blessed, and from there rode with her men to force the English to retreat from Orléans. So began their withdrawal from the whole of France. Later, as the kings of France moved restlessly from château to château, they often travelled with more than 10,000 people to Chambord and Blois.

BEAUGENCY**

🛈 Beaugency Tourist Office 3 pl. Dr Hyvernaud (or pl. de l'Hôtel de Ville); tel: 02 38 44 54 42, fax: 02 38 46 45 31, e-mail: tourisme.beaugency @wanadoo.fr; open daily all year.

Ⓦ www.ville-beaugency.fr/ (the town's useful and interesting official site).

Ⓟ It is difficult to drive or park in the town. It's easier to park by the riverside and walk.

It is best to approach Beaugency from the south, on the old bridge. The long, narrow, medieval stone structure that crosses the Loire, with its irregular arches and humped not in the middle but closer to the north bank, has determined much of the little town's history. When Loire bridges were few, they had great strategic importance. During the Hundred Years' War, Beaugency was frequently besieged, changing hands between English and French forces four times. In 1429, when Joan of Arc was marching from Blois to Orléans, she wanted to cross the river at Beaugency but was unable to do so because English soldiers held the bridge. Having driven the English from Orléans, she returned to Beaugency and defeated them here, too. Little more than a century later, the town and its bridge were again the focus of fighting, between Catholics and Protestants. In 19th- and 20th-century wars too, Beaugency's bridge was fiercely contested. The present structure is believed to date mainly from the 12th and 14th centuries.

Brou

Outarville

cheville 14

B E A U C E 7

Janville

Toury 9

0   25 km
0   10 miles

Orgères-
en-Beauce

D927

10

D927

Bazoches-les
Gallerandes

Logron

Loigny-la-
Bataille 7

13

Aschères-
le-Marché 7

Arrou

11

Terminiers

Neuville-aux-Bois 12

urtalain D927

18

D927 23

D935

Arrenay

Châteaudun

Patay 12

D5

21

24

D11

14

35

Chevilly

O R L É A N A I

Loury

Cloyes-sur-
le-Loir

11

D955 13

N20

D97

19

Traîn

La Ferté-Villeneuil

D925

D924

21

Épieds-
en-Beauce

D3

Saran

Fleury-les-Aubrais

St-Jean-de-Braye

N10

19

Ouzouer-
le-Marché 19

Coulmiers

13

6

St-Ay

St-Jean-de-la-Ruelle

Chécy

Morée

N157 12

Binas

7

Orléans

Jarç

rcs 14

12

St-Ay

7

Olivet

22

10

19

3

Sandillon

Oucques

D917

Marchenoir

19

23

Méung-
sur-Loire

Cléry-St-André

20

Marcilly-
en-Villette

19

27

Josnes

7

16

N20

13

D921

Talcy

A10

4

Beaugency

Lailly-
en-Val

D103 19

Jouy-le-Potier

Selommes

27

St-Laurent-Nouan

La Ferté-
St-Aubin

D957

D924

18

Mer

N152

13

13

31

20

31

31

19

Suèvres

D951

Vouz

E05/E60

Menars

Muides-
sur-Loire

La Ferté-St-Cyr

13

S O L O G N E

erbault

La Chaussée-St-Victor

Chambord

D925

29

Lamotte-
Beuvron

Blois

D766

Vineuil

18

10

D922

D923 19

St-Gervais-la-Forêt

Bracieux

D923

10

18

Nouan-
le-Fuzelier

houzy-sur-Cisse

14

9

Neung-sur-
Beuvron

A71

Onzain

D751

Cellettes

Cour-Cheverny

E09

Chaumont-
sur-Loire

21

11

15

D13

N20

oire

25

D765

23

D922

Marcilly-
en-Gault

23

Salbris

D764

Contres

Soings-en-Sologne

Pontlevoy

D956

Mur-de-
Sologne

13

Selles-St-Denis

La Ferté-
Imbault

9

Montrichard

D675

Chémery

D724

16

Romorantin-
Lanthenay

22

Pruniers-

Château Dunois, Musée des Arts et Traditions de l'Orléanais €€ *pl. Dunois; no phone; open Wed–Mon 1000–1100, 1400–1700 (1600 in winter).*

Markets: All day Sat. Big annual markets fill the streets on 1 May, 3rd Sun in June, and (wine and gastronomy fair) 3rd Sun in Sept.

Summer events: There is a programme of concerts, cultural events and *son-et-lumière* every summer – contact the tourist office for details.

Attractive cobbled streets and lanes, lined with old stone and timber houses, rise away from the river to the main square with its Renaissance town hall at the top of the town. A few paces higher up, Tour de l'Horloge is a remnant of medieval ramparts. Among pretty, smaller squares, pl. St-Firmin (together with pl. Dunois) has two huge towers – one is all that survives of a 15th-century church, the other, called Caesar's Tower, was a keep that formed part of the 11th-century fortifications. Old lamps give the squares a special charm after dark.

Lower down, **Chateau Dunois**✦ was converted in the 15th century from a small fortress into a luxurious mansion. Heavily restored, and with an interesting medieval garden at the back, it now contains the Musée Régional de l'Orléanais. This small museum of local culture and history has an eclectic assortment of furnishings, dolls and toys, and material on local celebrities. Alongside it, **Église Notre-Dame**✦ is a restored 11th-century Romanesque abbey church.

The devil's bridge

The legend has long been told in Beaugency, in song and in rhyme, of how it was the devil who first built the town's ancient bridge across the Loire. He built it in a single night, without the use of any tools, on condition that he could have and keep the first soul that crossed it. The wily folk of Beaugency agreed – and pushed a cat onto the bridge before anyone else. The cat ran across, too fast and too agile to be caught even by the devil.

Below
Vieux Beaugency

Accommodation and food in Beaugency

Hostellerie de l'Ecu de Bretagne €–€€ *5 r. de la Maille d'Or; tel: 02 38 44 67 60, fax: 02 38 44 68 07, e-mail: ecu-de-bretagne@wanadoo.fr, www.ecu-de-bretagne.fr* A long, low coaching inn just off the (quiet) main square, this atmospheric, creaky old 2-star hotel and excellent restaurant provide a very enjoyable stay at a modest price. The imaginative three-course set lunch menu is a bargain.

The Joan of Arc story

A focus for French nationalism, reverence for Joan of Arc reaches its height at Blois and Orléans. The main street of Orléans bears her name and a large equestrian statue of her stands at the centre of the main square. The cathedral has modern stained-glass windows devoted to her. Every year, on 7–8 May, the city celebrates its liberation by Joan of Arc.

Jehanne d'Arc was born to a peasant family in Domrémy, in northern France, in 1412. At the age of 17, while tending sheep, she began hearing voices, which she believed to be those of Saints Catherine and Michael. They told her that she would drive the English out of France (the Hundred Years' War had been continuing since 1337) and that the uncrowned king of France, Charles VII, would be crowned king in Reims. The English were at that moment besieging Orléans and looked likely to take the whole of France.

With six male companions, Joan set off to the Loire valley, arriving on 6 March 1429 at Chinon, where Charles was residing. She asked to be given an audience with him, and was admitted to the château. Although Charles was mixing with courtiers in the Great Hall, and not wearing royal robes, Joan identified him immediately and told him of the prophesy. She was taken to a religious court in Poitiers to determine whether she was inspired by the Devil. The court came to the conclusion that she was inspired by God, and she was taken to Tours to be provided with armour and troops. On 29 April, marching east from Blois, where her standard had been ritually blessed, she arrived at Orléans, then starving and demoralised after the long siege. Opposed by the town's officials, who tried to prevent her, Joan so roused the local people that they were able to expel the English forces the following week, on 7 and 8 May. Joan went on to defeat the English at Jargeau, Beaugency and Patay. On 1 July she accompanied Charles to Reims for his coronation.

Joan was then captured by Burgundians, allies of the English, to whom she was handed over. English authorities sentenced her to death by burning, carried out in Rouen in 1431. But the English were now retreating and, by 1453, they had been driven from France. Joan of Arc was finally made a saint in 1920.

CHAMBORD❖❖❖

Chambord Tourist Office *Centre d'Information, tel: 02 54 20 34 86 (Easter–Sept); at other times, try the Mairie de Chambord, tel: 02 54 20 31 53, fax: 02 54 33 31 01.*

www.chambord.org/ (the official site of the Chambord community, in French and English); www.unesco.org/whc/sites/161.htm (UNESCO's Chambord pages).

Chateau de Chambord €€ *tel: 02 54 50 50 00, fax: 02 54 20 34 69; open daily Jan–Mar, Nov–Dec 0900–1715 (no entry after 1645), Apr–June, Sept–Oct: 0900–1815 (no entry after 1745), July–Aug: 0900–1845. Closed 1 Jan, 1 May, 25 Dec.*

Below
Rooftops of Chambord

More than any other château, Chambord is fit for a king. Enclosed by a vast private oak forest, the pale castle is itself gigantically large, and covered with a huge black roof of wild, fantastic complexity. The sheer monumental madness of its grandeur and size seems to convey what it was to be monarch in 16th-century France. Construction of the Château de Chambord began in 1519, and took 15 years, thousands of men being employed on the site. It is entirely Renaissance in style. Erected for François I, it became his favourite château – even though he stayed there only 40 nights during 15 years. The building is three storeys high, and consists of a simple rectangular outer structure with round towers at each corner, and a massive square keep on the north-west side, also with towers.

Inside the château, everything is huge. Rising up through the centre of the keep is the vast *Escalier à Double Revolution*, an astounding idea, believed to be the work of Leonardo da Vinci, who was working for François I at the time. Two staircases in one (one above the other), it is so arranged that two people may use it at the same time without meeting. However, side openings would allow them to converse.

In the keep and the rest of the château, only about 80 rooms – a small proportion of the total – are open to the public. Though sparsely furnished, they are lavish enough in decoration and size to give an intriguing glimpse into château life.

On the first floor, the *Chambre du Comte de Chambord* contains a large, draped four-poster bed, under a ceiling of massive timbers, and a floor patterned with wood tiles. *The Chambre aux Lauriers-Rose* shows the 18th-century move towards greater decoration, refinement and

Entertainment at the château: Le Cheval Roi (equestrian display) – daily May–Sept 1145, www.chambord-horse-show.fr; Les Métamorphoses de Chambord (evening show) – every evening in summer; Son-et-Lumière – summer evenings. To book for these events, or for more information, tel: 02 54 50 40 00.

Visiting the château

It is best to arrive early at the château. A visit takes about two hours. Long queues build up during the day, and the building becomes more and more crowded. Tours in English are at 1100 daily (taking 1.5–2 hours); audioguides are available for a 1.5-hour self-guided tour. Also available is a *tour ludique* – a 1-hr tour 'led by a personality from the past'.

comfort. The Royal Apartments of the 17th century are decorated with huge tapestries. The *Chambre du Roi*, installed in 1681 for Louis XIV, is rich in sculpted, gilded wood and plasterwork. In contrast, the delicate *Chambre de la Reine* is decorated entirely in blue fabric, covering walls, ceiling and furniture. The *Chambre du Roi* in the François I apartments is heavy with red and gold fabrics, and a massive fireplace is still in use.

On the second floor, vaulted stone ceilings covered with carved coffers depicting royal emblems – notably the salamander and the letter F, both symbols of François I – are impressive. On that floor, a group of rooms is devoted to a Museum of Hunting and Nature. The central staircase climbs to the roof, where the profusion of windows and turrets resembles a lofty village with fine views over the parkland, the river Cosson, and the dark forest concealing game and wildlife. There is also a village of about 50 houses within the forest.

With 440 rooms, Château de Chambord is the largest of the Loire castles. Its estate of 5 440ha is the largest in Europe, and it is enclosed by the longest wall in France – 31km, which took from 1542 until 1645 to construct.

Accommodation and food in Chambord

There are several popular eating places just outside the château.

Hôtel du Grand Saint-Michel €€ *tel: 02 54 20 31 31, fax: 02 54 20 36 40.* Ideally situated just opposite the château entrance, yet moderately priced, this family-run 2-star hotel has comfortable rooms (three with views of the château) and a good restaurant with affordable menus. After the château is closed and the visitors gone, everything is entirely peaceful. Book months ahead.

CLÉRY-ST-ANDRÉ*

Cléry Tourist Office Pl. de l'Église; tel: 02 38 45 94 33, fax: 02 38 45 94 33, email: o-tourismedeclery @wanadoo.fr; open 0930–1230, 1430–1800.

The simple village is dominated by its large Flamboyant Gothic basilica* dedicated to the much-venerated Notre-Dame de Cléry. In 1280, a local peasant ploughed up ancient pottery shards, bones and other relics, including a figurine in female form which was promptly hailed as a miraculous appearance of the Virgin. Placed in a church, the statue attracted many pilgrims, and the church became a stop on the route to the shrine of St James at Compostela. The original Cléry church was destroyed by English soldiers as they passed through on their way to Orléans in 1428; a single tower which survived is incorporated into the present building. Dunois, the companion at arms of Joan of Arc, began the reconstruction of the church. Louis XI who had vowed to give his weight in silver to Cléry if he were

Overleaf
Château de Chambord

Basilica € Tel: 02 38 45 70 05; open daily all year (Apr–Nov guided tours pm).

Market: Sat am.

Events: Son-et-Lumière – end-July; pilgrimage of Notre-Dame de Cléry, with other events on the same day – 8 Sept.

victorious in the siege of Dieppe, and kept his vow – continued the work of building the Gothic basilica (it was completed under his son Charles VIII). Louis formed a close attachment to Cléry: he used to visit the church, going up the spiral staircase to a private oratory from which he could follow the service and, at his own wish, was buried there. His tomb, together with the statue of Our Lady of Cléry, was destroyed by Protestants in 1563. The wooden statue of the Virgin now over the altar is a later replacement, and the marble of Louis XI kneeling before her was made by Michel Bourdin in 1622. The rest of the king's tomb was a 19th-century addition. In vaults below it are the remains of Louis and his wife, except for their two skulls, which are in a glass case; on the other side of the nave is buried the heart of Charles VIII. A separate highly ornate Gothic chapel is dedicated to St James, while another houses the Dunois family vaults. Across the road from the basilica is the house where Louis XI used to stay while in Cléry.

MEUNG-SUR-LOIRE❖

Meung Tourist Office 42 r. Jehan de Meung; tel: 02 38 44 32 28, fax: 02 38 44 72 22, e-mail: touris.meung@wanadoo.fr; open summer daily (closed Sun pm), winter Mon pm–Sat. Free 1-hr guided tours of the town are bookable at the tourist office.

Château €€ Tel: 02 38 44 36 47, fax: 02 38 44 29 37, email: chateaudemeung@ worldonline.fr, www.chateaudemeung.com; open daily mid-Feb–mid-Apr, Oct–11 Nov: 1000–1200, 1400–1730, mid-Apr–end-Sept: 1000–1800, rest of year check opening times. Guided visits available.

Market: Sun am.

Penetrate the outskirts of this little town to reach the picturesque old riverside village at its heart. A stream, the Mauves, runs through the middle, with several old mills alongside (mostly now converted into apartments or houses). In the village centre there's a market square and a fine covered market with a timber-framed roof. The village has a large Romanesque and early Gothic church, and a large **château**❖, standing in a park at the foot of the village.

The château, from the 12th to the 18th century the residence of the Bishops of Orléans, is still occupied. Much updated over the years, it preserves almost every style, ranging from remnants of its medieval entrance to 19th-century interiors. It contains priceless furniture, some of it 14th-century, and several Aubusson and Flemish tapestries. Beneath the building's oldest section there is a surprising underground chapel. Also hidden below the castle are dungeons and torture chambers, and in the grounds is the oubliette where the Bishops of Orléans confined prisoners on a starvation diet until they did indeed die of starvation (as bishops, they felt it would be unchristian actually to sentence people to death). The oubliette was in the form of a deep well; prisoners were lowered down by rope onto a dark ledge, where they had to remain in the blackness, hoping that they would not fall off. A small amount of bread and water was lowered once a day – the same amount no matter how many prisoners were inside – and prisoners remained there until they died. Among the few ever to be brought out alive was the poet François Villon, known for his crimes of burglary and violence as well as for tender lyric verse. As Louis XI was passing through the town, he was told that the popular poet was in the oubliette, and ordered him to be released.

Accommodation and food in Meung

Auberge St Jacques €–€€ *60 r. Gén. de Gaulle, tel: 02 38 44 30 39, fax: 02 38 45 17 02.* It is claimed that the musketeer d'Artagnan lodged at this simple, inexpensive 2-star hotel on the main N152. Rooms are adequately equipped (although can be noisy on the main road side) and there is a good restaurant.

TALCY✣

ⓘ Tourist Office At *nearby village of Mer, in the Syndicat d'Initiative, tel: 02 54 81 70 21, fax: 02 54 81 70 21, e-mail: museemer@voilà.fr*

🏛 Château €€ *Tel : 02 54 81 03 01, fax: 02 54 81 03 01, e-mail: talcy@chateauxcountry.com open Apr–Sept daily 0930–1230, 1400–1830 (no midday closing July–Aug), rest of year Wed–Mon 1000–1230, 1400–1700. Closed national hols.*

✪ Festivals and events: The château is the setting for summer concerts and a literary festival in May. Contact château for details.

✪ Market: at Mer, Thur pm.

In a rural setting, behind a sober and dignified exterior, Talcy turns out to be one of the most comfortable and appealing of all the region's châteaux. It is richly decorated and furnished, mainly in Renaissance style but with a pleasing degree of restraint. Most notable are several medieval tapestries. A 16th-century kitchen also survives. Outside are attractive gardens, outbuildings and two courtyards. The first courtyard is galleried and has an old well, while the second has an extraordinarily large dovecote with 1 500 pigeonholes. There is a huge 300-year-old winepress too, still in working order and able to fill ten barrels in a single pressing. The château has the air of a grand farmhouse.

It was purchased in 1520 by a well-to-do Florentine financier, Bernardo Salviati, who had the castle rebuilt in its present style. His daughter Cassandre, when only 15, was the inspiration for Pierre de Ronsard's series of sonnets *Les Amours de Cassandre*, written over a ten-year period.

Suggested tour

Total distance: 65km, and a detour of 45km.

Time: The driving will take under 2 hours, but allow most of a day for the sightseeing.

Links: At Blois (*see page 204*) this route connects with the Grand Châteaux: Tours–Blois tour (*see page 54*), and at Orléans (*see page 242*) with that of the Upper Reaches (*see page 250*).

Route: Start out from **Blois** by crossing to the south side of the river on the main ring road and following signs, via Vineuil, to **CHAMBORD ❶** . The road follows the little river Cosson. Access to the château is on the private roads through the extensive, pretty woodland of the Parc de Chambord and Forêt de Boulogne. On leaving the château, follow signs to Orléans but, on reaching a junction where it is straight on for Orléans and left for Muides, take

 *www.chambordcountry. com* (website of the Loir-et-Cher *département*, with packages and special offers. English and French); *www.loiret.com* (for the Loiret *département*, magazine-style, full of information and news. French only).

 The *autoroute* A10 (from Paris) and N152 on the north bank, and the quieter D951 on the south bank, give access to Blois and Orléans and all points in between. There is a frequent rail service from Paris direct to Orléans and Blois. Local trains also run along the valley between the two towns.

the left. This road – from Chambord to Muides – is called the *Route François I*. Today the cooling towers of a nearby riverside nuclear power station, steam clouds streaming into the sky, dominate the view.

Detour: At Muides, continue over the Loire into **Mer**. From Mer turn back towards Blois on N152 to visit the **Chateau de Ménars**, a grand 17th- and 18th-century riverside palace which became one of the homes of Madame de Pompadour, the mistress of Louis XV. It has beautiful gardens. Returning to Mer, turn north, away from the river, on the rose-lined road to **TALCY ❷**. Return to Mer, and back over the river to Muides.

From Muides, turn towards Orléans on D951, the main south bank road. It would be equally possible to continue on the north bank – the drive is not very interesting on either side of the river – but the south bank gives a much better approach into **BEAUGENCY ❸**, which is entered by crossing the town's old bridge. Continue on the north bank to **MEUNG-SUR-LOIRE ❹**. From here, cross the Loire again, on the little suspension bridge, to **CLÉRY-ST-ANDRÉ ❺**. Stay on the D951 to Orléans.

Right
Boulangerie in
Meung-sur-Loire

Brou

cheville 14

BEAUC

Outarville

Janville 7

Toury 9

25 km

Orgères-en-Beauce 7

Loigny-la-Bataille

34

D927 10

Bazoches-le Gallerandes

10 miles

Logron

11

12

13

Aschères-le-Marché 7

Arrou

Terminiers

Neuville-aux-Bois 12

rtalain D927 18

D927 23

D935

Artenay

Patay

D5 21

Chevilly

ORLÉANA 24 DII

Châteaudun

11

12

35

Cloyes-sur-le-Loir 11

La Ferté-Villeneuil

D925

D955 13

N20

S Loury

D97 19 Traîn

D924

Épieds-en-Beauce

D3

Saran

N10

21

Ouzouer-le-Marché 19

Coulmiers 13

Fleury-les-Aubrais

19

St-Jean-de-Braye 21

cs 14

Morée 12

N157 12

Binas

19

7

St-Jean-de-la-Ruelle 6

Orléans

Chécy

Jarg

10

19

3

St-Ay 16

7

22

Olivet

Sandillon

Oucques D917

Marchenoir

27

Josnes

Meung-sur-Loire 19

4

5 23 Cléry-St-André

20

Marcilly-en-Villette

19

7

N20 13

D921

Selommes 27

Talcy 2

A10

3 Beaugency

4

Lailly-en-Val

D103 19

Jouy-le-Potier

La Ferté-St-Aubin

D957

D924 18

N152

Mer

13

St-Laurent-Nouan 13

31

16

31

20 Vouz

31 19

Suèvres 37

D951

Menars

Muides-sur-Loire

La Ferté-St-Cyr

E05/E60

La Chaussée-St-Victor

1 Chambord 13

D925

29

Lamotte-Beuvron

D766

Blois

Vineuil

D922

Onzain

St-Gervais-la-Forêt 17

18

Bracieux

10

10

D923 18

D923

19

Nouan-le-Fuzelier

ouzy-sur-Cisse 14

9

Neung-sur-Beuvron

A71

D751

Cellettes

E09

Chaumont-sur-Loire

Cour-Cheverny

15

D13

D922

N20

D764 25

21

11

D765

23

Marcilly-en-Gault

Salbris

Contres

Soings-en-Sologne

23

9

Pontlevoy

D956

Mur-de-Sologne 13

Selles-St-Denis

D724 15

La Ferté-Imbault

Montrichard

D675

16

Chémery 16

Romorantin-Lanthenay

22

E604

Pruniers-en-Sologne

Orléans

Ratings

Architecture	●●●●●
History	●●●●●
Gardens	●●●●○
Entertainment	●●●●○
Restaurants	●●●●○
Museums	●●●○○
Children	●●○○○
Winetasting	●○○○○

Orléans stands on the north bank of the Loire, at the most northerly point of the river's course, and is the nearest Loire Valley town to Paris. This positioning once gave it great commercial and strategic importance. An ancient, royal city, it has now become large and industrial. Its name is synonymous with Joan of Arc, the 'Maid of Orléans', object of fervent adoration since she was beatified in 1905. Although her only visit here lasted just a matter of days, the pivotal events of her patriotic mission occurred here. The superb cathedral at the heart of Orléans has become inescapably associated with her. The cathedral quarter and the area around the main square, pl. du Martroi, are majestic with fine avenues. Restoration of some of the town's many Renaissance houses is continuing, and work is starting on the older, more run-down neighbourhood between the cathedral and the riverside. New in the year 2000 was a modern tramway system running through the centre of Orléans. The city of Orléans, with its suburbs, has a population of about 270,000, of whom 27 per cent are under 20.

Getting there and getting around

ⓘ **Orléans Tourist Office** *6 pl. Albert 1er; tel: 02 38 24 05 05, fax: 02 38 54 49 84, e-mail: office-de-tourisme. orleans@wanadoo.fr; open Mon–Sat 0900–1900 (1830 in winter), Sun 1000–1200 (Sun in July–Aug 0930–1230, 1500–1830, national hols 1000–1300, 1430– 1800, except 1 Jan, 1 May, 1 Nov, 11 Nov, 25 Dec.*

By road

The main roads into Orléans are *autoroutes* A10 (Paris, Orléans, Tours, Bordeaux), A71 (Orléans–Clermont-Ferrand), N152 and N20. On reaching the town on the Loire's north bank, traffic is fed onto a ring-road of boulevards. Take any turn for *Centre Ville*.

By rail

At least 40 trains run daily from Paris to Orléans, taking about one hour. Other rail services run to the city from towns throughout the region. For rail information *tel: 08 36 35 35 35*.

Driving and parking

Driving and parking are difficult in the town centre. There are many one-way streets. Parking areas are small, and usually full. There is parking on some of the boulevards surrounding the centre, especially

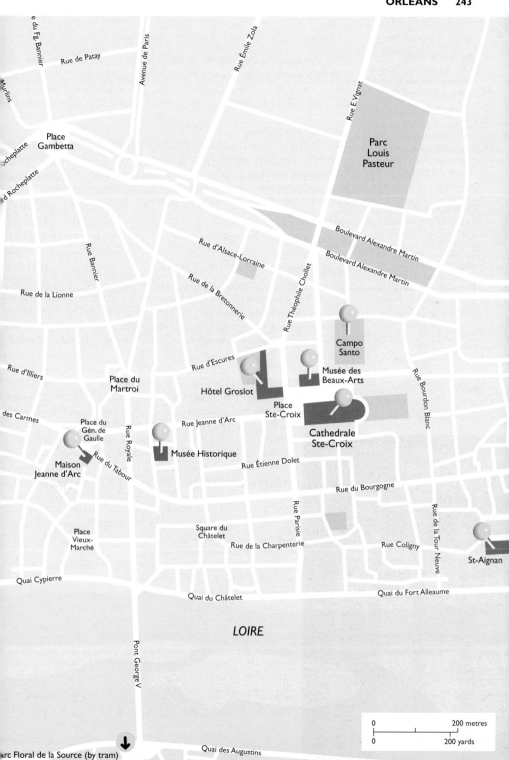

Rue de Patay

e du Fg. Bannier

Murlins

Avenue de Paris

Rue Émile Zola

Rue E. Vignat

Place Gambetta

ocheplatte

d Rocheplatte

Parc Louis Pasteur

Rue Bannier

Rue de la Lionne

Rue d'Alsace-Lorraine

Rue de la Bretonnerie

Boulevard Alexandre Martin

Boulevard Alexandre Martin

Rue Théophile Chollet

Rue d'Illiers

Rue d'Escures

Campo Santo

Place du Martroi

Musée des Beaux-Arts

Hôtel Groslot

Rue Bourdon Blanc

des Carmes

Place du Gén. de Gaulle

Rue Royale

Rue Jeanne d'Arc

Place Ste-Croix

Cathedrale Ste-Croix

Maison Jeanne d'Arc

Rue du Tabour

Musée Historique

Rue Étienne Dolet

Rue du Bourgogne

Rue de la Tour Neuve

Place Vieux-Marché

Square du Châtelet

Rue Parisie

Rue de la Charpenterie

Rue Coligny

St-Aignan

Quai Cypierre

Quai du Châtelet

Quai du Fort Alleaume

LOIRE

Pont George V

0   200 metres
0   200 yards

arc Floral de la Source (by tram)

Quai des Augustins

ℹ️ Annexe: Espace
d'Acceuil Touristique, 6
r. Jeanne d'Arc, tel: 02 38 53
33 44, open in season.

W️ www.ville-orleans.fr
(the city's official site,
in French and English);
www.tourismloiret.com/ (the
département's official site,
French and English)
www.orleanscity.org/ (useful
commercial site on
Orléans. French only);
www.coeur-de-france.com/
(regional site with pages
on Orléans).

🛒 Markets: Daily
covered market at Les
Halles, pl. du Chatelet.
Flower market in pl. de la
République, on Tue, Thur,
Sat and Sun am.

blvd Alexandre Martin, north of the cathedral. The underground car park at Campo Santo is convenient for the city centre. Other town centre car parks include St-Pierre Lentin, just behind the south side of the cathedral, and Châtelet, at the covered market near pont George V.

Getting around town

The old central area is small and easily accessible on foot. For longer journeys, consider using the bus or tramway. For local transport information contact:

Semtao–Transamo *12 r. Emile Zola, tel: 02 38 78 03 50, fax: 02 38 78 03 51.*

Espace Transports *4 r. de la Hallebarde, tel (freephone): 0800 01 2000.*

Sights

Campo Santo⁺

Just north of the cathedral, this 12th-century cemetery – known as the Martroi-aux-Corps until 1912 – is now a tranquil garden edged with elegant 16th-century arcades, entered by a Renaissance portal. It ceased being used for burials over 200 years ago, and today, the stonework beautifully renovated, it is the setting for many cultural events.

Cathédrale Ste-Croix⁺⁺⁺

Quite apart from its pale and ornate façade, and its two curious circular towers (popularly likened to a wedding cake decoration), most striking of all about the cathedral in Orléans is its grandiose 19th-century setting. A broad and handsome avenue in pale stone leads straight to the imposing west front, with an immense parvis in front of the building. Everything seems filled with light, space and majesty.

The town seems to revolve around the cathedral. Main streets converge on the building, and the administrative offices of the town and the *département*, as well as its Conservatoire de Musique and Musée des Beaux-Arts, are all around the cathedral square.

The architecture of the cathedral is a testament to the enduring appeal of the Gothic style. Although begun in the 13th century, at the height of the Gothic period, the construction continued over several centuries, and even into the 19th century – but all the work was done according to the original Gothic design. Almost all of the interior decorative work, seemingly medieval, was added in the 19th century. A series of ten stained-glass windows deals with the life of Joan of Arc. A new window devoted to her was added in the year 2000. Fine woodcarvings in the choir were a gift to Orléans from Louis XIV, the 'Sun

Below
Orléans Cathedral, Joan of Arc window showing Joan leading the troops

⚡ **Festivals and events:** *Grande Brocante* – big annual street market, 5–6 May; *Fêtes Johanniques* – celebrating the liberation of Orléans by Joan of Arc, 7–8 May; *Orléans Jazz* – international jazz festival, held in about June.

🏛 **Campo Santo €** *R. Fernand Rabier; for phone enquiries call tourist office; open Oct–Mar daily 0800–1730, rest of year 0730–2000.*

Cathédrale € *Pl. Sainte-Croix; for phone enquiries call tourist office; open Oct–Apr daily 0915–1200, 1415–1700, May, June, Sept until 1800, July–Aug until 1900:*

Église St-Aignan € *R. Neuve St-Aignan; for phone enquiries call tourist office; open July–Aug, 1400–1800. May also be open in Sept.*

Hôtel Groslot € *Pl. de l'Etape; open daily 0900–1800.*

Groslot Gardens € *Entrance in r. d'Escures; open Oct–Mar 0800–1730, rest of year 0730–2000.*

Maison Jeanne d'Arc € *3 pl. de Gaulle; tel: 02 38 52 99 89, fax: 02 38 79 20 82; open May–Oct Tue–Sun, 1000–1230, 1330–1800, rest of year pm only.*

Musée Historique et Archéologique € *Square Abbé Desnoyers; tel: 02 38 79 21 55; open Oct–Apr Wed, Sat and Sun 1400–1800, May, June, Sept Tue–Sun 1400–1800, July–Aug Tue–Sun 1000–1800.*

King'. In his honour, the rose windows in the transept have a radiant sun design.

Outside the cathedral on the north side, some remnants of the town's 4th-century ramparts have been uncovered.

Église St-Aignan*

One thousand years before Joan of Arc saved Orléans from the English, Aignan saved it from the Huns. He, too, became the object of intense reverence and was made the city's patron saint. The Gothic church dedicated to him is now much damaged, but the 11th-century Romanesque crypt is well preserved. It resembles a church in its own right. Some of its capitals have preserved the original colour with which they were painted in the year 1029. The crypt contains bones believed to be those of Aignan.

Hôtel Groslot**

Set back within a courtyard, almost opposite the cathedral, stands this red-brick Renaissance masterpiece erected in 1550 by Jacques Groslot. It became the principal residence of royalty in Orléans: François II died while here, and Charles IX, Henri III and Henri IV all had periods of residence here. After the Revolution, the mansion became the town hall, and remained so until the 1960s. It was extensively refurbished in the 19th century. Now open to the public, Hôtel Groslot not only gives a good insight into the extravagance of 19th-century French decor, it has also become a popular place for the town's grandest weddings and receptions. The Grand Salon d'Honneur is lavishly decorated, with gilded coloured walls, decorative coffered ceiling and chandeliers. The Council Chamber is especially richly decorated. The charming **gardens** are also open to the public.

Maison Jeanne d'Arc*

This is a picture-perfect medieval house of brick and timber. Joan of Arc spent ten days in Orléans, in May 1429, lodged at the home of Jacques Boucher, a treasurer of the Duke of Orléans. The house disappeared centuries ago, and even the area in which it had stood was entirely destroyed by bombing in 1940. In 1965, the Maison de Jeanne d'Arc was constructed from materials taken from various local old houses which had been demolished. The house contains a permanent exhibition honouring the girl soldier and saint (*see page 233*).

Musée Historique et Archéologique*

The lovely Renaissance mansion Hôtel Cabu, which houses an extensive collection of local historical artefacts, was badly damaged during the 1940 bombing. Its ornate, beautifully proportioned three-storey façade has been well restored. The museum displays a wide variety of items dating back to the Roman period, with many medieval wooden religious pieces and interesting pre-industrial

Musée des Beaux-Arts € 1 r. Fernand Rabier; tel: 02 38 79 21 55, fax: 02 38 79 20 08; open Sun, Mon, Tue 1100–1800, Wed 1000–2000, Thur, Fri, Sat 1000–1800.

domestic household objects. The highlight is a large number of **Gallo-Roman bronzes**✧✧✧ found at Neuvey-en-Sullias (east of Orléans).

Musée des Beaux-Arts✧✧

One of the best provincial collections of French painting is housed across the road from the cathedral. Some of the works are those confiscated from religious establishments during the Revolution. Subsequently, the Orléans Fine Arts Museum became a repository for many great state-owned works, as well as being given numerous donations. This priceless collection was partly destroyed during the 1940s bombing of the town, but thousands of important works remain. In total the museum possesses some 52,000 works, although it can only display about 700 at any one time. While French works from the 16th century to the 19th, displayed on the second floor, form the greater part of the collection, the first floor is devoted to other European schools, notably Italian, Spanish and especially 17th-century Flemish. In the basement is a good modern collection, starting with Gauguin's *Fête Gloanec*, including a room devoted to Max Jacob, and with a contemporary collection focusing on the 1980s. There is also a considerable sculpture collection, including works by Rodin and Maillol.

Parc Floral de la Source €€ Olivet, about 5km south of the Loire, accessible by tramway; tel: 02 38 49 30 00, fax: 02 28 49 30 19, email: info@parcfloral-lasource.fr, www.parcfloral-lasource.fr; open Apr–11 Nov 0900–1800, rest of year 1400–1700 (the park remains open until one hour after final entry time). Guided tours are available.

Parc Floral de la Source✧

These pleasant and interesting gardens of some 35ha lie south of the city at suburban Olivet. They were originally laid out in 1967 in the grounds of a château for the Floralies gardens exhibition. Neat gravel paths meander among flower beds and lawns shaded by some unusual trees. Botanists will be fascinated, while others may enjoy a visit for the agreeable setting around the source of the Loiret river (which in reality is not a separate river but an underground branch of the Loire that resurfaces here). One of the most surprising features is the giant butterfly house, with interior heat and humidity mimicking the tropics, and exotic butterflies with 15-cm wingspans. The park also includes a vegetable section, an animal farm, a little railway and other attractions such as mini-golf and a play area. Emu, deer and flamingos can be seen.

Accommodation and food in Orléans

Chain hotels in all price ranges are well represented at Orléans, but are often several kilometres from the city centre on the N20 or close to the autoroute exits often several kilometres from the city centre on the N20 or close to the *autoroute* exits.

Les Antiquaires €€ *2 r. au Lin, tel: 02 38 53 52 35, fax: 02 38 62 06 95.* In a backstreet close to the river, Philippe Bardeau's restaurant is the best in town, noted for an exceptionally light, deft touch with seafoods, sauces and seasoning, and excellent local farm-made ingredients. Good selection of Loire wines.

L'Archange €–€€ *6 faubourg de la Madeleine, tel: 02 38 88 64 20.* A little way from the centre, as you head west, this highly respected local restaurant is charming and comfortable, with a pretty courtyard. The very moderately priced menus feature classic, well-prepared, exquisitely seasoned fish dishes with a light, imaginative approach.

Le Brin de Zinc € *62 r. Ste-Cathérine, tel: 02 38 53 38 77.* On this pedestrian section of r. Ste-Cathérine, just off pl. du Martroi, several inexpensive brasseries specialise in quick, low-cost meals served at outdoor tables, which almost fill the narrow street. Le Brin de Zinc is one of the best of them, with inexpensive salad, fish and seafood dishes.

Hôtel d'Arc €€ *37ter r. de la République, tel: 02 38 53 10 94, fax: 02 38 14 77 47.* Convenient for the railway station, this rather old-fashioned and basic hotel (with no restaurant) makes an adequate base and is just a short walk from the main square and the sights of Orléans. It's in a section of street with no traffic except for the tramway.

Entertainment

Orléans has a full programme of shows, exhibitions, concerts and other events throughout the year. Major venues include the Zénith (*tel: 02 38 25 05 05*) and its Parc des Expositions (*tel: 02 38 56 97 10*), the Carré St-Vincent theatre and Centre d'Art Contemporain (*tel: 02 38 62 75 30*), and the Astrolabe concert hall (*tel: 02 38 54 20 06*). For listings of discos, late-night bars with music, cabaret and other nightlife, ask the tourist office for a copy of the latest edition of *Orléans Jour et Nuits*, which also includes hotels and restaurants.

Suggested walk

Total distance: About 2km, or 8km including the tramway detour.

Time: Allow 2–3 hours, or a full day with the detour.

Route: Start at **pl. du Martroi**, the large and open main square. It has café tables in its corners, a carousel, and a central equestrian statue of Joan of Arc wearing her armour. Walk a few paces down arcaded 18th-century r. Royale, where William Wordsworth lodged in 1791 (he and a girlfriend, Annette Vallon, had an illegitimate child here, named Caroline). Reaching the equally handsome main street, r. Jeanne

d'Arc, which runs majestically towards the front of the cathedral, turn right (away from the cathedral) to pl. du Général de Gaulle and the **MAISON JEANNE D'ARC ❶**.

Turn down r. du Tabour passing, on the right, the Centre Charles Péguy in a fine Gothic-Renaissance mansion. The Centre is devoted to the study of the life and work of this Catholic Socialist thinker (1873-1914). Reaching r. Royale again, cross over to continue into r. de Bourgogne; this is the oldest street in the city, running through the middle of the once-walled 5th-century Orléans. A mainly pedestrianised shopping street today, it has many interesting old buildings. Turn to the right for **Église St-Pierre le Puellier**, a deconsecrated church that originally dated from the 6th century. The much-renovated interior now provides a light, clear, white space used for exhibitions and concerts. The deserted area all around it was once a very active part of medieval Orléans, busy with river traders and students. Continue along r. des Africains and r. Coligny to **ÉGLISE ST-AIGNAN ❷**.

Return to St-Pierre le Puellier and turn back away from the river on r. de la Poterne and r. Parisie until you reach the south side of the **CATHEDRAL ❸**. On the north side of the building, the **MUSÉE DES BEAUX-ARTS ❹** is across the road. A short distance behind it is the **CAMPO SANTO ❺**. Also adjacent to the north side of the cathedral, diagonally across the road from the west front, is **HÔTEL GROSLOT ❻**.

Take r. Jeanne d'Arc away from the cathedral. Turn left into r. Ste-Cathérine to see Hôtel Cabu, with its **MUSÉE HISTORIQUE ET ARCHÉOLOGIQUE ❼**. There are many other Gothic-Renaissance houses in this area. Return the other way along r. Ste-Cathérine to reach pl. du Martroi.

Detour: From pl. du Martroi catch a tram to **PARC FLORAL DE LA SOURCE ❽**. The tramway stop is called Université-Parc Floral; the entrance to the park is a well-signposted 300-m walk.

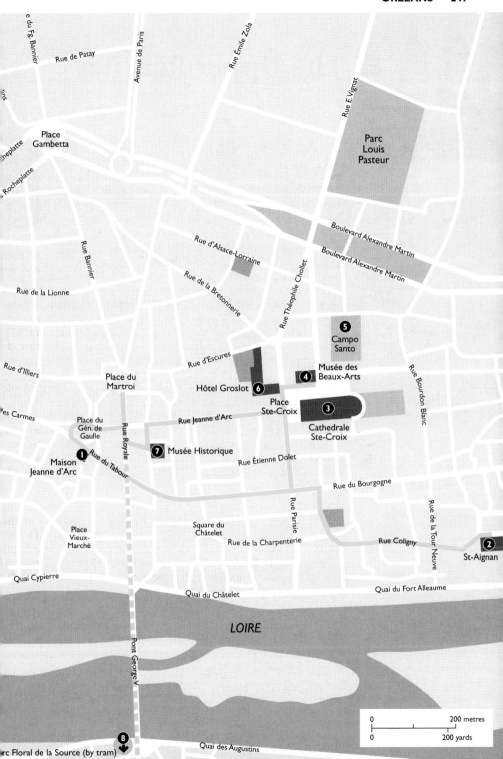

Rue du Fg Bannier

Rue de Patay

Avenue de Paris

Rue Émile Zola

Rue E. Vignat

Place Gambetta

Rocheplatte

heplatte

ins

Parc Louis Pasteur

Boulevard Alexandre Martin

Boulevard Alexandre Martin

Rue Bannier

Rue d'Alsace-Lorraine

Rue de la Bretonnerie

Rue Théophile Chollet

Rue de la Lionne

Rue d'Illiers

5 Campo Santo

Rue d'Escures

Place du Martroi

Hôtel Groslot **6**

4 Musée des Beaux-Arts

Rue Bourdon Blanc

es Carmes

Place du Gén. de Gaulle

Place Ste-Croix

3

Rue Jeanne d'Arc

Rue Royale

Cathédrale Ste-Croix

1

Maison Jeanne d'Arc

Rue du Tabour

7 Musée Historique

Rue Étienne Dolet

Rue du Bourgogne

Place Vieux-Marché

Square du Châtelet

Rue Parisie

Rue de la Tour Neuve

Rue de la Charpenterie

Rue Coligny

2

St-Aignan

Quai Cypierre

Quai du Châtelet

Quai du Fort Alleaume

Pont George V

LOIRE

0		200 metres
0		200 yards

8

rc Floral de la Source (by tram)

Quai des Augustins

The Upper Reaches

Ratings

History	●●●●●
River views	●●●●●
Winetasting	●●●●○
Wildlife	●●●●○
Architecture	●●●○○
Activities	●●●○○
Children	●●●○○
Gastronomy	●●●○○

Upstream from Orléans, the Loire Valley has a different character. Instead of the broad, meandering Loire of flood plains, opulent châteaux and royal history, the river flows with determination between the stone embankments of handsome old towns. All the way up to Sancerre, the river is wide and brisk, spanned by fine old bridges, edged by industrious small towns with dignified mansions and quaysides. Once teeming with small businesses and busy docks, and inhabited by boatmen with their own colourful lifestyle, today the upper Loire runs peacefully under its pearly skies. To either side the land rises into green hills. Nature lovers find plenty of birdlife on the way, while gourmets delight in discovering the elegant wines of the Loire Valley's oldest vineyards. Most of the route is in the Sancerre district, known especially for its great whites, and occasionally crosses the Loire into Burgundy to taste the local vintages on that side of the river.

BRIARE✦✦✦

ⓘ Briare Tourist Office / Pl. Charles de Gaulle; tel: 02 38 31 24 51, fax: 02 38 37 15 16; open: Apr–Sept Mon–Sat 1000–1830, Sun 1000–1200, Oct–Mar Mon–Sat 1000–1200, 1400–1800.

ⓜ La Maison des Deux Marines € 58 blvd Buyser; tel: 02 38 31 28 27, fax: 02 38 37 07 45; open June–Sept 1000–1230, 1330–1830, Oct–Dec, Mar–May 1400–1800.

A tranquil little town clinging to the east bank of the Loire, at the meeting point of handsome 17th-century canals, Briare (now calling itself, sometimes, Briare-le-Canal) has become a centre for boating. Its loveliest sight is the great **Pont-Canal (Canal Bridge)**✦✦✦ that carries the calm waters of a canal over the fast swirl of the River Loire. Some 662m-long, the imposing wrought-iron bridge dates from 1890, and has an elegance and style that belies its purely functional purpose. The waterside pavement makes a pleasing and unusual stroll to the other side of the Loire and back.

The waterways, which linked the Atlantic, the Mediterranean and Paris, made Briare a prosperous small town. **La Maison des Deux Marines (House of the Two Waterways)**✦ is all about the role of the canals and the river in the fortunes of the town which, in the 18th and 19th centuries, became a great centre of trade and transportation as every type of merchandise was carried through here. The museum

Musée de la Mosaïque et des Emaux €€ *Blvd Loreau; tel: 02 38 31 20 51; open daily June–Sept 1000–1830, Oct–Dec and Mar–May 1400–1800.*

looks at the canal culture and boating trades of the people of Briare up to the time of the steamships. About a century ago, Briare's wealth came from high-quality enamelware. In particular, it had a factory that could mass-produce buttons – an innovation with which other firms around the world could not compete. Another development here was the use of machinery to create artworks, especially in ironwork and in mosaic, heralding the beginnings of Art Nouveau. A still-operating enamel factory is the setting for the town's interesting **Musée de la Mosaïque et des Emaux (Museum of Mosaic and Enamel)***, including a mosaic by Art Nouveau artist Eugène Grasset.

Accommodation and food near Briare

Hôtel des Voyageurs €–€€ *10 Grande Rue, Bonny-sur-Loire (12km south, on the right bank); tel: 02 38 27 01 45, fax: 02 38 27 01 46. Closed 27 Aug–10 Sept, 19 Feb–12 Mar, and Mon.* Enjoy astonishing value for money at this simple, traditional, family-run country hotel, and excellent dining in its restaurant. Imaginative presentation of classic dishes, and good local wines.

Wildlife on the Loire

The Loire, threatened by upriver dams and development, is home to 240 species of birds. River swallows dart from the banks, crested warblers drift on the stream, herons and partridges and hoopoes fly by. Under the surface, catfish, eels, bream and perch number among myriads of fish. Beside the river, wildlife thrives in shallow lakes and streams and deciduous woods. The Forêt de Bertranges, upriver from Sancerre, is a forest of oak, beech, maple, cherry and other varieties, providing shelter for deer, wild boar, badgers and wild cats.

Above Right
Briare Pont-Canal

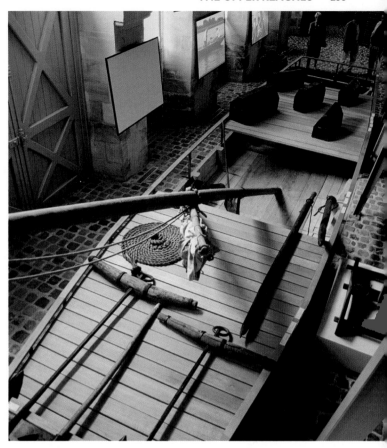

Right
Musée de la Marine,
Châteauneuf-sur-Loire

CHÂTEAUNEUF-SUR-LOIRE❖

ⓘ Châteauneuf Tourist Office *3 pl. Aristide Briand; tel: 02 38 58 44 79, fax: 02 38 58 52 83; open all year Mon–Sat 0930–1230, 1400–1900 (in summer also Sun 0930–1230).*

ⓜ Musée de la Marine de la Loire *In château stables; tel: 02 38 46 84 46, fax: 02 38 46 41 01; open Apr–Oct Wed–Mon 1000–1800, Nov–Mar 1400–1800.*

A pleasant market town, Châteauneuf is named for a castle which no longer exists. On the site of it, an exact copy of Versailles was built in miniature but that, too, was partly demolished in the Revolution. Among what survives are a fine rotunda, gallery and pavilions (now housing the town hall). The former château stables are occupied by the **Musée de la Marine de la Loire (Loire Nautical Museum)**❖, which contains a mass of interesting material about the Loire boatmen and their way of life. The château grounds are now a moated park with a fine display of rhododendrons. In the town's church lies the superb Baroque marble tomb of Phélypeaux de la Vrillière (d. 1681), who had the château built.

GIEN❖❖

ⓘ Gien Tourist Office
*Centre Anne de
Beaujeu, pl. Jean-Jaurès; tel:
02 38 29 85 54, 02 38 67
25 28, fax: 02 38 29 80 09;
open all year (Mon pm only).
Closed Sun in winter.*

Ⓜ Markets: Wed am in
pl. Jean-Jaurès, Sat am
in pl. de la Victoire.

Ⓕ Festival: *Carnaval –*
3rd weekend in July.

**Ⓒ Château de Gien
and Musée
International de la
Chasse** €€ *Pl. du Château;
tel: 02 38 67 69 69, fax: 02
38 38 07 32; open daily
Nov–Apr 0900–1200,
1400–1700, May–Oct
0930–1830.*

Église Ste-Jeanne-d'Arc
€ *Pl. du Château; open daily.*

**Musée de la Faïencerie
(Chinaware Museum)**
€€ *78 pl. de la Victoire; tel:
02 38 67 00 05, fax: 02 38
67 44; open May–Sept daily
0900–1830 (opens at 1000
on Sun), Oct–Dec, Mar–Apr
Mon–Sat 0900–1200,
1400–1800 (opens at 1000
on Sun), Jan–Feb Mon–Sat,
1400–1800.*

Curiously, the town's noble château is built mainly of bricks, while the ordinary houses and cottages all around are built mainly of handsome stone. Flower-filled cobbled streets and restored historic town houses – all recreated after heavy wartime destruction – make the town attractive. The best view is from the handsome pale stone bridge that spans the Loire. The River Loire is at its best here, stately and wide, yet not inaccessibly vast. Ordinary little bars line its quayside, and you can walk right beside the flowing river.

Traditionally, the Gien Faïence Works was one of the world's leading manufacturers of *faïence*, or glazed earthenware. The factory is still in business, and this important part of the town's art and history can be explored at its excellent **Musée de la Faïencerie (Chinaware Museum)❖❖**. Housed in atmospheric cellars beneath the workshops, the museum explores the range from inexpensive household crockery to the most elegant chinaware commissioned by aristocratic families. Little other industry survives at this once busy town, and there are surprisingly few tourists.

Flights of steps lead up to Gien's star attraction, the very striking 15th-century **Château de Gien❖❖** with its geometric pattern of red and black brickwork. Originally 9th-century, the castle was reconstructed in this way by Anne of Beaujeu, daughter of Louis XI, in 1484. Here young King Louis XIV, along with his new queen, Anne of Austria, took shelter during the turmoil of the aristocratic Fronde rebellion of 1652. Inside the castle today is a comprehensive **Musée International de la Chasse (International Hunting Museum)❖❖**. If hunting upsets you, don't go in – the museum looks lovingly at the whole process of chasing and killing animals and birds, how it has inspired, entertained and fed people, which creatures have been hunted, and the methods and weapons used. Over 3000 artworks depicting the hunt are displayed, and numerous stuffed specimens. Don't miss the entrance hall, however, with its 17th-century painting of St Hubert – hunting's patron saint – and his vision of a 'holy stag'.

While in the town, also visit the modern reconstruction of the 15th-century **Ste-Jeanne-d'Arc church❖** (incorporating a tower from its bombed predecessor), which has beautiful stained glass by Max Ingrand.

Accommodation and food in Gien

Hotel-restaurant du Rivage €€ *1 quai de Nice; tel: 02 38 37 79 00, fax: 02 38 38 10 21.* Have a cocktail at the bar and enjoy dinner on the terrace at this outstanding restaurant specialising in local dishes skilfully made from the best of fresh ingredients. It's also a small hotel, set in a handsome building a few minutes from the town centre and looking out across the Loire.

Above
Vineyards near Pouilly

POUILLY-SUR-LOIRE✢

ℹ **Pouilly Tourist Office** 61 r. Waldeck-Rousseau; tel: 03 86 39 03 75, fax: 03 86 39 18 30; open Mon–Sat 1000–1200 (except July–Aug 1000–1200, 1500–1800). Closed Oct.

🏛 **Caves de Pouilly Le Moulin à Vent** Av. de la Tuilerie; tel: 03 86 39 10 99; open Mon–Sat 0800–1200, 1400–1800.

🎡 **Festival:** Foire aux Vins (a major regional festival of wine and food) 15 Aug.

🛒 **Market:** Fri am.

Though the unassuming little town of Pouilly is technically in Burgundy, it has vineyards on both sides of the river and its wine is considered a 'Loire'. Don't confuse it with the other Pouilly, near Mâcon, whose wine really is Burgundy. The town's name is given to its lesser wine, made using Chasselas grapes. Its better wines, using Sauvignon, are called Pouilly-Fumé. Compare the two at the Caves de Pouilly wine cellars.

Accommodation and food in Pouilly-sur-Loire

Le Relais Fleuri and Restaurant Le Coq Hardi €€ 42 av. de la Tuilerie; tel: 03 86 39 12 99, fax: 03 86 39 14 15. Good classic cooking without pretensions, and a dozen comfortable rooms at this reliable, well-established, family-run Logis. Once a popular inn on the busy N6, it has become quieter now that through-traffic is diverted around the edge of town.

Saint-Benoît-sur-Loire✦✦✦

Specialities

Les Moinillons are boiled-sugar sweets first devised by the monks (moines) at the abbey.

ℹ St-Benoît Tourist Office Maison Max Jacob, 44 r. Orléanaise; tel: 02 38 35 79 00, fax: 02 38 35 79 00; open Mar–Oct Tue, Thur, Fri and Sat 0900–1200, 1430–1800, Mon 1430–1800, Wed 0900–1200.

Below
Capital in Basilica, St-Benoît

At this ancient riverside village stands one of France's finest Romanesque treasures, the imposing **Romanesque Basilica**✦✦✦ dedicated to St-Benoît (St Benedict in English). Known as the 'Father of Monasticism', Saint Benoît (d. 547) was the founder of the Benedictine Order, which had vast influence throughout Europe during the Middle Ages. Curious, diverse, richly carved capitals in the belfry-porch, which originally stood apart from the rest of the building, are considered a masterpiece of Romanesque stonework. Originally founded in the 7th century, an abbey was constructed on a site of great importance for the pre-Christian Druidic religion. Most of the existing majestic abbey church in pale stone dates from the 11th century, though an older crypt contains the remains of Benedict himself. Benedict had no associations with this place, and did not die here; 125 years after his death his remains were brought here from Italy with a view to attracting pilgrims and prosperity. The abbey was sacked by Protestants during the Religious Wars, and its treasures sold – including a 700-year-old library of manuscripts. After the Revolution, the abbey was destroyed, leaving only the church, but the buildings were restored in the 19th century, and the abbey itself revived in 1944. The distinguished poet and artist Max Jacob lived for several years in the village. A permanent exhibition of his work is now on display at the **Maison Max Jacob**✦, and he is buried in the local cemetery.

Basilica €€ *Tel: 02 38 35 72 43; open for 45-min guided visits at 1030, 1500, 1630, summer daily (except during services, in Holy Week), winter Sun only. Closed Jan, Feb and 1st Fri each month.*

Maison Max Jacob € *See tourist office.*

Max Jacob at St-Benoît

Born in 1876 and brought up as a Jew, Max Jacob became a convert to Catholicism in 1915. He moved to the village of St-Benoît and, when monks returned to the abbey in 1944, he took up residence there. Almost at once, he was arrested for being of Jewish descent and sent to Drancy, the Nazi detention camp for Jews. Many famous writers and artists of the day launched a petition for his release – it was notable that his close friend Picasso refused to sign, being fearful of the consequences for his own safety – but by the time it had been agreed to release him, Jacob was already dead as a result of the brutal conditions of the camp. As an acknowledgement of the order for his release, his body was returned to St-Benoît for burial.

Food in St-Benoît-sur-Loire

Restaurant du Grand Benoît €€ *7 pl. St André; tel: 02 38 35 73 27, fax: 02.38.35.13.79.* One of the better eating places here, with good menus at very reasonable prices.

SANCERRE❖❖

Sancerre Tourist Office *Nouvelle Place, r. de la Croix de Bois; tel: 02 48 54 08 21, fax: 02 48 78 03 58, e-mail: ot.sancerre.cher@en-france.com; open Mar–Oct daily 1000–1230, 1430–1800.*

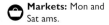

www.sancerre.net/otsi

Markets: Mon and Sat ams.

Events and exhibitions: Art shows, exhibitions and concerts all summer. *Fête du Crottin de Chavignol –* Weekend nearest 1 May, Sancerre Wine Fair – Pentecost (Whitsun); French Wine Festival – last weekend in Aug; Oyster Fair – last weekend in Oct.

This exceptionally good-looking town is poised on a round hill gazing across the expanse of its neat vineyards, its tangled old streets and lanes guarded by a 14th-century tower. It's well known for world-class fragrant dry white wines, fortunately regarded as the local wine everywhere along this route. It can be tasted at wine cellars in and near the town. Try, too, some of the district's highly praised goats' cheese called Crottins de Chavignol, perfectly delicious despite the name (*crottins* means 'goat droppings').

Food in Sancerre

Restaurant de la Tour €€ *31 Nouvelle Place; tel: 02 48 54 00 81, fax: 02 48 78 01 54.* An attractive local gastronomic favourite, and a long-established feature of Sancerre, the Tour has an easy, reliable way with traditional regional dishes, and represents exceptional value for money.

Restaurant La Pomme d'Or €-€€ *1 r. Panneterie / pl. de la Mairie; tel: 02 48 54 13 30, fax: 02 48 54 19 22.* Straightforward menus of classic local fare, expertly prepared, are served here. Wines of Sancerre and Pouilly are a speciality, and available by the glass – a good way of trying out a few. Very good value

SULLY-SUR-LOIRE✧✧✧

ⓘ Sully Tourist Office
Pl. de Gaulle; tel: 02 38 36 23 70, fax: 02 38 36 32 21; open all year Mon–Sat, also Sun in July–Aug.

Ⓜ Market: Mon, all day.

Ⓕ Festivals: St-François Fair – Easter weekend; International Classical Music Festival – weekends in June.

Opposite
Sully Château

This pretty little town is a popular holiday spot and riverside resort, conveniently and attractively placed close to the forests of Orléans and Sologne, offering fishing, walking, and river trips. It has an awesome 14th-century **Château**✧✧✧, solidly rectangular, guarded by mighty towers and turrets, and cleverly 'moated' by the river Sange. Voltaire spent long periods here as a guest of the Duke of Sully. The keep has a remarkable 600-year-old wooden roof. Designed by the Louvre's architect, Raymond du Temple, the castle fell into ruin and has been impeccably restored since World War II, when the town suffered much damage from bombing – once by the Germans and once by the Allies. The château makes a wonderful setting for frequent indoor and outdoor evening entertainments held through the summer months.

Accommodation and food in Sully-sur-Loire

Hôtel de la Poste € *11 r. du faubourg St-Germain; tel: 02 38 36 26 22, fax: 02 38 36 39 35.* The good, exceptionally low-priced menus at this long-established, family-run inn are very popular with locals. The unpretentious, comfortable hotel rooms, too, are good value. Ask for the river view.

Suggested tour

ⓘ Regional tourist offices:

Comité Départementale de Tourisme du Cher
5 r. de Séraucourt, Bourges; tel: 02 48 48 00 10, fax: 02 48 48 00 20, e-mail: tourisme.berry@wanadoo.fr

Comité Départementale de Tourisme de Loiret
8 r. d'Escures; tel: 02 38 78 04 04, fax: 02 38 77 04 12, e-mail: tourisme.loiret@wanadoo.fr

Comité Départementale du Tourisme de la Nièvre
(in Burgundy) 3 r. du Sort, Nevers; tel: 03 86 36 39 80, fax: 03 86 36 63, e-mail: cdt-nièvre58@wanadoo.fr

Total distance: 120km.

Time: Allow 1–2 days.

Links: At Orléans (*see page 242*) this tour links with the Blois to Orléans route (*see page 230*).

Route: Start out from **Orléans**, taking the N460 (or bigger N60), or perhaps the small and pretty south bank riverside road, to **CHÂTEAUNEUF-SUR-LOIRE ❶**. Close by, at **Germigny-des-Près** on the D60, there's a lovely small church which, astonishingly, dates from the year 806. It was originally built as a private chapel adjoining the home of Theodulf, Abbot of St-Benoît. On the roof of the east apse, there's a superb mosaic believed to be as old as the oldest parts of the building. Stay on D60 to reach **ST-BENOÎT-SUR-LOIRE ❷**. Continue on the same road, and cross the river into **SULLY-SUR-LOIRE ❸**. Stay on the river's left bank (there's a nuclear power station on the other side) as far as the bridge into **GIEN ❹**, on the right bank.

Staying on the same side of the river, take D952 to **BRIARE ❺**. After seeing the canal-bridge, drive as far as the next river bridge, into **Châtillon-sur-Loire**, 7km from Briare. This is a likeable and

www.rivernet.org/loire/loire.htm (economics, politics and ecology are the issues here. English and French); www.lvo.com/ (Loire Valley Online, a commercial site about the whole region, in English); www.berrylecher.com (site of the Cher *département* tourist office. English and French); www.tourismloiret.com (site of the Loiret *département* tourist office. English and French).

The main highway N7 and the *autoroute* A77, coming from Paris, meet the Loire at Briare. TGVs run direct from Paris to Orléans, taking 1h 30min. Frequent local trains run from town to town along the Loire. There are internal flights to Orléans.

picturesque historic town with many charming old houses of stone or timber, and rooftops at chaotic angles. Follow the river road on either side of the river – on the right bank the busy N7 or, on the left bank, the quieter D951, pretty in parts – to **Cosne-sur-Loire**, a largeish and busy but likeable riverside town (*www.mairie-cosnesurloire.fr/* is the official Cosne website). Leave Cosne, cross the river if necessary, and take the attractive vine road into **SANCERRE** ❻.

The road continues up beyond Sancerre through vineyards and pretty countryside. Take the Loire's left bank road and cross the bridge into **POUILLY-SUR-LOIRE** ❼.

Also worth exploring: A little further upriver is **La Charité-sur-Loire**, a picturesque former monastic town, once a bustling river port, with old ramparts (*www.mairie-charite-sur-loire.icar.fr/* is its website). Here a good red wine, rather than a typical Loire white, is produced. Quiet and attractive, well-sited on the river's edge, La Charité is the last town, heading upriver, where the grandeur and beauty of the Loire Valley can be experienced.

Right
Church interior,
Germigny-des-Près

Bourges

Ratings

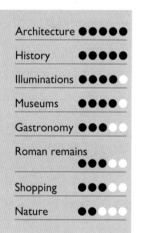

Architecture	●●●●●
History	●●●●●
Illuminations	●●●●
Museums	●●●●
Gastronomy	●●●
Roman remains	●●●
Shopping	●●●
Nature	●●

Two thousand years ago Julius Caesar lauded Bourges as '...the most beautiful in all of Gaul...'; he wouldn't be far wrong today. Known to Caesar as *Avaricum*, Bourges is strategically situated at the centre of *la hexagone* (the French nickname for France), accounting for the fact that it continued to maintain its importance long after the Empire fell. Its most prosperous era was, however, between the 13th and 16th centuries, when the town expanded, the magnificent cathedral was built, royalty resided and when palatial mansions and attractive gardens were laid out on its earlier, sometimes Roman, remains. Today this historic area constitutes the *Vieille Ville*, just north of the cathedral. On narrow streets, old houses and palaces have been restored and provide the extraordinary ambience that characterises its medieval heart. With its spring music festival, summer arts programme, and the cultural wealth in the surrounding Berry area, Bourges is one of France's most prized destinations.

Getting there and getting around

ⓘ Bourges Tourist Office *21 r. Victor-Hugo; tel: 02 48 23 02 60, fax: 02 48 23 02 69, e-mail: tourisme@ville-bourges.fr; open Oct–Mar Mon–Sat 0900–1800, Sun & hols 1400–1700, Apr–June & Sept Mon–Sat 0900–1900, Sun & hols 1000–1900, Jul–Aug Mon–Sat 0900–1930, Sun & hols 1000–1900. Closed 1 Jan, 5 May & 25 Dec.*

By road
At the centre of France, Bourges is skirted by the north-south A71–E11 motorway. Paris is 246km (2.5hr) to the north, Clermont-Ferrand 178km to the south. The N76 links the city to Tours (155km, about 2hr 30min) to the west.

By rail
Fast trains connect Bourges with Paris (Austerlitz) in a minimum of 1hr 50min.

Parking
The best free parking is in pl. Sérraucourt (linked to the cathedral by a free shuttle bus) and Cours A. France, or along the blvd de la

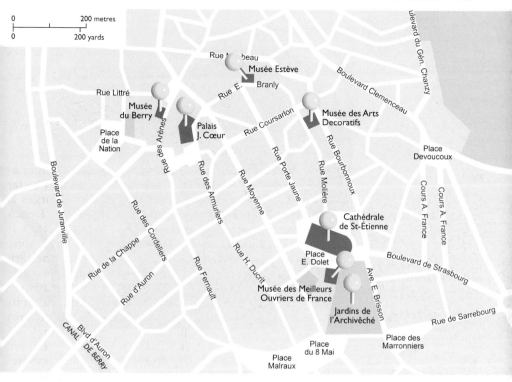

Map legend:

0 | 200 metres

0 | 200 yards

Rue Mirbeau
Musée Estève
Branly
Rue E.
Rue Littré
Musée du Berry
Rue des Arènes
Palais J. Cœur
Place de la Nation
Rue Coursarlon
Musée des Arts Decoratifs
Rue Bourbonnoux
Place Devoucoux
Rue des Armuriers
Rue Moyenne
Rue Porte Jaune
Rue Molière
Cours A. France
Cours A. France
Boulevard de Juranville
Rue des Cordeliers
Rue de la Chappe
Rue d'Auron
Rue Fernault
Rue H. Ducrit
Cathédrale de St-Étienne
Place E. Dolet
Boulevard de Strasbourg
Musée des Meilleurs Ouvriers de France
Ave. E. Brisson
Jardins de l'Archivêché
Rue de Sarrebourg
Blvd d'Auron
CANAL DE BERRY
Place Malraux
Place du 8 Mai
Place des Marronniers
Boulevard Clemenceau
Boulevard du Gén. Chanzy

République near the superb Jardin des Près-Fichaux. The heart of old Bourges is compact. Having parked, walk or take the *Train Touristique* €€ for a 45-min tour departing from the cathedral.

Sights

Cathédrale de Saint-Étienne***

Not just one of Bourges' most impressive monuments, but one of France's most treasured religious works and a UNESCO heritage site, this cathedral was begun at the turn of the 12th century. Take in its western portal first – not just one but five finely-carved entrances, decorated with saints and apostles, pencil-thin columns and arcades rising to five-pointed arches. These lead into the five-nave cathedral, an anomaly for the building has no transept. It is essentially bullet-shaped: the naves lead up to the choir and the rounded apse behind. In these apse chapels are the fabulous stained-glass windows. Executed between 1215–25 by three different workshops, they at first appear as a kaleidoscope of colour. But as you look up and begin to discern the windows, you'll pick out the individual figures from both the Old and New Testaments. Before exiting the cathedral, pass by the Chapelle Jacques-Cœur with more spectacular stained glass. A ticket to the crypt (where an effigy of the once-powerful Duc de

Bourges by Night

This is an unique son-et-lumière experience. During summer and over holiday weekends at other times, Bourges diffuses music and illuminates parts of its major monuments (and the gardens of the Archbishopric), giving the city quite a different feel. The route between the main monuments is much the same as our suggested walk (see page 267). If you have the chance, do it by night (from 2130 in autumn and from 2200 or 2230 in spring and summer) as well as by day.

Cathédrale de Saint-Étienne €
Open Oct–Mar daily 0900–1745, Apr–Sept daily 0830–1915. **Crypt and North Tower €€** crypt open daily (except Sun am) for guided visits at 0945, 1100, 1430, 1545 (& 1700 during summer) and mid-July–mid-Aug for individual visits; North Tower open daily, times as cathedral. Both closed 1 Jan, 1 May, 1 & 11 Nov, 25 Dec.

Jardins de l'Archivêché
€ Open 0700–2400.

Musée des Arts Decoratifs € 6 r. Bourbonnoux; tel: 02 48 57 81 17; open daily except Sun am & Mon 1000–1200, 1400–1800, July–Aug 1000–1830, closed 1 Jan, 1 May, 1 & 11 Nov, 25 Dec.

Above
Portal, Bourges cathedral

Berry lies) will also offer access to the Renaissance North Tower. After climbing 396 steps in corkscrew fashion to a height of 65m, you'll have a great view over the *Vieille Ville* and the marshy Marais area to the northeast.

Jardins de l'Archivêché*
On the southeast flanks of the apse are the lozenge-shaped gardens of the Archbishopric. Beautifully laid out over 300 years ago, full of shady walks, and containing a delightful little bandstand, the gardens are a fine place to relax. The views of the cathedral's apse and south flank are particularly good.

Musée des Arts Decoratifs**
This interesting museum, dedicated to the decorative arts, is housed in the fine Hôtel Lallemart. Note its elegant façade (a beautiful, and finely proportioned, early Renaissance work) before wandering through the collections of French furniture, 16th- and 17th- century tapestries, cabinets intricately inlaid with wood, Oriental lacquerwork and some exquisite examples of faïence and ivorywork.

Musée des Meilleurs Ouvriers de France*
The former Archbishop's Palace, an imposing building from the 17th century, shelters this unusual and fascinating collection of crafts which changes as craftsmen from some 200 disciplines enter the museum's prestigious yearly competition.

Right
Musée des Arts Decoratifs, interior

Right
Musée des Arts Decoratifs, interior

Musée des Meilleurs Ouvriers de France € Pl. Étienne Dolet; tel: 02 48 57 82 45; open daily except Sun am & Mon 1000–1200, 1400–1800, July–Aug 1000–1830, closed 1 Jan, 1 May, 1 & 11 Nov, 25 Dec.

Musée du Berry € 4 r. des Arènes; tel: 02 48 57 81 15; open daily except Sun am & Tue 1000–1200, 1400–1800, in July & Aug 1000–1830, closed 1 Jan, 1 May, 1 & 11 Nov, 25 Dec.

Musée Estève € 13 r. Edouard Branly; tel: 02 48 24 75 38, fax: 02 48 24 29 48; open daily except Sun am & Tue 1000–1200, 1400–1800, in July & Aug 1000–1830, closed 1 Jan, 1 May, 1 & 11 Nov, 25 Dec.

Palais Jacques-Cœur €€ 10bis r. Jacques-Cœur; tel: 02 48 24 06 87; open daily 0900–1200, 1400–1700 (until 1800 Apr–June & Sept–Oct), July–Aug 0900–1300, 1400–1900, closed 1 Jan, 1 May, 1 & 11 Nov, 25 Dec.

Musée du Berry✝✝
Located in the impressive **Hôtel Cujas**, a Renaissance mansion (look at the wonderful bulging corner towers – so popular at that period – capped by their slate pepperpot roofs) houses relics from the Roman days of *Avaricum*, parts of the Duc de Berry's mausoleum and a large collection of pottery.

Musée Estève✝✝
This is a museum – in old surroundings – for modern art lovers. The Hôtel des Échevins was used for over three centuries as the municipal headquarters. Its stairwell, in the form of a tower with light, lacy sculptural decoration on its monochrome exterior, does little to prepare one for the vast and colourful works of a French contemporary artist. Maurice Estève (1904–2001) was a self-taught painter who, influenced by Braque and Cézanne, hovered between the figurative and abstract, before heading in the 1950s towards a highly colourful, abstract world of painting. The 130 oil paintings, watercolours and sketches in this museum are imbued with the vibrant colours and strong sense of form that made his reputation.

Palais Jacques-Cœur✝✝
Charles VII's protégé silversmith, Jacques Cœur (*see page 281*) rose to fame and considerable wealth from a humble start in life. He commissioned this lovely Gothic mansion for himself. Delicate stone tracery, ornate towers, and beautiful balustrades enhance the creamy stone façade, while the interior is richly decorated with superb sculptural elements around its chimneys and doors, and paintings, woodwork and ceilings. Cœur invested lavishly and introduced decorative elements gathered on his considerable travels in the East. It was finished in 1451 but, as Cœur was by then in exile, he never inhabited it and the palace passed to his heirs on his death in 1457.

Right
Façade, Musée du Berry –
Hôtel Cujas

Vercingétorix v. Caesar

The nigh-indomitable Gaul leader, Vercingétorix, met his match in Julius Caesar. As the Romans moved north, conquering and absorbing the locals into their expanding empire, this leader stood his ground and, rather than relinquish Gaul to the invaders, burned all the towns and villages. The citizens of Bourges begged him to spare the town and he made an exception. Bourges' safety was not long-lived, however. Caesar came and conquered, reputedly slaying all its 40,000 citizens.

Accommodation and food in Bourges

Hôtel de Bourbon €€–€€€ *blvd de la République; tel: 02 48 70 70 00, fax: 02 48 70 21 22, e-mail: h1888@accor-hotels.com* Incorporating the remains of the Abbaye Saint-Ambroix, this fine hotel is exceptionally comfortable. The historic centre is within walking distance. The hotel restaurant (*see below*) is outstanding.

Hôtel d'Angleterre €€ *1 pl. des Quatres-Piliers; tel: 02 48 24 68 51, fax: 02 48 65 21 41*. In the middle of the *Vieille Ville*, this medium-sized hotel is located in an elegant 19th-century building. Comfortable, private (paying) parking and restaurant offering traditional French cuisine.

Inter-Hôtel Les Tilleuls €€ *7 pl. de la Pyrotechnie; tel: 02 48 20 49 04, fax: 02 48 50 61 73; e-mail: Antoine.Falleur@wanadoo.fr* Just ten mins from the cathedral, this smallish hotel is comfortable, friendly and well-maintained.

Abbaye Saint-Ambroix €€€ *Hôtel de Bourbon* (*see above*). In the remains of the nave from what was once the Abbaye Saint-Ambroix's church, this award-winning gastronomic restaurant has innovative modern cuisine and an outstanding wine cellar.

Philippe Larmat €€–€€€ *62bis blvd Gambetta; tel: 02 48 70 79 00, fax: 02 48 69 88 87; closed Sun pm, Mon and last 2 wks Aug*. One of Bourges' top restaurateurs, Larmat has created a fine restaurant with an exceptional cuisine. Traditional but innovative, his menus range from the affordable to the gourmet.

Restaurant Le Beauvoir €€ *1 av. Marx Dormoy; tel: 02 48 65 42 44, fax: 02 48 24 80 84; closed Sun pm*. In the direction of Les Marais, but not far from the centre, this restaurant with modern decor has established a reputation for high-quality and creative cuisine at reasonable prices.

Suggested walk

Total distance: About 1.95km.

Time: 2 hours, not counting time spent in museums.

Route: Start in place **Étienne Dolet** in front of the south door of the **CATHÉDRALE DE ST-ÉTIENNE ❶** and walk along its flanks to the magnificent western portals. Keep to its northern side, taking **r. des 3 Maillets**. On the left between r. Molière and the pedestrian r. Bourbonnoux, are the remains of Bourges' **Roman ramparts**.

Continue via r. Bourbonnoux down to the Hôtel Lallemant, the **MUSÉE DES ARTS DÉCORATIFS** ❷ on your left. From here continue to **pl. Gordaine**, full of half-timbered houses, one of the most beautifully-restored squares in town.

Detour: To the east of pl. Gordaine, via r. de la Poissonnerie, blvd Clémenceau and r. Neuve des Bouchers, you'll reach **Les Marais**, the marshland attached to the River Auron. This fascinating area, a breath of fresh air for the city, has been cultivated for over 300 years.

Go back along the pedestrianised **r. Mirabeau** and turn left up the stairs, coming out in r. Branly. On your right is the Hôtel des Échevins, which houses the **MUSÉE ESTÈVE** ❸. Retrace your steps (and mind your head down the stairs) to r. Mirabeau and follow this

Right
Carved window and
figure, Bourges

lovely road with its half-timbered buildings around to **pl. de la Barre**, where you take the r. Pelvoysin, named for the local architect, through pl. Planchat to Hôtel Cujas, and the **MUSÉE DU BERRY** ❹. Walk down r. des Arènes, that used to lead to the Roman amphitheatre, as far as the steep stairs, **escalier Jacques-Cœur**, on your left, that climbs up to the r. Jacques-Cœur and, again on your left, the imposing **PALAIS JACQUES-CŒUR** ❺.

Leaving the palace, walk past the escalier Jacques-Cœur, and into the **pl. des 4 Piliers**, where imposing 17th- to 18th-century mansions are grouped around a fountain, and head down the **r. des Armuriers** towards the Prefecture. On the corner of **r. d'Auron** is a fine half-timbered house known, erroneously, as the 'house of Jacques-Cœur': in fact the house was built long after the silversmith's demise but was on the site of his birthplace. Cross the pl. M Plaisant and walk along r. Ducrot, past the Prefecture, turning left into **r. V Hugo**, past the **tourist office** and back to the south side of the cathedral. Turn right, and you'll see the entrance to the **MUSÉE DES MEILLEURS OUVRIERS DE FRANCE** ❻. After the last museum, it is time to relax. Turn right out of the museum and enter the **JARDINS DE l'ARCHIVÊCHÉ** ❼ and explore this pleasant garden.

The Berry

Ratings

History	●●●●●
Medieval towns	●●●●○
Religious architecture	●●●●○
Porcelain	●●●●○
Gastronomy	●●●○○
Scenery	●●●○○
Local produce	●●○○○
Children	●●○○○

The Berry is a vast plateau area straddling central France – indeed the geographical centre of the country falls within this region. It rises through forests and descends to marshes, extends through important agricultural land and touches the broad band of the Loire Valley in the east. It is not one of the country's most crowded tourist areas, so getting around is fairly easy. In fact, Berry does a fairly good job of hiding its assets. As one of its famous sons, Alain-Fournier, wrote: you need to 'part the branches to get to know the area'. But the rewards of doing so are rich. Although the Romans conquered the Celtic tribes of the Berry, the most complete historical legacy here is from the 11th and 12th centuries, the Romanesque era. The religious architecture and the many wall paintings from this period form one of France's greatest treasures. Famous Berry residents include George Sand, Alain-Fournier, Honoré de Balzac and contemporary actor, Gerard Dépardieu.

BOUGES-LE-CHÂTEAU✦✦✦

ⓘ Comité Départemental de Tourisme du Cher 5 r. de Séracourt, Bourges; tel: 02 48 48 00 10, fax: 02 48 48 00 20, e-mail: tourisme.berry@wanadoo.fr, web: www.berrylecher.com; open Mon–Fri 0900–1230, 1330–1700.

Comité Départemental du Tourisme de l'Indre 1 r. St-Martin, Châteauroux; tel: 02 54 07 36 36, fax: 02 54 22 31 21; Mon–Fri 0900–1200, 1400–1800,

It is something of a surprise to see the elegant, Italianate **Château de Bouges✦✦** rise amid Berry pastureland. But this rectangular stone building, devoid of towers and with grey slate roofs, has symmetry and proportion not usual in this part of France. It is often compared to the Petit Trianon, in Versailles, to which it has a strong resemblance. It was built in 1759, probably by architect Jacques-Ange Gabriel, for Charles Le Blanc de Marnaval, who was the manager of Châteauroux's royal factory for bed linen, and was later owned by Talleyrand. Smallish but very well furnished, the château doesn't have that musty, museum feel to it that some other small mansions do. During the guided visit you'll see a remarkable collection of good 18th-century furniture (added by the last private owner, Henri Viguier) and pass through Louis XVI's bedroom. The well-maintained 80-ha park also has a formal French garden, while the courtyard, with its elegant stone buildings capped by steep slate-tiled Mansard roofs, contains the

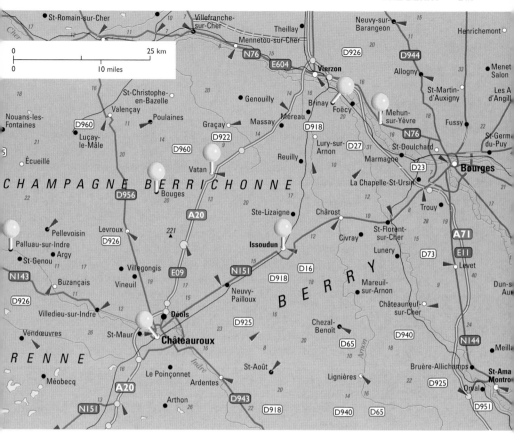

closed public hols.
www.berrylindre.com

Château de Bouges
€–€€ tel: 02 54 35 88
26, fax: 02 54 35 16 96;
open for guided tours, Mar,
June & Nov 1100, 1500 &
1600, Apr, May, Sept & Oct
1100, 1500, 1600 & 1700,
July–Aug 1000, 1200, 1500,
1600, 1700 & 1800, closed
Dec–Feb and 1 May.

stables and tack rooms, complete with harnesses and saddles. Don't miss the good collection of horse-drawn carriages.

Food in Bouges-le-Château

Auberge du Château € *Opposite château entrance; tel: 02 54 35 68 73.*
A simple but pleasant and inexpensive place to stop for a bite.

Berry lentils

Seven times richer in iron than spinach, full of protein, vitamins, fibre and natural sugar, green Berry lentils are of excellent quality. The best lentils carry the *Label Rouge* denoting adherence to a stringent criteria of cultivation.

BRINAY❖❖

🏛 **Église St-Aignan €**
Open daily 0900–1900.

🏪 **Market:**
Foëcy, Fri am.

Below
Frescoes, Église St-Aignan,
Brinay

Highlight of this tiny Berrichonne village is its 11th-century **Église Saint-Aignan**❖❖❖, hidden from immediate view by the prolific shrubbery and old trees. This small Romanesque building, with a somewhat triangular façade and topped by an odd little steeple, was sited on the remains of a former proto-Christian church and is in the simplest of forms: a rectangular nave and a smaller rectangular choir. It has a wooden barrel-vault ceiling held in place by crossbars, ancient wooden pew stalls and a well-worn brick floor. However, its highlights are the substantial remains of its paintings, decorating the apse in vivid hues of ochre, red, white, green and even some touches of blue. The paintings represent, amongst others, the *Labours of the Months* (unique as it's the only complete Romanesque cycle of this subject still extant in France), *The Prophets and Apostles* and the *Life of Christ*. They are executed with unusual realism and certain vigour – a late Carolingian style with some Byzantine touches. The *Massacre of the Innocents*, a scene which is often represented in later art, is quite gruesome in its depiction and intentionally evokes emotion. Amazingly, the work has withstood the ravages of nine centuries, possibly because the wall paintings were covered with later layers of painting and the original 12th-century work was only discovered in 1911. It remains one of the finest examples of French Romanesque art.

Route de Porcelaine

An itinerary has been organised in this area of the Berry to link the factories that produce porcelain. Known as the *Route de Porcelaine*, it gives information on 14 participating manufacturers, museums or workshops located in the 6 local communities between Viezon and Bourges. Although only introduced in the beginning of the 19th century, the industry has prospered and garnered a reputable name for its decorative and household products.

CHÂTEAUROUX✦✦

ℹ️ **Châteauroux
Tourist Office** 1 pl.
de la Gare, Châteauroux; tel:
02 54 34 10 74, fax: 02 54
27 57 97; open June–Sept,
Mon–Sat 0900–1900, Sun
& hols 1000–1530,
Oct–May, Mon–Sat
0900–1230, 1400–1815.

ℹ️ **Déols Tourist
Office** 7 r. de
l'Abbaye, Déols; tel: 02 54
07 58 87; open Mon–Sat
0900–1230, 1400–1815.

🌐 www.ville-
châteauroux.fr

🏛️ **Musée Bertrand €**;
2 r. Descente des
Cordeliers; tel: 02 54 61 12
30, fax: 02 54 61 12 31;
open June–Sept, Tue–Sun
1000–1200, 1400–1800,
Oct–May, Tue–Sun
1400–1800.

**Musée du Berry,
Maison des Arts et
Traditions Populaires**
parc Balzan, 44 av. François
Mitterand; tel: 02 54 61 12
30; open by telephone
appointment. A fine
collection of items relating
to the local arts, crafts and
cultural traditions in the
Berry.

Église de Saint-Etienne
€ open daily for guided tour
mid-June–mid-Sept 1500,
rest of year open daily
except Sun.

🛒 **Markets:** Pl. Voltaire,
Châteauroux, Sat all
day; Déols, Tue & Fri all
day.

As the regional capital of southern Berry, the substantial hilltop town of Châteauroux is imposing. It rises above the large oak forests to the south and the vast stretches of agricultural land which gave it prosperity, and sits at an important north-south crossroads. It grew around the fortress built at the end of the tenth century by the Seigneur of Déols, who required a safer address than his previous one. The site at Châteauroux was a great improvement. The oldest – and most pleasant – part of Châteauroux is around the former main street, the r. Grande, which runs into the r. de l'Indre, one-time haunt of the town's tanners, weavers and dyers. The town's **Musée Bertrand**✦✦✦ (also known as the Musée de Châteauroux) is in the 18th-century Hôtel Bertrand, a fine mansion belonging to Napoleon's faithful companion, General Henri-Gatien Bertrand. It is notable for its Napoleonic memorabilia, including paintings and decorative arts. Looking out over the countryside at one edge of the old town is the handsome Couvent des Cordeliers, now a venue for local exhibitions. Not to be missed, either, is the **Musée du Berry, Maison des Arts et Traditions Populaires**✦.

The town of **Déols**✦✦ has been absorbed into the suburbs of Châteauroux with the result that there is no obvious distinction for tourists. The heart of ancient Déols fans out from the sparse remains of its Abbaye Notre-Dame dating from 917. The gracious stonework of its clocktower is all that still stands of a once-important abbey (a sister abbey to the great Abbaye de Cluny and the most important monastery in the Berry), though current excavations are revealing the foundations of the former complex. Part of the remains can be seen in the Musée Bertrand. If early Christian sculpture fascinates, then don't miss the parish church of **Saint-Etienne**✦ on Place Carnot (a short walk northwards from the Abbey remains), for here there is an extraordinarily beautifully carved sarcophagus belonging to Saints Ludre and Léocarde, dating from the fourth century. The delicacy and realism of its figures harks back to the best sculpture of the Roman Empire some 300 years earlier.

Back in the centre, the 15th-century Porte du Pont-Perrin is an elegant entrance town gate which once guarded the Pont-Perrin, crossing point over the Indre while, at the other end of the street, the fine twin-towered Porte de l'Horloge has, for over 550 years, housed the town clock.

Accommodation and food in and around Châteauroux

Le Relais Saint Jacques €€ *Exit 12 from A20; tel: 02 54 60 44 44, fax: 02 54 60 44 00; open year round.* Nearer Déols than the centre of Châteauroux (5km), this good, modern hotel and restaurant is a favourite with local gourmands.

La Ciboulette €–€€ *42 r. Grande, tel/fax: 02 54 27 66 28; closed Mon & public hols, 2 wks in Jan, 4 wks in July/Aug.* A central address and attractive rustic decor in this restaurant serving local specialities and fine wines.

ISSOUDUN✧✧

Issoudun Tourist Office *Pl. St-Cyr; tel: 02 54 21 74 02, fax: 02 54 03 03 36; open June–Sept daily 0930–1200, 1400–1900, Oct–May, Mon–Sat 1000–1200, 1500–1800.*

La Tour Blanche € *tel: 02 54 03 22 15; open May–Sept Mon–Sat 1400–1900, Sun & public hols 1000–1200, 1400–1800, Oct–Apr Wed–Sun 1400–1800. May–Sept, self-guided son-et-lumière tours in pm.*

Issoudun is a pleasant, unhurried town in the midst of farming land and oak woods. As you climb up into the old town, its sense of history begins to unfurl. Because of its strategic location, Issoudun prospered in the Middle Ages as the capital of Lower Berry and became a royal city in 1240. Its 27m-high **Tour Blanche**✧ (not really white but of light-coloured stone) is an imposing, Medieval tower begun in 1195 and, as part of Issoudun's defensive system, rises high above the town, piercing its skyline. It was once part of English-occupied France; Richard the Lionheart and Philippe-Auguste came to blows (yet again) here, but Philippe-Auguste won the town back on Richard's death in 1199, and finished constructing the tower. It is now open to latter-day travellers who find it at its best during a *son-et-lumière* presentation. Next door is a fine topiary garden, with yew trees manicured into the form of chess pieces. The Belfry also dates from a similar era and, despite its use as a prison and a later renovation, remains a fine

Right
Issoudun, Tour Blanche

Museé de l'Hospice
Saint-Roch € 23 r. de
l'Hospice St-Roch; tel: 02 54
21 01 76, fax: 02 54 21 88
56; open 2 Nov–Mar Mon,
Wed, Thu, Fri 1400–1800,
Sat & Sun 1000–1200,
1400–1800, Apr–Oct Mon
& Tue 1400–1900,
Wed–Sun 1000–1200,
1400–1900, closed 1 May,
1 & 11 Nov.

Market: Fri am, Sat
all day.

building. The Église Saint Seer stands a stone's throw from the main square (it's just beside the half-timbered, tourist office) and dates from the 10th to 12th centuries. It has an unusually long nave and, above the west door (where you enter), a good, but poorly-lit, *Descent from the Cross* by Jean Boucher dating from 1625. The modern building (housing temporary exhibits) that forms part of the **Museé de l'Hospice Saint-Roch**✦✦✦ is a surprise beside the handsome hospice that, as the Hôtel-Dieu de Issoudun, once sheltered pilgrims and beggars on their way to Santiago de Compostela. This 15th- to 18th-century building now houses the eclectic but interesting museum tracing Issoudun's Roman and Renaissance heritage. The hospice's chapel is decorated with two magnificent sculptural interpretations of the *Tree of Jesse*, a unique feat of three-dimensional workmanship, while another section holds the hospice's fascinating 17th- to 19th-century pharmacy. The surgical instruments once used in the hospice are a salutary reminder of the progress made in medicine. Lastly, don't miss the modern painting of the medieval healing saint, Roch (*see page 276*), complete with his life-saving dog. He's dressed rather like a *brasserie* waiter and has dropped his trousers to show the plague pustules!

Accommodation and food in Issoudun

La Cognette €€ *Blvd Stalingrad; tel: 02 54 21 21 83, fax: 02 54 03 13 03, web: www.chateauxhotels.com/cognette* Built in 1789 as an inn, and frequented by Balzac. The renowned restaurant offers Berry specialities and contemporary dishes in a refined atmosphere.

Saint Roch

Saint Roch is a popular holy man, hailing from Montpellier, France. During the plague years in the mid-14th century, he renounced his worldly goods and set off on a pilgrimage to Rome. He healed many fellow pilgrims en route by making the sign of the cross over their ailing bodies. He, too, succumbed to the plague and famine and collapsed in a wood. Roch was kept alive by a dog who brought him a hunk of bread daily until its owner discovered the man and sheltered him. His short life ended in prison in 1379. He has been adopted as the patron saint of beasts by many guilds and is often depicted in paintings accompanied by a dog.

MEHUN-SUR-YÈVRE✧✧

Mehun Tourist Office *Pl. du 14 juillet; tel: 02 48 57 35 51, fax: 02 48 57 13 40; open June–Aug Mon–Sat 0915–1215, 1330–1800, rest of year 0900–1200, 1330–1700.*

Église Notre-Dame *€ Open daily 0830–1800.*

Pôle de la Porcelaine € *Jardins du Jean de Berry; tel: 02 48 57 06 19, fax: 02 48 57 34 16; open May, June & Sept 1400–1800, except Mon, July–Aug 1000–1200, 1400–1800, Mar–Apr & Oct–Nov weekends only 1000–1200.*

Musée Charles VII € *Tel: 02 48 57 36 84; open May, June & Sept 1400–1800, except Mon, July–Aug 1000–1200, 1400–1800, Mar–Apr & Oct–Nov weekends only 1000–1200.*

Market: Wed am.

It was Jean, Duke of Berry, son of King Jean II le Bon, who reconstructed the château in Mehun in the late-14th century. Perhaps better known as a patron of arts, Jean de Berry commissioned the famous *Les Très Riches Heures* (*see page 278*), one of Europe's most beautiful, illustrated medieval manuscripts. At his death in 1416, the castle passed into the hands of his nephew, King Charles VII, who was to receive, amongst others, Joan of Arc here in 1429 and 1430. The king died in Mehun, and the castle survived another couple of centuries before being dismantled during the Revolution. What is left is minimal – however, it must have been a sumptuous castle if the illustration in *Les Très Riches Heures* is accurate.

The **Musée Charles VII**✶ is housed in one of the remaining towers and, amid its exhibits, is a reproduction of the famous Book of Hours.

Medieval Mehun is rather scant, too, although the **Église Notre-Dame**✶, former collegiate church dating from the mid-1000s, still stands, and the attractive r. Jeanne d'Arc, named for the heroine who stayed in this street, still has some historic homes. At its end is the dignified town gateway Porte de l'Horloge which dates from the 14th century.

Mehun is best known today for its porcelain industry – it has six porcelain companies that welcome visitors. Since this industry was established 200 years ago in the valley of the Yèvre it has prospered, making this one of France's prime areas of production. Apart from visiting exhibitions and museums that trace the history, the bonus for visitors is the possibility of buying items at factory outlets. The **Pôle de la Porcelaine**✶✶ in Mehun displays some beautiful items which aptly capture the breadth of this craft.

Porcelain factories in Mehun

Porcelaine Cerame *16 av. Raoul Aladenize; tel: 02 48 57 48 05; open Tue–Sat 0900–1230, 1400–1900, Sun & hols 1000–1230, 1430–1900,*

Porcelaine Jacques Cœur *Route de Foëcy; tel: 02 48 57 30 56, fax: 02 48 57 16 88; open Mon–Sat 1400–1800.*

Porcelaine Pillivuyt *Av. de la Manufacture; tel: 02 48 67 31 00; fax: 02 48 57 13 00; ceramic shop open Tue–Sat 1000–1200, 1430–1830. Locally produced porcelain.*

Right
Folk dancers in front of
château, Mehun

Accommodation and food in Mehun-sur-Yèvre

Hôtel La Croix Blanche € *164 r. Jeanne d'Arc; tel: 02 48 57 30 01, fax: 02 48 57 29 66, hotel closed Jan, restaurant closed 22 Dec–22 Jan, and Oct–Easter Fri and Sun pm.* A smallish and friendly hotel with good facilities.

Restaurant Les Abiès €€ *Av. Jean-Châtelet, route Vierzon; tel: 02 48 57 39 31; fax: 02 48 57 00 70; closed end-Oct, Feb & Mon, Wed pm & Sun pm.* Local produce used to produce traditional French fare of consistently high standards.

Les Très Riches Heures du Duc de Berry

This exquisite work was commissioned by the Duke and executed by the three Limbourg brothers, Paul, Hermann and Jean, a trio of celebrated illustrators from Flanders who had also worked for the Duke of Burgundy. This Book of Hours outlines the liturgical text for each hour of the day and includes psalms, prayers and calendars. The finely-executed illustrations in the calendar part of this Très Riches Heures probably comprise the book's finest section, and the importance of this example of medieval art is arguably on a par with any of Raphael or Leonardo da Vinci's works. The original is now kept at Chantilly in northern France.

PALLUAU✦

ⓘ Palluau Tourist Office Pl. Frontenac; tel: 02 54 38 53 03; open July–Aug 1000–1200, 1430–1830. Other times contact the Mairie; tel: 02 54 38 45 55.

Market: Sun am, pl. des Marronniers.

Église Saint-Laurent € open 0745–1930. To visit, ask for key either at the nearby shops, at the Tourist Office or from the Mairie.

Palud means *swamp* in Latin, and no doubt the marshy areas around the Indre gave their name to this small medieval village built above the river. Its history is traceable with certainty to the ninth century, but most of what one sees today is 15th-century and later. The stone Château de Palluau (not open to the public) was built by the Count of Anjou, Foulques le Rechin, at a strategic position on the Indre. It was a much sought-after castle and gave rise to many a battle, the most notable of which was the successful siege against the English in 1188, when Philippe-Auguste managed to outwit Richard the Lionheart's men by cutting off their water supplies. The deconsecrated **Église Saint-Laurent✦✦**, once part of the Prieuré Saint-Laurent, has extremely fine frescoes in its apse. The church has been divided up, and parts of it are used for domestic purposes. Ask for a key at the nearby shops.

VATAN✦

ⓘ Vatan Tourist Office Pl. de la République; tel/fax: 02 54 49 71 69; web: www.vatan-en-berry.com; open July–Aug Mon–Sat 0900–1230, 1400–1730, Jun & Sept Mon–Sat 0900–1230, 1400–1800, Oct–Feb Mon–Sat 1000–1200, 1400–1700, open every Sun 1000–1200.

Amid kilometres of undulating hills defined by golden cereals or rapeseed flowers, lies the agricultural town of Vatan. It must surely have one of the country's more unusual museums: the **Musée du Cirque✦✦**, unique in France. It grew from the private collection of Dr. Alain Frère who had amassed an extraordinary assortment of posters, costumes, maquettes and accessories. Through video footage visitors learn much about the behind-the-scenes life of itinerant circus artists. In the centre of town, the place République is where the old Wheat Hall is still located. Once used for the public auctions of grain and for public festivals, it now shelters the tourist office. In the north of town, the 15th-century Église Saint-Laurian faces the ancient

Musée du Cirque € *Square de la Libération;* tel: *02 54 49 77 78; open July–mid-Sept daily 1000–1200, 1400–1800, rest of year, daily except Mon and Tue am 1000–1200, 1400–1800.*

Market: Wed am.

Above
Porcelain painter, Mehun

Porcelaines Philip Deshoulières *5 r. Louis Grandjean, Foëcy; tel: 02 48 53 04 55; fax: 02 48 52 60 50; open daily 0900–1200, 1400–1900.*

Relais Saint-Hubert *€–€€ 53 av. Maréchal Foch; Massay; tel: 02 48 51 91 37; fax: 02 48 51 92 58, closed in winter.* Attractive, traditional little hotel in this untouristy village.

Hotel Relais de la Cloche *€ 3 r. National, Levroux; tel: 02 54 35 70 43, fax: 02 54 35 67 43; closed Feb, Sun pm, Mon pm and Tue.* Equidistant between Villegongis and Bouges, this small family-run hotel in Levroux has a warm welcome and includes a traditional restaurant.

Granary. This was used to store grain representing a levy of 10 per cent of a farmer's annual output, which was destined to swell the church coffers.

Accommodation and food in Vatan

Hôtel de la France € *16 pl. de la République; tel: 02 54 49 74 11; open year round except first week Dec, last 2 weeks in Feb, first week Sept, restaurant closed as above and each Tue pm and Wed, excepting public hols.* A simple but pleasant place to lodge or eat. The restaurant serves local specialities.

Suggested tour

Total distance: About 240km or, with the detour, 300km.

Time: 1 or 2 days, depending on how much time you want to spend at each stop.

Links: From Vatan, it is 24km on the D960 between this market town and Valençay, on the tour of South Touraine (*see page 92*), while Palluau is around 14km from Châtillon-sur-Indre on the same tour.

Route: Exit **Bourges** (*see page 262*) by the N76 marked to Viezon, and you'll arrive in **MEHUN-SUR-YÈVRE** ❶, one of the major stops on the **Route de Porcelaine**, the Porcelain Route. Continue on the same road towards Viezon but turn off to the left as you enter **Vignoux-sur-Barageon** onto the D30, which crosses both the Yèvre and the motorway and enters the village of **Foëcy**, site of an important porcelain factory. Continue on the D30 for a couple of kilometres, crossing the Cher, and take the D27 road off to the right at Beauregard, marked Viezon and **BRINAY** ❷. It is a winding set of roads that leads onwards.

Leave Brinay on the D18E via the village of Méreau, passing the large and impressive **Abbaye St Martin de Massay**, with its interesting Église St-Martin in the village of the same name, before taking the small, and not particularly busy, D320 which hugs the motorway, passing from side to side until it enters **VATAN** ❸.

The D926 toward Levroux is a fast road. Dolmens are off the road to the left just before entering the village of Liniez. Here you take the D66 to the right, marked to **BOUGES-LE-CHÂTEAU** ❹. The château itself is just on the north side of the village. From Bouges, the D2, southwards, follows the valley of the River Renon and goes via **Levroux**. Continue on the D926 in the direction of **Châteauroux** before turning off 7km later onto the D27, which leads to the **Château de Villegongis**, site of a Renaissance château, closed for the

The 'village of lovers'

In the triangle between Vatan, Châteauroux and Issoudun is the small village of **Saint-Valentin**, the only village in the country bearing the saint's name. Dubbed *Le Village des Amoureux* it trades on its sobriquet to hold an annual festival for sweethearts and attracts visitors from all over France. The date? 14th February, St Valentine's Day, of course.

foreseeable future. This road changes into the D7B and then D63 as it skirts the Forêt de Villegongis, passing through the hamlet of Fouillereau and crossing the D926 in the direction of **Argy**, noted for its 15th- to 16th-century château. Turn right here onto the D11 in the direction of Ecueillé and pass through **Pellevoisin** where the D15 leads to **PALLUAU-SUR-INDRE ❺**, situated on the northern banks of the Indre. The best views of this Medieval hillside town are as you cross the Indre, leaving for the N143 to the south. Turn left on this highway and follow the directions to **CHÂTEAUROUX ❻**.

ⓘ Maison de George Sand € *tel: 02 54 31 06 04, fax: 02 54 27 65 98; open daily Apr–June Sept–mid Oct 0900–1215, 1400–1830, July–Aug 0900–1930, rest of year 1000–1215, 1400–1630, closed 01 Jan, 01 May, 01 & 11 Nov, 25 Dec.*

Detour: Literary aficionados might like to include a tour to **Maison de George Sand** at Nohant-Vic, 27km south of Châteauroux on the D943. The 19th-century author's home is arranged much as it was when she inhabited it, and now fulfils a role as an interesting museum of memorabilia, from the life of this prominent author. The house was originally constructed in the 12th century, but was restored and modernised in the 17th century. George Sand (born Aurore Dupin in 1804) spent her youth and adolescence here, and later inherited the large house, a *'modeste demeure'*, as she referred to it. It provided her with a much-loved refuge. Among the luminaries of the 19th-century music, artistic and literary world to visit her home were Balzac, Lizst, Delacroix, Gautier, Flaubert and, of course, her lover Chopin. George Sand was also responsible for helping restore the exquisite Romanesque frescoes in Nohant-Vic's **Église Saint-Martin**, a church that was under the jurisdiction of the abbey at Déols. Take a few minutes to visit this well-known little church, open daily.

The old town of **Déols**, on the D151 to the north, was once a separate entity but has now been absorbed by the suburbs of Châteauroux. It is a straight road, the N151, onwards to the less busy but equally interesting town of **ISSOUDUN ❼**. Bourges is just 37km from here, back along the N151.

The Berry region map showing towns including Vierzon, Bourges, Châteauroux, Issoudun, Valençay, Reuilly, and numbered tour stops 1–7. Road numbers shown: D675, D4, E604, D944, N76, D960, D922, D918, D27, D23, A20, D956, D926, N143, E09, N151, D16, D73, E11, A71, D925, D940, N144, D65, D943, D990, D951, among others.

Reuilly wine

This tour encircles the Reuilly wine-producing district. Sauvignon, Pinot Noir and Pinot Gris are the three grape varieties used in the cultivation of AOC Reuilly wine. This area has a history of some 1500 years of vinification, notably producing its fine Pinot Noir red wine, and now extends over 137ha with a total output of some 8000hl annually.

Jacques Cœur

In the Berry region, north and south of Bourges, you'll come across the symbol marking the Route de Jacques Cœur. It might seem that you're following a comical child's cartoon character but in fact you're tracing the footsteps of Jacques Cœur, the wealthy merchant and master silversmith who was employed by King Charles VII. He was born in Bourges (see page 262) around 1400 and rose to prominence for his fine craftsmanship. Apart from being present in many of the royal châteaux along the Loire and in the heart of the Berry, he also travelled to the Orient to trade. In a hideous plot to discredit him, he was accused of treason and of poisoning the king's mistress, Agnès Sorel – offences punishable by the death sentence. In an unfair trial he was found guilty of subsidiary crimes but not guilty of the murder, and was exiled. He died on the Greek island of Chios.

Language

Although English is spoken in most tourist locations it is courteous to attempt to speak some French. The effort is generally appreciated, and may even elicit a reply in perfect English! The following is a very brief list of some useful words and phrases, with approximate pronunciation guides. The *Thomas Cook European Travel Phrasebook* (£4.95/$7.95) lists more than 300 travel phrases in French (and in 11 other European languages).

- **Hello/Goodbye**
  Bonjour/Au revoir *Bawngzhoor/Ohrervwahr*

- **Good evening/Goodnight**
  Bonsoir/Bonne nuit *Bawngswahr/Bon nwee*

- **Yes/No**
  Oui/Non *Wee/Nawng*

- **Please/Thank you (very much)**
  S'il vous plaît/Merci (beaucoup) *Seelvooplay/Mehrsee (bohkoo)*

- **Excuse me, can you help me please?**
  Excusez-moi, vous pouvez m'aider s'il vous plaît? *Ekskewzaymwah, voo poovay mahyday seelvooplay?*

- **Do you speak English?**
  Vous parlez anglais? *Voo pahrlay ahnglay?*

- **I'm sorry, I don't understand.**
  Pardon, je ne comprends pas. *Pahrdawng, zher ner kawngprawng pah.*

- **I am looking for the tourist information office.**
  Je cherche l'office de tourisme. *Zher shaersh lohfeece de tooreezm.*

- **Do you have a map of the town/area?**
  Avez-vous une carte de la ville/région? *Ahveh-voo ewn cart der lah veel/rehzhawng?*

- **Do you have a list of hotels?**
  Vous avez une liste des hôtels? *Vooz ahveh ewn leesst dez ohtehl?*

- **Do you have any rooms free?**
  Vous avez des chambres disponibles? *Voozahveh deh shahngbr deesspohneebl?*

- **I would like to reserve a single/double room with/without bath/shower.**
  Je voudrais réserver une chambre pour une personne/pour deux personnes avec/sans salle de bain/douche. *Zher voodray rehsehrveh ewn shahngbr poor ewn pehrson/poor der pehrson avek/sawns sal der banne/doosh.*

- **I would like bed and breakfast/(room and) half board/(room and) full board.**
  Je voudrais le petit-déjeuner/la demi-pension/la pension complète. *Zher voodray ler pewtee-dehjewneh/lah dermee-pahngsyawng/lah pahngsyawng kawngplait.*

- **How much is it per night?**
  Quel est le prix pour une nuit? *Khel eh ler pree poor ewn nuwy?*

- **I would like to stay for . . . nights.**
  Je voudrais rester . . . nuits. *Zhe voodray resteh . . . newyh.*

- **Do you accept travellers' cheques/credit cards?**
  Vous acceptez les chèques de voyages/les cartes de crédit? *Voos aksepteh leh sheck der vwoyazh/leh kart der krehdee?*

- **I would like a table for two.**
  Je voudrais une table pour deux personnes. *Zher voodray ewn tabl poor der pehrson.*

- **I would like a cup of/two cups of/another coffee/tea.**
  Je voudrais une tasse de/deux tasses de/encore une tasse de café/thé. *Zher voodray ewn tahss der/der tahss der/oncaw ewn tahss der kafeh/teh.*

- **I would like a bottle/glass/two glasses of mineral water/red wine/white wine, please.**
  Je voudrais une bouteille/un verre/deux verres d'eau minérale/de vin rouge/de vin blanc, s'il vous plaît. *Zhe voodray ewn bootayy/ang vair/der vair doh mynehral/der vang roozh/der vang blahng, seelvooplay*

- **Could I have it well-cooked/medium/rare please?**
  Je le voudrais bien cuit/à point/saignant s'il vous plaît. *Zher ler voodray beeang kwee/ah pwahng/saynyang, seelvooplay?*

- **May I have the bill, please?** L'addition, s'il vous plaît! *Laddyssyawng, seelvooplay!*

- **Where is the toilet (restroom), please?**
  Où sont les toilettes, s'il vous plaît? *Oo sawng leh twahlaitt, seelvooplay?*

- **How much does it/this cost?**
  Quel est le prix? *Kehl eh ler pree?*

- **A (half-) kilo of . . . please.**
  Un (demi-) kilo de . . . s'il vous plaît. *Ang (dermee)keelo der . . . seelvooplay.*

Index

Acknowledgements

Project Management: Fay Franklin
Series design: Fox Design
Front cover design: Pumpkin House
Layout: PDQ Digital Media Solutions Limited
Map work: Polly Senior Cartography
Repro and image setting: PDQ Digital Media Solutions Limited
Printed and bound in Spain by: Grafo Industrias Gráficas, Basauri

We would like to thank **Ethel Davies** for the photographs used in this book, to whom the copyright belongs, with the exception of the following:
John Heseltine (*page 151*).

Front cover: Spectrum Colour Library
Back cover: John Heseltine

Feedback form

If you enjoyed using this book, or even if you didn't, please help us improve future editions by taking part in our reader survey. Every returned form will be acknowledged, and to show our appreciation we will give you £1 off your next purchase of a Thomas Cook guidebook. Just take a few minutes to complete and return this form to us.

When did you buy this book? ....
....

Where did you buy it? (Please give town/city and, if possible, name of retailer)
....
....

When did you/do you intend to travel in the Loire Valley?..
....

For how long (approx)? ....

How many people in your party? ....

Which cities, national parks and other locations did you/do you intend mainly to visit?
....
....
....
....

Did you/will you:
❑ Make all your travel arrangements independently?
❑ Travel on a fly-drive package?
Please give brief details: ....
....

Did you/do you intend to use this book:
❑ For planning your trip?   ❑ Both?
❑ During the trip itself?

Did you/do you intend also to purchase any of the following travel publications for your trip?
A road map/atlas (please specify) ....
Other guidebooks (please specify) ....

Have you used any other Thomas Cook guidebooks in the past? If so, which?
....
....
....

Please rate the following features of 'Signpost Loire Valley' for their value to you (Circle VU for 'very useful', U for 'useful', NU for 'little or no use'):

The Travel Facts section on pages 14–23	VU	U	NU
The Driver's Guide section on pages 24–29	VU	U	NU
The touring itineraries	VU	U	NU
The recommended driving routes throughout the book	VU	U	NU
Information on towns and cities, châteaux, etc	VU	U	NU
The maps of towns and cities, etc	VU	U	NU

Please use this space to tell us about any features that in your opinion could be changed, improved, or added in future editions of the book, or any other comments you would like to make concerning the book:

....
....
....
....
....
....
....
....

Your age category: ❏ 21-30   ❏ 31-40   ❏ 41-50   ❏ over 50

Your name: Mr/Mrs/Miss/Ms ....
(First name or initials) ....
(Last name) ....

Your full address: (Please include postal or zip code)

....
....
....
....
....

Your daytime telephone number: ....

Please detach this page and send it to: The Project Editor, Signpost Guides, Thomas Cook Publishing, PO Box 227, Thomas Cook Business Park, Units 19–21, Coningsby Road, Peterborough PE3 8XX, United Kingdom.

Alternatively, you can e-mail us at: *books@thomascook.com,* or *editorial@globe-perquot.com* **for the US.**

We will be pleased to send you details of how to claim your discount upon receipt of this questionnaire.